William Henry Davenport Adams

Before the Conquest

English Worthies in the Old English Period

William Henry Davenport Adams

Before the Conquest
English Worthies in the Old English Period

ISBN/EAN: 9783337372842

Printed in Europe, USA, Canada, Australia, Japan

Cover: Foto ©ninafisch / pixelio.de

More available books at **www.hansebooks.com**

OR,

ENGLISH WORTHIES IN THE OLD ENGLISH PERIOD.

BY

W. H. DAVENPORT ADAMS,

AUTHOR OF 'THE CIRCLE OF THE YEAR,' 'SWORD AND PEN,' 'BURIED CITIES OF CAMPANIA,' ETC.

'*Multi fortes vixere ante Agamemnona.*'

WITH ILLUSTRATIONS BY F. BARNARD.

EDINBURGH:
WILLIAM P. NIMMO.
1873.

IN history, all that belongs to the individual is exhibited in subordinate relation to the commonwealth; in biography, the acts and accidents of the commonwealth are considered in their relation to the individual, as influences by which his character is formed or modified, as circumstances amid which he is placed, as the sphere in which he moves, or the materials he works with. The man with his works, his words, his affections, his fortunes, is the end and aim of all. He does not, indeed, as in a panegyric, stand alone like a statue; but like the central figure of a picture, around which others are grouped in due subordination and perspective, the general circumstances of his times forming the back and foreground. In history, the man, like the earth on the Copernican hypothesis, is part of a system; in biography, he is, like the earth in the ancient cosmogony, the centre and final cause of the system.

HARTLEY COLERIDGE.

PREFACE.

THE present volume is the first of a series, in which it will be the writer's design to illustrate certain important periods of English history, by the assistance of English biography; in other words, to assist the young student in obtaining a closer acquaintance with the great events of his country's annals, by showing him what manner of men were they who had the chief part in bringing them about. Of the reign of Henry II., for instance, and the influence it exercised on the current of our history, no reader can obtain an accurate idea, unless he knows the character and life of Thomas à Becket. As little can he understand the reign of Henry III., without a full appreciation of the genius and policy of Simon de Montfort. These worthies, however, in the historical works usually accessible to the young, and even to the general reader, are but mere names—*voces, et preterea nihil.* They pass across the crowded stage like shadows, and their actual lineaments are never realized. The writer therefore hopes that a series of volumes, in which their lives shall be told with some degree of fulness, especially in their connection with English history, will prove acceptable, and be regarded as no unfitting introduction to works of a more elaborate character.

With this view, the writer has been careful to resort to the best authorities, and to embody in his pages, as far as possible, the valuable results of modern critical inquiry. Nor has he neglected the stores of information placed at the student's disposal by the publications issued under the direction of the Master of the Rolls,—those old, quaint, but interesting chronicles, which often illuminate so vividly the 'obscure passages' of past times.

In the present volume the writer deals with four of the worthies who flourished 'before the Conquest,'—the great Ælfred, Dunstan, Harold II., and Archbishop Stigand. The latter, it is true, survived the liberties of his country, but may fairly be regarded as belonging to that old English period which terminated on the field of Senlac.

Each biography is connected with its successor by a carefully compiled chronological summary; so that, in effect, the volume now before the reader gives a condensed, but, it is hoped, an intelligible view of English history, from the first settlement of the Angles to the rise of Thomas à Becket.

It will be seen that, in his sketches of Harold II., the writer has adopted the views of Mr. Freeman, to whose elaborate *History of the Norman Conquest* he has been largely indebted. He has generally followed the same accurate authority in his spelling of the old English names, as it seemed to him desirable that the young reader should be familiarized with their correct forms. Numerous quotations have been introduced from the old chroniclers, for the purpose of giving life and freshness to the narrative; and especially from the *Roman de Rou*,—a heroic poem, with which every Englishman ought surely to be as well acquainted as with the *Iliad* or the *Æneid*.

In conclusion, the writer may be allowed to state, that his work has been done conscientiously, and with an earnest desire to do justice to the memories of the heroes whose lives it records. Whatever its shortcomings, it is not wanting, he believes, in a true English spirit; and it aims, from first to last, at encouraging in its youthful readers a genuine love and admiration of that grand old fatherland, of which they are fortunate enough to be the sons.

W. H. DAVENPORT ADAMS.

CONTENTS.

BOOK I.

ÆLFRED THE GREAT.

A.D. 849-901.

CHRONOLOGICAL LANDMARKS.

	PAGE
From the Roman Invasion to the Accession of Ælfred the Great,	3

CHAPTER I.

Ælfred's Youth—His Accession to the Throne—Condition of England at this Period—The Danish Invasions—Athelney—Reappearance of Ælfred—Victory over the Northmen, ... 7

CHAPTER II.

Battle of Ethandune—Treaty with the Danes—The Danelagh—Consequences of the Peace of Wedmore, ... 33

CHAPTER III.

Concluding Years of Ælfred's Reign—Formation of a Navy—Later Danish Invasions, ... 40

CHAPTER IV.

Asser's Character of Ælfred—His Love of Learning—His Architectural Works—His Piety—His Economy of Time—His Impartiality—His Death, ... 52

BOOK II.

DUNSTAN, ARCHBISHOP OF CANTERBURY.

A.D. 925 (?)–988.

CHRONOLOGICAL LANDMARKS.

	PAGE
From the Death of Ælfred the Great to the Accession of Eadgar,	77

CHAPTER I.

Birth and Birthplace of Dunstan—His Early Years—Character of his Genius—Struggle between Love and Ambition—Brain Fever—The Married Clergy—A Revolution contemplated—Dunstan's share in it—Becomes Abbot of Glastonbury—Is called to Court, . . . 81

CHAPTER II.

Accession of Eadred — His Character — Dunstan's Influence — A Legend—Accession of Eadwig—Scene at his Coronation—Banishment of Dunstan—His Recall—Accession of Eadgar—Dunstan as a Statesman — His Policy — What he accomplished — Eadgar's Vices—A Penance—The Story of Ælfrida, . . . 100

CHAPTER III.

Æthelred the Unready—A Shameful Reign—Writings of Dunstan—His Canons of Canterbury—His Death—His Burial—His Tomb re-opened by Archbishop Warham, ... 115

BOOK III.

HAROLD, THE 'LAST OF THE SAXON KINGS.'

A.D. 1023 (?)–1066.

CHRONOLOGICAL LANDMARKS.

PAGE

From the Death of Dunstan to the Accession of Eadward the Confessor, ... 129

CHAPTER I.

His early Years and Parentage—A Portrait—His first Appearance on the historic Stage—Becomes Earl of the East Angles—His Brother Swegen—An atrocious Act—Harold's Influence—The Normans in England—Eustace of Bretagne—The Affray at Dover—King Eadward's Anger—Godwine refuses to interfere—He is charged with Rebellion, and, through Norman influence, he and his Sons are banished—Temporary Downfall of the House of Godwine, . 139

CHAPTER II.

William the Norman visits the English Court—Eadward's Promise—Gradual Rise of a Patriotic Spirit—Harold raises an Army in Ireland, and crosses to England—Godwine raises a Fleet—Harold and Godwine sail up the Thames, and are warmly welcomed by their Countrymen—King Eadward is forced to submit—A great Witán is held—Godwine and his Sons restored to their Estates—Exodus of the Normans—Death of Godwine—The Truth and the Fiction—Godwine's Character—Harold becomes Earl of the West Saxons—He repels a Welsh Invasion, ... 159

CHAPTER III.

Death of the Ætheling Eadward—Harold recognised as future King—Magnificent Position of the House of Godwine—Ancestry of Godwine—Harold's Pilgrimage to Rome—He founds the Minster at Waltham—Invasion of the Welsh under Gruffydd—Harold's great Campaign—Death of Gruffydd, and Subjugation of the Welsh—The Northumbrian Revolt against Earl Tostig—It is put down through Harold's prudent Policy—Eadward's Illness—His last Hours—His prophetic Visions—Nominates Harold as his Successor—His Death and Burial—His Character, . . . 176

CHAPTER IV.

Election of Harold as King—An Episode in his Life—His Visit to Normandy—How he was received by Duke William—A Crafty Plot—Harold's Oath and the Sacred Relics—Harold's Coronation—His Popularity—How the Tidings were received in Normandy—A Striking Scene—William and his Barons—Preparations for the Invasion of England, ... 190

CHAPTER V.

Harold organizes his Kingdom—Shadows of Coming Events—The Hairy Star—England invaded by Harold Hardrada of Norway—Scandinavian Visions—March of the English, . . . 213

CHAPTER VI.

The Battle of Stamford Bridge — Harold and his Brother — The Struggle—Death of Hardrada—Victory of the English—King Harold at York—The Messenger from the South, . . 225

CHAPTER VII.

Duke William's Preparations—Seeks for Allies—Mysterious Fate of Conan of Brittany—The Norman Army and Fleet—Waiting for a Fair Wind—The Invasion of England, . . . 231

BOOK IV.

HAROLD II.—*continued.*

A.D. 1066.

CHAPTER I.

The Battle of Senlac, or Hastings—The Morning ot Battle—Speeches of William and Harold—The Norman Charge—Repulse by the English—Deeds of Valour—William's Stratagem—Harold's Death —Disorder of the English—The Battle Lost and Won, . . 257

CHAPTER II.

The Battle of Hastings—*continued,* 278

CHAPTER III.

Night on the Field—Harold's Character considered—Search for his Body—Its Interment at Hastings—Removal to Waltham Abbey —Harold and Edward the First, ... 294

BOOK V.

STIGAND, ARCHBISHOP OF CANTERBURY.

A.D. 1013 (?)-1070.

Stigand's early Career—King Eadward's Court—Stigand promoted to the See of Winchester—Is elevated to the Primacy—Consecration of Westminster Abbey—Death of Eadward—Coronation of Harold —Coronation of William—Stigand's Policy—Visits Normandy in the Conqueror's Train—Retires into Scotland—The Camp of Refuge—Stigand made prisoner and deposed—His Death—His Character, ... 305

NOTES.

	PAGE
Death of Earl Godwine, ...	328
The Seven Sleepers, ...	332
Death of King Eadward, ...	334

APPENDIX.

I. Table of Contemporary Sovereigns, for the Reigns of William I., William II., Stephen, and Henry I., ... 341

II. Chronological Landmarks, from the Battle of Hastings to the Rise of Thomas à Becket, ... 343

English Worthies.

BOOK I.—ÆLFRED THE GREAT.

'Truth-teller was our English Alfred named.'
                                        TENNYSON.

'The pious Ælfred, king to justice dear!
Lord of the harp and liberating spear,
Mirror of princes! indigent renown
Might range the starry ether for a crown
Equal to *his* deserts, who, like the year,
Pours forth his bounty,—like the day doth cheer,—
And awes, like night, with mercy-tempered frown.'
                                        WORDSWORTH.

CHRONOLOGICAL LANDMARKS.

FROM THE ROMAN INVASION TO THE ACCESSION OF ÆLFRED THE GREAT.

B.C. 55. First invasion of Britain by Julius Cæsar. He lands near Deal.
B.C. 54. Second invasion of Cæsar, who defeats Cassivellaunus.
A.D. 43. Renewal of the Roman projects of conquest under Aulus Plautius and Vespasian. Arrival of the Emperor Claudius.
A.D. 52. Heroic but fruitless struggle of Caractacus, who is captured and sent to Rome.
A.D. 61. Suetonius Paulinus captures Anglesey. Insurrection of the Britons under Boadicea. Roman London destroyed. Victory of Suetonius, and death of Boadicea.
A.D. 78. Agricola made governor of Britain. He pushes the Roman conquests to the Frith of Forth, and divides Roman Britain into six departments.
A.D. 120. The Emperor Hadrian visits Britain, and builds a wall from the Tyne to the Solway Frith.
A.D. 208. Visit of the Emperor Severus, who builds a new rampart along the line of Hadrian's wall.
A.D. 211. Severus dies at York (Eboracum).
A.D. 281. First appearance in British history of the 'Saxons' or Northmen.
A.D. 286. Carausius, a Roman general, assumes the sovereignty of Britain, and builds a fleet. Is assassinated, in 292, by his confidential minister, Allectus, who reigns for three years, until defeated by the Cæsar, Constantius Chlorus.
A.D. 297-306. Constantius makes York his capital.
A.D. 303-305. Persecution of the Christians. Martyrdom of St. Alban.

A.D. 306. Constantine the Great acknowledged emperor at York.
A.D. 363. The Picts ravage Northern Britain.
A.D. 368. The Picts driven out of England by Theodosius.
A.D. 400-408. Intestine troubles, and election of successive 'emperors,' —Marcus, Gratian, Constantine.
A.D. 410. The Emperor Honorius renounces the allegiance of Britain.
A.D. 411. The Northern immigration, which has already continued for many years, now assumes a marked prominence.
A.D. 450. The Northmen spread themselves all over England, partly by conquest, and partly by colonization. They are formed into various independent kingdoms (erroneously called the 'Heptarchy'), Cornwall being still held by the Britons or Romanized Celts, as well as North and South Wales, Cumbria, and Strathclyde. These, at a later date, also fall under the sway of the Northmen. 'There is every reason to believe that the Celtic inhabitants of those parts of Britain which had become English at the end of the sixth century, had been as nearly extirpated as a nation can be.' The women, however, were largely spared, and became the wives of the Teutonic conquerors.
A.D. 449. The earliest permanent Teutonic settlement in Britain was the Jutish kingdom of Kent. The Jutes also formed a small principality out of the Isle of Wight and part of Hampshire (530).
A.D. 477. The South Saxon kingdom (Sussex) founded by Ælla.
A.D. 526. The East Saxon (Essex) founded.
A.D. 519. The West Saxon (Wessex) founded by Cerdic; like Aaron's rod, it swallowed up all the others.
A.D. 571. East Anglia founded by Offa.
A.D. 547. Northumbria founded by Ida.
A.D. 584. Mercia (the *march* or border-land against the Welsh) founded by the junction of several small states.
A.D. 590. Occasionally the sovereign of one of these kingdoms obtained a decided supremacy, and was recognised as *Bretwalda*.
A.D. 597. Kent, under its sovereign Æthelbehrt, embraces Christianity, which is preached by Augustine.
A.D. 681. All Britain Christian, Sussex being the last state to be received into the fold of the church.
A.D. 577-584. Ceawlin, the West Saxon Bretwalda, enlarges his kingdom.

A.D. 652. From this date the progress of West Saxon conquest becomes continuous. 'Step by step the English frontier advanced from the Axe to the Parret, from the Parret to the Tamar. Taunton at one stage, Exeter at another, were border fortresses against the Welsh enemy. Step by step the old Cornish kingdom shrunk up before the conquerors, till at last no portion of land north of the Bristol Channel was subject to a British sovereign.'

A.D. 577–823. Rivalry between Mercia, Northumberland, and Wessex. The most flourishing period of Mercia appears to have extended from 716 to 819, under its three great kings, Æthelbald, Offa, and Cenwulf. The permanent supremacy of Wessex was secured by Ecgbehrt, who became king

A.D. 823. in 823, and assumed the style of King of the English. 'In a reign of thirty-six years he reduced all the English kingdoms to a greater or lesser degree of subjection.' He was undoubtedly the founder of English unity; for, though Mercia retained her kings for another half-century, yet 'they now received their crown at the hands of the West Saxon over-lord.'

A.D. 787. The incursions of the second migration of Northmen or Danes begin. They proved so successful, because England at this time had no maritime force, and her inhabitants displayed no partiality for maritime pursuits.[1]

A.D. 835. Battle of Hengestesdun, in Cornwall, in which Ecgbehrt defeats the Northmen and revolted Welsh.

A.D. 836. On the death of Ecgbehrt, his son Æthelwulf succeeds to the throne.

A.D. 855. The Northmen for the first time winter in the Isle of Sheppey.

A.D. 867. Northumberland conquered by the Danes.

A.D. 868. Mercia invaded. They seize Nottingham.

A.D. 870. East Anglia conquered.

A.D. 871. Wessex first invaded in the reign of Æthelred.

A.D. 871. In this year begins the reign of Ælfred the Great.

---

[1] Mr. Freeman distinguishes three periods of Danish invasion: the first, of simple plunder (787–855); the second, of settlement (855–897); the third, of political conquest (980–1015). Eventually the Danes became absorbed in the Teutonic population.

CHRONOLOGY OF ÆLFRED'S REIGN.

A.D. 872. After a series of great battles, peace is made with the Northmen.

A.D. 878. Second invasion of Wessex. Ælfred flies for concealment to the marshes of Somersetshire.

A.D. 878-880. Having recruited his army, Ælfred attacks the Danes, and concludes the peace of Widmore. Guthrum and his followers embrace Christianity; and Guthrum, under the name of Æthelstane, reigns in East Anglia.

A.D. 887. Ælfred recovers London.

A D. 886-873. Interval of peace. Ælfred promotes the education of his subjects, codifies the laws, removes unjust judges, builds a fleet, and re-organizes the kingdom.

A.D. 893-897. Later Danish wars. Ælfred, after five years of struggle, restores peace.

A.D. 901. Death of Ælfred.[1]

CONTEMPORARIES OF ÆLFRED THE GREAT.

Emperor of the East, . Leo the Philosopher (886–911).

Emperors of the West, . Charles the Bold (840–877); Louis the Stammerer (877–879); Louis III., and Carloman (878–884); Charles the Fat (884–887); Arnold (887–899); Louis IV. (897–911).

Kings of France, . Eudes, Count of Paris (887–898); Charles the Simple (898–923).

---

[1] 'Opening with the great days of Charlemagne, it is right that the ninth century should close with the far more glorious days of Ælfred, the patriot and sage,—a century illuminated at its two extremes, but in its middle period dark with disunion and ignorance, and not unlikely, unless controlled to higher uses, to give birth to a state of more hopeless barbarism than that from which the nations of Europe had so recently emerged.'—REV. JAMES WHITE, *The Eighteen Christian Centuries,* p. 201.

BOOK I.

ÆLFRED THE GREAT.

A.D. 849–901.

CHAPTER I.

Ælfred's Youth—His Accession to the Throne—Condition of England at this Period—The Danish Invasions—Athelney—Ælfred's Reappearance—Victory over the Northmen.

WE are about to tell the story of the life and reign of Ælfred, or Alfred, not unjustly surnamed the Great;—of him who first made England an actual living nation; who first created an English literature; who laid the foundation of English naval power; and who was not less eminent for his virtues as a man, than for his high qualities as a king.

It has been his singular good fortune to have extorted the laudations of historians of widely different views; and those writers who have laboured to clear away the mists enveloping our earlier annals, whatever may have been their divergence on other points, and however great the devotion of each to his own peculiar theory, have all united in a tribute of praise to this remarkable monarch. It will be worth our while, before entering on the narrative of his career, to compare these panegyrical opinions, and to gather from them some idea of the man around whom they have accreted. We shall then have an opportunity of determining whether, in the formation of such opinions, any prejudices and prepossessions have had a part; how far, in fact, the Man and the King deserved the homage of his eulogists.

Turning to our latest and our best authority on early English history,[1] we find Mr. Freeman warmly characterizing Ælfred as a saint without superstition, a scholar without ostentation, a warrior all whose wars were fought in the defence of his country, a conqueror whose laurels were never stained by cruelty, a prince never cast down by adversity,—never lifted up to insolence in the day of triumph. He asserts that no other name is comparable to his. Saint Lewis of France—he who perished in an unprofitable crusade against the Saracens at a time when his own kingdom urgently needed his presence and active government—seems to have resembled him in the union of a more than monastic piety with the highest civil, military, and domestic virtues. But Ælfred rightly attended to the sphere of duty which lay around him, and forbore from wasting his own or his country's strength on Quixotic expeditions to Egypt or Tunis. With an inquiring spirit, says Mr. Freeman, which embraced the whole world, for purposes alike of scientific inquiry and of Christian benevolence, he never forgot that his first duty was to the people over whom he ruled. With a mind in advance of his age, he sent out fleets to explore the Northern Ocean, and he despatched alms to the distant churches of India, but not until he had

[1] E. A. Freeman, *History of the Norman Conquest*, pp. 51-55.

secured peace in his kingdom, and established the commonweal on a safe foundation.

The virtue of Ælfred, continues our authority, consisted in no marvellous displays of superhuman genius, but in the simple, straightforward discharge of the duty of the hour.—A great poet of our own time, we may add, has, with true poetic insight, recognised in him this distinguishing quality, and associated him in the same record with a later English hero of like character.[1]

> 'Not once or twice in our fair island story,
> The path of duty was the way to glory. . . .
> Truth-teller was our England's Alfred named.'—

Mr. Freeman, in this respect, compares him with the American Washington; but Washington, though illustrious as soldier, statesman, and patriot, was not, like Ælfred, a saint and a scholar.

William of Nassau, surnamed William the Silent, was equally great as the saviour of a people, but he possessed no literary merits, and 'in his career, glorious as it is, there is an element of intrigue and chicanery, utterly alien to the noble simplicity of both Ælfred and Washington.'

A similar union of devoutness and learning, combined with the highest gifts of the warrior and the statesman, is found in Charles the Great; but the glory of the western emperor is not so pure as that of Ælfred. Amidst all the splendours of conquest and legislation, we cannot be blind, as Mr. Freeman remarks, to an alloy of personal ambition, of personal vice, to occasional unjust aggressions, and occasional acts of cruelty.

Among our later English sovereigns, the only one who can bear comparison with Ælfred is Edward the First. The great

[1] Tennyson, *Ode on the Death of the Duke of Wellington*, p. 147.

Plantagenet was superior as a legislator and a soldier, but not his equal in manly virtues, in purity, simplicity, and honour. Ælfred, therefore, remains 'a singular instance of a prince who has become a hero of romance, who, as such, has had countless imaginary exploits and imaginary institutions attributed to him, but to whose character romance has done no more than justice, and who appears in exactly the same light in history and in fable.'

We turn to Professor Pearson,[1] and find him describing our hero as 'the typical English king.' Of Ælfred's political capacity, he says, there can be no doubt. Wielding only the resources of a third of the kingdom, he contended against the most powerful foe then known to the nations of Europe, exacted honourable peace, and literally enlarged his dominions by Mercia, which had been free rather than dependent under his brothers, and under him became dependent rather than free. To him especially belongs the credit of having first recognised the fact that the best defence of an island is the water surrounding it; and his establishment of a national navy is in itself a sufficient proof of his statesman-like sagacity.

His zeal for learning is justly particularized as one of his most honourable titles to remembrance. He was not only himself an author, but he encouraged scholars and teachers with a wise liberality, founded schools, and stimulated a love of scholarship.

In days,—says Pearson, speaking of the great king's private virtues,—in days when charity had grown cold, and when religion no longer restrained the powerful, their king was the one man to whom the needy could apply for support, and the

[1] Professor Pearson, *Early and Middle Ages of England*, pp. 118-122.

injured for redress. His shrewd sense was the terror of evil-doers; and though the sternness of his early years was tempered, as he grew older, by courtesy, his wish to conciliate never so far prevailed as to make him swerve from the truth.

'In one or two minor points,' continues Mr. Pearson, 'we may have a curious resemblance between the views of Ælfred and those of later English society. His character was of that striking conservative type which bases itself upon old facts, but accepts new facts as a reason for change. Recognising slavery, he was yet careful in his will to provide for the liberty of his old servants. It is in his laws that we first find the principle of entail maintained; and in his will he declares his intention of following his grandfather's example, and leaving his lands on the spear-side. His laws confirmed the authority of the noble as well as that of the king. That he opened the ranks to the ceorl who enriched himself, or to the merchant who had made three voyages, proves indeed that his love of order was not the narrow and senseless love of caste, but does not weaken the presumption that he was aristocratic in his sympathies. The watchwords of modern democracy would have sounded strangely in his ears.[1] Some regard him as a Protestant before Luther. It is the fondest of speculations to discover such absolute tendencies in Ælfred. It is possible that a more original thinker might, if called upon to legislate, have anticipated the modes of thought that are common in our own days; but it is at least doubtful whether such high speculative talent could have been combined with the tact, the statesmanship, and the success of Ælfred.'

---

[1] Surely this is only equivalent to saying that Ælfred did not live in the nineteenth century. Democracy was simply impossible under the conditions that prevailed in Ælfred's time.

Sir Francis Palgrave,[1] after enumerating those virtues of the great king which all his biographers agree to recognise, is yet inclined to believe that he did not approach to that *ideal* perfection sometimes portrayed by his panegyrists. Certainly he began with good intentions, but he did not always bear them in mind (which is only saying that, after all, he was human); and during the first portion of his reign he was proud, tyrannical, and almost as much hated as he was afterwards beloved.[2] Still he preserved within him the only germ of real improvement, the consciousness of his own entire insufficiency; and the same tendency which, before he yielded to the temptations of authority, had rendered him unwilling to accept the throne, enabled him afterwards to reform from his errors. Yet, after every allowance has been made for such of Ælfred's faults as may be discovered in the accounts which we possess, and still greater deductions for the faults and sins of which the memory has been buried with him, we are justified in asserting that he affords a brighter model for the character of a good king than can be found in any other age or realm. He really and truly sought wisdom from her only source, and employed her various gifts in assisting him to discharge with strict conscientiousness the duties of his high and difficult position. As a legislator, he was guided by three main principles: the first, a tolerant (and, let us add, a truly English) endurance of institutions, not theoretically perfect, but incapable of alteration without the risk of greater evil; the second, an incessant endeavour to supply any deficiency in the theory of his laws, by the prompt and equitable

---

[1] Sir F. Palgrave, *History of England—Anglo-Saxon Period*, pp. 186-192.
[2] It is presumption to differ from so great an authority, but we must confess that for this sweeping assertion we can find no foundation.

administration of them in practice;—instead of introducing new machinery, he addressed himself to the task of making the old work well by constant care and watchfulness;—and, third, he earnestly and unremittingly sought to introduce the true spirit of the divine law into the secular legislation of his kingdom.

'We commonly say,' continues Palgrave, 'that Christianity is a part of the law of the land. Ælfred had a clearer perception of the part which religion ought to perform in a Christian commonwealth. He would have wished to render Christianity the law itself. The necessity for any human law exists simply and solely in proportion to our neglect of the divine law; and if we were enabled to write that law in our hearts, nothing whatever would be left for human legislation to perform.'

Lastly, we shall borrow the sketch of Ælfred's character furnished by Sir Edward Creasy.[1]

History, he says, has justly associated with his name the epithet of 'The Great;' and many are the other phrases of affection and admiration with which he is spoken of in his country's annals. Perhaps the title most grateful to a spirit so pure, so fearless, so averse from all fraud and meanness, must have been that which we find used by one of his biographers,—the title of 'Ælfred the Truth-teller.'

Some of the old writers, he adds, mention blemishes in Ælfred's character during the early part of his reign, which may in part account for the national want of zeal in his behalf at his season of peril. He is said to have shown haughtiness and impatience, when suitors for justice and petitioners for redress of grievances approached him. The vehemence of

[1] Sir E. Creasy, *History of England*, pp. 141-150.

disposition which gained for him in the Saxon camps, while a mere lad, the surname of the 'wild boar of the battle,' and which made him in the chase the keenest and most daring of hunters, may, before experience and sorrow taught him self-control, have made him hasty in demeanour, and petulantly negligent of the dull routine of official duty. But even if we should adopt all that is asserted by old, and insinuated by some modern, writers, against the character of Ælfred in his youth, we should find the greater reason to admire him when we take him for all in all, and review the whole, instead of an exceptional part, of his career. If such tales show that Ælfred had strong passions to subdue, they also show that he *did* subdue them. For it is beyond all doubt, that in his manhood he was pure, and gentle, and enduring; and that he preserved a noble equanimity of soul amidst the frequent attacks of agonizing and debilitating physical disease.

These estimates, by different but competent and discriminative critics, should furnish the reader with a tolerably full and accurate conception of the character of Ælfred the Great. They are mainly founded upon facts—facts which no one can dispute, and which are happily free from any legendary or mythical surrounding; and they show us a man reaching almost to the ideal of humanity; a king sensible of the importance of his duties, and energetic in their due discharge; a Christian with gentle tolerance for the views of others, but earnest and emphatic in acting upon his own. High thoughts were his,

'And amiable words,
And courtliness, and the desire of fame,
And love of truth, and all that makes a man.'

Like Tennyson's Arthur, he seems to have charged himself with a noble and sacred enterprise :

> 'To break the heathen and uphold the Christ,
> To ride abroad redressing human wrongs,
> To speak no slander,—no, nor listen to it,—
> To lead sweet lives in purest chastity.' [1]

His desire of knowledge was strong and keen, not only for himself, but for others, and he sought to elevate his subjects to the high standard he had himself attained. In adversity never desponding, in prosperity he was never rash. Obstacles could not daunt, and successes were unable to elate him. His mind was so well balanced that it spontaneously threw off the faults of youth ; and though he was of an ardent and daring disposition, he could bide his time with a heroical patience. Incapable of envy, he generously rewarded merit ; of a tender though resolute heart, he felt an active compassion for the widow and the fatherless. Though his genius was eminently progressive, he made no changes for the mere sake of change, but, availing himself of the machinery at his hands, so improved it by gradual modification as to adapt it for the fit performance of the work it had to do. Naturally endowed with æsthetic tastes, he nevertheless shrank from a regal splendour which might have oppressed his subjects, and in all things displayed the moderation of a noble and self-restrained nature. His military talents fitted him to shine in war, but he cultivated peace, because peace was needful for the prosperity of his kingdom. Tortured by an agonizing malady, he endured its paroxysms with composure, and never suffered them to impede him in the performance of the task he had undertaken.

Such a character seems to be almost too good for human

[1] Tennyson, *Idylls of the King: Guinevere.*

nature's daily food. The picture is so charged with light that we can hardly look upon it as an accurate transcript from nature. The ideal beauty of the statue seems to have sprung from a poet's imagination. As if conscious of this very perfection, his biographers have endeavoured to introduce an occasional shadow into the picture, to point out a flaw or two in the exquisite marble. But the errors of which they accuse the great king only serve to bring his virtues into bolder and more striking relief. We are told of the passions of his youth; yet we find his self-control so great that he completely mastered them. And surely this is a proof of a nobler nature than the insipid saintliness of an Eadward the Confessor. Ælfred did not stand aloof like an anchorite from the storm, and strife, and sinfulness of the world, but plunged deep into the press, and yet bore himself throughout like a pure and stainless knight.

Ælfred the Great was born at Wantage, in Berkshire, on the 29th of October, in the year of our Lord 849. He was the youngest child of King Ethelwulf and Queen Osburga, whom the old chronicles describe as 'a religious woman, noble both by birth and nature.'[1] At an early age he distinguished himself above his brethren by the quickness of his talents. He was permitted, however, to reach the age of six without learning his letters. It happened then that he was playing one day around his mother, who was reading a book of Saxon ballads, emblazoned, as was then the custom, with rich ornamental devices and brilliantly illuminated initial letters. The gay colouring caught the children's attention, and Osburga placed it in their hands to examine, with the promise that he who

[1] She was the daughter of a Jutish noble, the king's cup-bearer.

first learned what was written in its pages, and repeated it to her, should be rewarded with the book,—no small reward in days when books were literally worth their weight in gold !

'Will you really give it,' said Ælfred, 'to the one of us who learns it most quickly, and says it by heart?'

Osburga repeated her assurance that she would do so ; and the princely boy, immediately taking the book from her hands, repaired to an instructor, who made him acquainted with its contents, either by teaching him to read it, or by reciting it to him until his memory thoroughly retained its contents.[1]

He was dearly loved by his parents, partly, we may suppose, on account of his talents, and partly on account of his beauty of person. If he was slow in being instructed to read and write, he was quickly accustomed to wind the horn and bend the bow; and, as became the son of a bold and martial king, he displayed great skill in hawking and the chase. His love of poetry was absorbing, and he committed to memory the ballads which were chanted in the royal hall by the minstrels and the glee-men—the masters of old English song. He became, moreover, a proficient on the harp.

He was still in his youth (A.D. 855) when he accompanied his father on a pilgrimage to Rome, where he remained for a twelvemonth, alive (we may well believe) to all the spirit-stirring influences which belong to the Imperial City. And, as Sir Edward Creasy suggests, he may have watched with unforgetting enthusiasm the living example exhibited by Leo IV.

---

[1] According to Dr. Pauli (*Life of Alfred*, p. 85), Ælfred only learned it from dictation. Asser, the king's friend and biographer, says that he did not know how to read in his youth, yet in recording the above anecdote he uses the strong word '*legit.*' At all events, the king must eventually have acquired this useful art, or he could not have carried out his literary labours.

in his contests against the Saracens, of how much the personal energy of a ruler may effect in rescuing both Church and State from destruction by pagan invaders, and in reviving the splendour of civilisation in a desolated and half-barbarized community.

At a later period he again visited Rome, and was received by the Pope with a noble welcome, and anointed as Prince Royal of England.

Of the remainder of his youth we possess very few details. His thirst for knowledge was great, but, owing to his ignorance of Latin, could not be readily gratified. In those days all science and all wisdom were shut up in Latin books, like treasures in a cave which can only be opened by a magician's spell. The land lay asleep in the darkness of ignorance; and so few were the grammarians, or Latinists, in Wessex, his father's kingdom, that Ælfred could discover no competent teacher. In his later life he frequently deplored as the greatest of all the misfortunes of his career, this compulsory idleness of his youth. He endeavoured to remedy the evil in the little leisure which he could snatch from the cares of royalty and the tortures of physical pain, by arduous application; and probably he valued knowledge all the more highly, from the toil he underwent and the difficulties he conquered in its acquisition.

In his twentieth year Ælfred married Ealhswitha, the daughter of Æthelred 'the Big,' Earl of the Gainishmen[1] (Gainsborough, in Lincolnshire). At this time the throne of Wessex was occupied by his brother Æthelred, and he himself held the rank of 'Secundarius,' which may probably mean either heir-presumptive to the crown, or viceroy of the king-

---

[1] Pauli, *Life of Alfred*, p. 121.

dom. His energy and ability were, at all events, of the highest service to Æthelred in the struggle he was carrying on against the Danish invaders—

> 'For now the heathen of the Northern Sea
> Began to slay the folk, and spoil the land.'

The second period of the Danish invasion began in 867, the second year of Æthelred's stormy reign. At first the Northmen busied themselves in ravaging and subjugating the kingdoms tributary to Wessex. The conquest of Northumberland occupied them from 867 to 869. Then with fire and sword they harried Mercia and captured Nottingham (868); nor could Æthelred dispossess them of this stronghold. East Anglia was their next prey—its king, Eadmund, perishing by a martyr's death (878). And, lastly, the storm broke upon Wessex itself.[1]

The Danes were strongly opposed by the West Saxons, and four great battles were fought at Reading, Ashdown, Basing, and at Merton. At Ashdown[2] alone were the enemy defeated; their defeat being generally ascribed to Ælfred's courage and military skill. The young prince began the fight by charging vigorously up the slope[3] covered by the Danish forces. Sword met battle-axe in swift exchange of blows, and both English and Danes fought with a courage worthy of their common stock; but at first the issue of the contest was doubtful, for Æthelred was hearing mass in his tent, on the spot now called Hardwell Camp, and left Ælfred unsupported. In due time, however, the main body of the

---

[1] Freeman, *History of the Norman Conquest*, p. 47.

[2] In Hampshire, according to some authorities, but more probably in Berkshire.

[3] Now called Uffington Castle.

English came to the assistance of their countrymen, routed the Danes, slew most of their leaders, and pursued the fugitives to the very walls of Reading.[1]

Among the slain were King Baeseg, Sidroc the elder and Sidroc the younger, and Earls Osbern, Harold, and Frena; names which, if uttered in the hearing of an Englishwoman, had long possessed the power to blanch her face with terror. A single thorn bush, growing in the midst of the battle-field, continued for generations to mark the spot where the fight had been hottest; but from the hard-won victory no permanent advantages flowed. Fresh reinforcements, pouring in from the lands of the Northmen, soon swelled their army to its original numbers; while the English, weary and spent with the protracted warfare, were unable to supply the terrible gaps in their ranks. The land echoed with lamentations; every household had father or son to mourn for; and we cannot wonder that Ælfred, when called to the throne on his brother's death (A.D. 872), should have taken upon himself the burthen of royalty with reluctance, 'for he did not think that he alone could sustain the multitudes and the fierceness of the pagans.'

---

[1] Asser gives the following account of this great battle:—'Now the Christians had determined that Æthelred with his men should attack the two heathen kings, but that his brother Ælfred and his forces should take the chance of war against the two jarls. Matters being thus arranged, the king remained a long time in prayer, and the heathens came rapidly to the fight. Then Ælfred, though possessing a secondary authority, could no longer support the charge of the enemy, unless he retreated or attacked them without waiting for his brother. At length he bravely led his troops against the foe, as had been before arranged, but without waiting for his brother's arrival, for he relied on the divine counsel; and forming his men into a dense phalanx, marched on at once to meet the enemy.

'But here I must inform you that the field of battle was not equally

Some idea of the troubles the young king was called upon to confront, may be gathered from the few simple but emphatic words of the Saxon chronicler:[1]

'A.D. 872.—Then Ælfred, the son of Æthelwulf, succeeded to the kingdom of the West Saxons. And about one month after this, King Ælfred, with a small band, fought against the whole army at Wilton, and put them to flight for a great part of the day; but the Danes had possession of the place of carnage. And this year nine general battles were fought against the army in the kingdom south of the Thames, besides which, single ealdormen and king's thegns oftentimes made invasions on them, which were not counted; and within the year nine ealdormen and one king were slain. And that year the West Saxons made peace with the (Danish) army.'

Sore need had they of peace, though it was rather an armed truce than any more settled pacification. Their king availed himself of the breathing time to build castles and construct ships, and draw together his levies for a new army. He found occasion, moreover, to correct the abuses which had crept into the administration of the law, and with a heavy hand he meted out justice to the wrongdoer, whether noble

---

advantageous to both sides. The heathen occupied the higher ground, and the Christians advanced from below. There was also a single thorn tree (*unica spinosa arbor*) of stunted growth, but we ourselves have never seen it. Around this tree the opposing armies came together with loud shouts from all sides; the one party to pursue their wicked course, the other to fight for their lives, their country, and all they held dear. And when both armies had fought long and bravely, the heathen at length, by the divine judgment, were unable longer to bear the attacks of the Christians, and having lost the greater portion of their army, took to disgraceful flight.'—ASSER, *Life of Alfred*, edited by Giles, p. 55.

[1] *Anglo-Saxon Chronicle*, ed. Giles, in anno 872.

or peasant. Meanwhile the Danes were consolidating their conquests in Mercia and Northumbria. They established their headquarters in Lincolnshire, until a favourable opportunity for attacking Burhred, the Mercian king, arrived. Having easily defeated him, they divided his territories among themselves; while he, escaping beyond sea to Rome, ended in the papal city his weary life, and was buried in the so-called 'school' or 'college' of the English (874).

The whole country was now divided between the Danes and the West Saxons; and the former, as soon as they had completely subjugated Mercia and Northumbria, proceeded to renew their hostilities against the latter. They had chosen a favourable time, for it seems impossible to doubt that Ælfred had temporarily lost the confidence of his subjects, and could with difficulty bring a decent force into the field. It is not improbable, though we confess ourselves unwilling to believe it, that his severe administration had disgusted both thegn and ceorl. Certain it is that, from some not easily explained cause, he spent the first seven years of his reign in comparative inaction. When the Danes renewed their attacks, he endeavoured to obtain a brief truce,—'a momentary repose,'—either by submission, or by some violent but spasmodic efforts. It must nevertheless be admitted that Ælfred had early come to the determination of meeting his tenacious enemy by sea. In 875 he equipped a few ships, manned them with mercenaries, and, sailing in quest of the enemy, fell in with a Danish fleet of seven vessels, engaged them, and captured one, while the others escaped. Encouraged by this success, he built some new ships and galleys, and succeeded in forming an English navy. He laboured to this end with a perseverance and an energy which show that his inertness in the beginning of his reign arose from no individual lethargy. And in 877 the advantage of his policy was very clearly demonstrated.

Exeter at this epoch was a free and prosperous city, which owned but a nominal allegiance to the kings of Wessex. The Britons were in revolt, and the Danish leaders therefore saw in such a conjunction of circumstances an irresistible inducement to attack Ælfred where he was necessarily weakest. They embarked their foot on board their fleet, which steered for the Exe, while their cavalry marched by land, and in due time took possession of Exeter. Thither they were closely pursued by Ælfred, who shut them up in the city, and proceeded to invest it. His fleet at the same time followed up the Danish; but the latter had scarcely ventured to sea, before a storm drove them on the coast of Hampshire, where they lost half their ships; the others, shattered by the gale, recovered their course, but found themselves opposed, off the mouth of the Exe, by the Saxons, and, after a well-foughten fight, were entirely destroyed. Guthrun, the Danish leader, on learning this disaster, negotiated a truce with Ælfred, and retired into Mercia.

But the Danes were still masters of half the island; and new arrivals from northern Europe constantly augmented their numbers or repaired their losses. Spurning all the bonds of treaties, Guthrun, in January 878, again advanced into Wessex, and attacked the strong and prosperous city of Chippenham, in Wiltshire. The Saxons were celebrating the feast of Epiphany, and, taken by surprise, could offer no availing resistance. Planting his standard on its walls, Guthrun next broke like a thunderstorm into the very heart of the kingdom,[1]

[1] 'They rose from the earth like locusts (*operientesque terram quasi locustæ*),' says Henry of Huntingdon (v. 739).

marking his course with suffering and devastation. The English, weary of the protracted struggle, lost heart and pith; and as many as were able, flying to the sea-coast, took refuge in France, in Wales, or in the Isle of Wight.

Some of the Danish ships, commanded by Hubba or Adda, the brother of Hingwar and Halfdene, had, in this same year, ravaged the coast of Devonshire. It fell to their lot to awaken in the English some gleams of the grand old spirit which had borne them through so many years of adversity. Finding the castle of Kynwith, on the river Taw, surrounded by massive walls, and secure on all sides except the eastern, they refrained from an assault, but attempted to starve its garrison into surrender. The issue, says Asser,[1] was not what they expected; for the Christians, inspired by Heaven, and judging death or victory better than the cruel agonies of famine, sallied forth in the early dawn against the unready Norsemen, and cut them to pieces. Only a few stragglers reached their ships; a thousand Danes lay dead before the walls of Kynwith. A very large booty was captured, and a precious trophy,—the standard called 'the Raven,' which was made in one morning by the three daughters of Regnar Lodbrog for their brothers Hingwar and Hubba, and in whose centre the mystic bird fluttered its wings, as if alive, when victory was at hand, or drooped them in shame when defeat impended.

This solitary gleam of success, however, brightened but for a moment the deep darkness which hung over the land. The heart of the people was touched by the cold hand of fear, and they no longer came together at the summons of their king. It appears, says Pauli, not only from the general aspect of the affairs of the country, and the sudden surprise of all the West

---

[1] Asser, *Life of Alfred*, pp. 61, 62.

Saxon district, but also from the testimony of the chronicler Ethelward, that in this hour of national peril bitter strife prevailed among the inhabitants themselves. The discords originating in differences of race and descent broke out afresh: the Celts of the west remembered what oppression they had undergone at the hands of their former conquerors; and now that these were threatened with a similar fate, they showed no disposition to make common cause with them. On the contrary, their wishes were probably on the side of the Northmen, whom they unwisely taught themselves to regard as the avengers of their former wrongs.

While this rebellious spirit was at work among Ælfred's British subjects, his English or Teutonic population had grown weary of the prolonged and apparently hopeless resistance, and bowed their necks to the yoke of the Danish robbers. Mr. Sharon Turner attributes their defection to the harsh government of Ælfred, but on no satisfactory data; and the fact is more plausibly and rationally accounted for by supposing that Saxon England was suffering from the reaction which often ensues on a prolonged and unequal struggle; and that it was stricken by one of those accesses of despair which frequently befall both individuals and nations. It wanted rest, and even the rest of servitude and humiliation was preferable to none. Its resources were exhausted; the bones of its warriors lay upon a hundred fields; it could no longer send forth its youth, resolute and hopeful, to the banners of its king. The spell of despondency had enfeebled its limbs, and a pause was necessary that it might recover from the depression which weighed so heavily upon it.

Ælfred's position at this epoch was one of bitter trial. He was a king without subjects—a chief without warriors. He saw his kingdom ravaged by fierce invaders, and yet was utterly powerless to defend it. At such a moment he might almost have been forgiven had he abandoned his throne, and, like the Mercian king, retired to the sacred shades of Rome, to close his career in peace. But had he done so, the Christian faith in England must have perished.[1] The Northmen would have proselytized with fire and sword, and compelled all the land to bow down before the bloody altars of Thor and Woden. Even as it was, the religion of the Cross was rapidly dying out, and the old idol-worship once more lifted up its head.

How different had been the course of English history, if Ælfred had shrunk from further sacrifice, and withdrawn from the scene of strife! How different had been the course of English history, if the Northmen had at this epoch made good their hold upon the kingdom, and swept away the old English civilisation and literature, replacing them by their own rough and semi-barbarous polity! That a fairer fate befell our land is wholly due, under Providence, to the heroic patience of Ælfred, under circumstances which must assuredly have broken down a less resolute will.

But Ælfred lived, says one of his best biographers, and in him lived the firm conviction that Providence had chosen him to be the protector and champion of the doctrines of the Cross, and the shield and sword of the noble English race. It was only because he was inspired by this belief that he could conquer the desire he must have occasionally felt, of endeavouring to provide for his own safety, and for the safety of the few still bound to him by the ties of blood or fidelity. His sagacity, too, may have prompted in him a well-founded

[1] Dr. Pauli, *Life of Alfred the Great*, p. 98.

assurance that the fit of lethargy which had seized his people would soon pass away, and that in due time he would again be saluted as Ælfred the King, and implored to lead them against their heathen oppressors. But for the present, armed resistance was impossible, and it became necessary to select some place of retreat, where he might await in security the awakening of the nation.

He chose a remote and almost inaccessible spot in the wild and marshy districts of Somersetshire,—a few acres of sodden ground, overhung by alders, surrounded on one side by the river Parrett, on the other side by the river Thone, just above their point of confluence, and protected in the front by an extensive morass. This spot was and is still known, though the swamps have disappeared, and corn-fields ripen where waved the alder wood, as the Isle of Athelney.[1] He must have endured great hardships in this remote asylum. His supplies of food were scanty, and to renew them he and his small band of followers were compelled to make frequent forays among the Danish settlements. Meanwhile, neither Dane nor Englishman could conjecture what fate had befallen the English king, though the latter, as he groaned under the stranger's tyranny, and felt the old warlike spirit reviving in his heart, often breathed a wish that Ælfred might ere long return to lead his subjects in victorious battle.

A more romantic episode in a royal life can scarcely be found than this retirement of Ælfred's to the marshes of Athelney. And it is certainly no wonder that in after time the minstrels should have invested it with a poetical halo, and woven about it a glittering network of legend and tradition. One of the most popular tales connected with it has not im-

---

[1] 'Æthelinga-eig,' the prince's island.

probably a foundation in truth. It first occurs in the *Life of St. Neot*,[1] written towards the end of the tenth century; is next copied into the *Annals;* and has since been repeated in every biography of Ælfred.

One day it chanced that the king had taken shelter in the hut of a cowherd, who was acquainted with the fact of his concealment. The man, however, was abroad, and engaged in his daily labour; his wife, who was occupied in baking bread, knew not the real quality of her visitor. Supposing him, from his poor and worn habiliments, to be a serf, and one of her husband's companions, she bade him watch the cakes while she went out to see after the cattle. Intent upon the making of a bow and arrows, Ælfred forgot his important charge; and the good wife, on return, found the bread burned and spoiled. In great indignation she addressed the unconscious king:

> 'Hulloa, companion!
> Dost not see that the cakes here are burning? Why lazily sit, and not turn them?
> Ready enough wilt thou be to take thy share and devour it.'

To this volley of wrath Ælfred listened with great composure, replying never a word, and turning the cakes as he was bidden.

Our historians, says Palgrave, must have considered this obedience to be a great trial, for it holds a prominent position in all their narratives. We know that Ælfred was accustomed, when happier times arrived, to relate his adventures to Asser and other friends;[2] and it is not impossible that on some actual occurrence was founded the tradition we have here recorded.

---

[1] See *Life of St. Neot*, edited by Gorham.
[2] William of Malmesbury, ii. § 121. '*Solebat ipse postea*,' etc.

Florence of Worcester relates an anecdote in reference to the elevation of Denewulf to the bishopric of Winchester, which must not be omitted.

'This man,' he says, 'if we may trust the report, had in his early days been a swineherd, and knew nothing of the art of reading. When Ælfred lived in exile in the forests, he became acquainted with Denewulf, as he drove his swine to the oak woods to feed upon acorns. The man's natural talent interested the king, who took pains with his instruction, and afterwards promoted him to a high dignity.'

A marvellous legend, belonging to the same period of the king's life, is told by the biographer of St. Cuthbert.[1]

'The king was dwelling among the alder shades of Athelney in urgent need. His followers had gone to fish in a neighbouring stream, and he was sitting in his hut alone with his wife. He was endeavouring to seek consolation among his many sorrows, in reading the Book of Psalms, when a poor man appeared in the doorway, and asked for a piece of bread. A solitary loaf was all that remained for the king and his companions, but his heart could not deny the beggar's prayer, and he divided the loaf with him, and a scanty portion of wine that still remained in the pitcher. Then the guest suddenly disappeared; and, lo, the bread was unbroken, and the pitcher full of wine to the brim. Shortly afterwards the fishermen returned from the river, charged with a great booty. In the ensuing night St. Cuthbert appeared to him in a vision, and made known to him that the end of his sufferings was approaching. The king rose mightily refreshed at dawn, crossed over to the mainland in a boat, and blew his horn three times,—the

[1] *Hist. St. Cuthberti,* pp. 71, 72.

sound inspiring his friends with courage, and his enemies with terror. By noon five hundred warriors had gathered round him, and acquainting them with the divine promise, he led them to victory.'

A different version of this beautiful legend, which one is ill inclined to dismiss from the historic page, we owe to William of Malmesbury:—

St. Cuthbert appeared to the king in his sleep, and informed him that, he and his subjects having now expiated their sins, the king would shortly be restored to his throne, and the people to freedom. As a token that God had not forgotten him, his companions, who had gone abroad to fish, should return with nets well filled, though the water was at that time covered with a thick crust of ice. Ælfred awoke, and found that his wife had dreamed the same dream; and while both were wondering at the coincidence, the fishermen returned with a heavy burden, sufficient to have fed a large army.

Another story, evidently of poetic origin, is also to be found in the later chronicles.

Having collected a band of faithful followers in his fastness at Athelney, Ælfred disguised himself as a minstrel or gleeman, and repaired to the camp of the Danish king. There he was received with a rude welcome,—for the Norsemen were ever partial to minstrelsy,—and he wandered from tent to tent, singing his best ballads, and acquainting himself with the plans and condition of the heathen army. Then returning to Athelney, he assembled his warriors, led them by secret paths to the Danish camp, and falling suddenly upon it, gained a complete victory.

About Easter 878 Ælfred had completed a strong entrenchment in his forest-girt island, which served as a rallying point for all true English patriots. The land had already begun to throw off its incubus of lethargy and despair, and as soon as it became known that the king was alive and in safety, an army speedily gathered round him. At an opportune moment he unfurled his banner of the Golden Dragon, and strengthened the hopes and courage of his men by occasional excursions, which, from their suddenness, struck terror into the hearts of the Danes. New reinforcements constantly poured into the camp at Athelney, and a spirit of patriotic fervour was awakened, which Ælfred may well have deemed in itself an omen of assured success. At length, between the 5th and 12th of May, he determined on recommencing hostilities in the open field, and moved towards Egberts-stan (now Brixton Deverill), through the leafy shades of Selwood Forest.[1] Here he was joined by the men of Somersetshire, Wiltshire, and the southern counties, who greeted their new-found king with shouts of loyal welcome. 'They were joyful at his presence.'[2]

> 'Co est del hest de Selewode
> Ceolmer vint contre le e Chude,
> Od les barons de Sumersete,
> De Wilteschire e de Dorsete.
> De Hamteschire i vint Chilman,
> Ki les barons manda per ban.'[3]

And after a day spent in resting his men, and making the necessary preparations, he moved towards the Danes, who still

---

[1] Coit-mawr, or 'the great forest.'
[2] *Anglo-Saxon Chronicle*, A.D. 878.
[3] Gaimer, v. 3168. The chronicler, however, is confirmed by no other authority.

held their post at Chippenham. For one night he halted at Okely, in the morning resuming his march along the green line of the Wiltshire hills. At length he came in sight of the enemy at a place called Ethandune, the modern Edington, near Westbury.

CHAPTER II.

Battle of Ethandune—Treaty with the Danes—The Danelagh—Consequences of the Peace of Wedmore.

THE great battle of Ethandune, which it is not too much to say rescued England from the supremacy of the pagan creed of the Northmen, is described by Asser in few but emphatic words:

'There Ælfred fought in a dense phalanx against all the army of the pagans, whom, with the divine help, he defeated with great slaughter, and pursued them flying to their fortifications.'[1]

From other sources we learn that the fight began with a discharge of arrows. The Northmen then, according to their customary tactics, swept down upon Ælfred's army in a succession of furious charges; but the English stood locked together in serried ranks, which would not yield to the onset, but which, when the foe had spent himself with his Berserkir fury, turned upon his straggling and disordered army, and slaughtered without mercy. The fugitives were pursued to the very gates of Chippenham, and all who were taken captives put to the edge of the sword.

Encouraged by this great victory, Ælfred laid siege to the Danish fortress, which, after a blockade of fourteen days, was

[1] Asser, *Life of Alfred*, p. 62.

starved into surrender. The fulness of the king's success is shown by the terms which for the first time he exacted,—that he should receive from the Danes as many hostages as he chose, while he should give them none. He also made them swear to keep the peace and quit the kingdom. Their leader, Guthorm or Guthrun, the most powerful Viking who had yet appeared in England, undertook to embrace Christianity. There is no reason to suppose, says Pauli,[1] that Ælfred had made this step one of the conditions of the treaty; its first idea, even though insincere, and impeded only by present necessity, seems to have arisen in the mind of the heathen. We confess that this idea seems to us improbable; and it is our belief that one of the stipulations imposed by the conqueror was the acceptance by Guthorm and his captains of the Christian faith.

At all events, peace was concluded, and the Danes departed northwards. And about three weeks later, as the Saxon chronicler tells us, Guthorm, and thirty of his noblest warriors, repaired to Ælfred's camp at Aller, and were solemnly baptized; the English king standing sponsor for his former enemy, who assumed the name of Æthelstane. The Danes tarried twelve days with their conquerors, and on the eighth the ceremony of the chrism-loosing—that is, of the removal of the chrismal or fillet of white linen bound round the head at baptism—was performed at Wædmor or Wedmore, where the full conditions of pacification were afterwards ratified by the Witenagemót, or Parliament of the West Saxon kingdom.[2]

---

[1] Dr. Pauli, *Life of Alfred the Great*, pp. 108, 109.

[2] Kemble, *Saxons in England*, vol. ii. c. 6, p. 251; *Saxon Chronicle*, A.D. 878.

The nature and consequences of the Treaty of Wedmore[1] have been very concisely stated by Mr. Freeman.

The Northmen agreed to evacuate Wessex and that part of Mercia lying south-west of the Watling Street, thus placing Ælfred in possession of the important city of London. The country beyond Watling Street they held as vassals of the West Saxon king.

In this wise, a large portion of England was formally colonized by Danish inhabitants, who gave their name to their conquest; and the country was thenceforth divided into Wessex, Mercia, and *Danelagh*,—that is, the Dane-law.

This Danish occupation, says Freeman,[2] was a real settlement of a new people in the land. There is no reason to think that any extirpation or expulsion of the native inhabitants took place, such as that which accompanied the English conquest. But the displacement of landowners and the general break-up of society must have been far greater than anything that was afterwards effected by the Normans. How extensive the Danish occupation was, is best seen in the local nomenclature. The West Saxon counties retain to this day the names and the boundaries of the principalities founded by the first successors of Cerdic. In some of them there is no one dominant town in a shire: several shires contain a town bearing a cognate name,[3] but in one case only is the shire called directly and solely after a town. That shire is the first seat of the conquest,—the shire which contained the capital. No doubt it originally bore no name but that of *West Seaxnance;* when it became needful to distinguish it

---

[1] The treaty is given in Thorpe's *Saxon Laws and Institutes*, p. 152.
[2] Freeman, *History of the Norman Conquest*, pp. 47-50.
[3] As Somersetshire and Dorsetshire in Somerton and Dorchester.

from the other West Saxon principalities, it received the name of *Hamptonshire*. In short, the local divisions of Wessex were not made, but grew. Mercia, on the other hand, has every appearance of having been artificially mapped out. The shires, with two exceptions,[1] are called after towns, and in most cases the county groups itself round its capital, as round an acknowledged and convenient centre. The names of the old principalities vanish, and their boundaries are often disregarded. One principality (the Hwiccas) is divided among several shires, and another shire (Lincolnshire) is made up of several ancient principalities. We can hardly doubt that the old divisions were wiped out in the Danish invasions, and that the country was divided again, either by the Danish conquerors, or, more probably, by the English kings after the re-conquest.

Again, says Mr. Freeman, the names of the towns and villages throughout a large part of the ceded territory show the systematic way in which the land was divided among the Danish leaders. Through a large region, stretching from Warwickshire to Cumberland, but most conspicuously in Yorkshire, Lincolnshire, and Leicestershire, the Danish termination *by* marks the settlements of the invaders, and in a vast number of cases the name of the manor still retains the name of the Danish lord to whom it was assigned in the occupation of the ninth century. Names like Carlby, Haconby, Kettilby, Thorkillby, tell their own story. In two cases, at least, the Danes gave new names to considerable towns. Streoneshulh and Northweorthig exchanged their names for the new ones of Whitby and Derby (Deornby).

[1] Shropshire and Rutland. The latter did not become a shire until after the compilation of the Domesday Roll.

This last town is one of considerable importance in the history of the Danish settlement. It formed, along with Lincoln, Leicester, Nottingham, and Stamford, a member of a sort of confederation of Danish towns, which, under the name of the Five Boroughs, often plays a part in the events of the tenth and eleventh centuries.

A peace which gave a large portion of England to a foreign prince, seems, at the first glance, a singular result to be attained by a great victory, and by no means a subject for much congratulation. Yet, if calmly examined, the Treaty of Wedmore will be found to have gained for Ælfred no inconsiderable advantages. Had the King of the West Saxons been king of all England, there can be no doubt that such a peace would have been the foulest dishonour; but Ælfred was simply a ruler over a portion of the realm, and his hold over that portion so precarious, that for months he had been a fugitive in the marshes of Somersetshire. It is true that the victory of Ethandune seems to have been so complete as to have justified Ælfred in compelling the Danes to withdraw altogether from England. But as they had entire command of the sea, he could not have prevented them from returning in the following year with increased numbers, and a ferocity inflamed by the pang of recent defeat. As it was, by peaceably settling them in the land, they afforded him a security against fresh invasions for at least a number of years.

But a more direct advantage was attained. Mercia had long been separated from Wessex; a considerable portion of it was now reunited, and the supremacy of the King of the West Saxons was at the same time more firmly established over Kent and Sussex, which became provinces instead of dependent kingdoms. And the fact of the foreign occupation of the rest of England prepared the way for its easier incorporation, — as was afterwards the case in France and Normandy, — with the one independent and homogeneous kingdom governed by a native prince. The wars of Wessex with the Danes of Mercia and Northumbria were, as Mr. Freeman points out, wars of a very different character from the old border strife between the English inhabitants of the several kingdoms. In the strictest sense, they were *national* wars, — wars of religion and patriotism. The West Saxon kings were regarded by all Englishmen as the champions of the national independence, as the defenders of the national faith, just as the Prussian kings would be regarded by all Germans if the French held the north bank of the Rhine. They were not conquerors, but deliverers; the provinces they subdued, they rescued from the Danish yoke; and wherever their arms penetrated, the subject English population received them with open joy. Thus the successors of Ælfred were enabled, in the course of years, to win back the supremacy first established by Ecgbehrt, and to enlarge it into 'an actual sovereignty over all England, and an acknowledged supremacy over all Britain.' And if the compact realm thus founded was at last overcome by a Danish conqueror, it was overcome, says Freeman, by a very different process from the settlement of any wandering sea-rover. It was the transfer of 'the crown of a consolidated English kingdom to the head of the king of a no less consolidated kingdom of Denmark.'

It should also be remembered that England had been so depopulated by protracted wars, that but for this Danish colonization, a great portion of it must have been abandoned to the kite and the wild boar. And, further, that the peaceful settlement of the Danes rendered possible the spread of Christianity from the English Channel to the Forth.

Regarded from these points of view, the Treaty of Wedmore appears a signal proof of the political sagacity of Ælfred.

CHAPTER III.

Concluding Years of Ælfred's Reign—Formation of a Navy—Later Danish Invasions.

NORTHUMBRIA, though nominally included in the Dane-law, was a separate kingdom; and one of Ælfred's first acts, after peace had been restored, was to fill its then vacant throne. Several years before, Guthred, the son of Hardacnute, King of Lethra, had been kidnapped and sold into slavery by the sons of Regnar Lodbrog (the famous 'Hairy Breeches'). At the period of which we are now writing, he was serving as a thrall to an aged widow of Northumberland. His royal lineage, however, was not unknown; and on the death of King Halfdene, Eadred, Bishop of Lindisfarn—acting, as he said, under the direction of St. Cuthbert, who had appeared to him in a dream—brought him before the Northumbrians, and prevailed upon them to receive him as their king.

Conducting him with joyous shouts to Oswin's Dune, or the Hill of Oswin, they invested him with the golden bracelets, the insignia of royalty, and did homage to him. The appointment was approved by Ælfred, and Guthred acknowledged himself as his vassal. Like his fellow-countryman Guthrun, he remained faithful to his vow throughout his reign; and Ælfred ruled as lord paramount over all England south of the Tweed. Mercia was virtually under his direct control, though he placed over it, as Ealdorman, his son-in-law Æthelred. Wherever his power extended, it is certain, as Sir Francis Palgrave says, that he applied himself with all his heart and soul to secure the welfare of his subjects.

From internal convulsions his kingdom, during the remainder of his reign, was happily exempt; but it occasionally suffered from the inroads of the Northmen. These fierce and restless rovers still plotted the subjugation of Christendom, and sought to establish the worship of Odin over the whole of Europe. They were apparently ubiquitous, and always descended where they were least expected; and always, even if defeated, left ineffaceable marks of their presence. It was evident that no part of western Europe would be safe from their attacks so long as there were slaves to be captured or plunder to be secured, or until the western nations grew strong enough for the efficient defence of their own coasts.

In 879, soon after the Treaty of Wedmore, a large fleet of Danish vessels appeared in the Thames, with the view of joining Guthred against the English. But Guthred was now a Christian, and had learned enough of the new faith to shudder at the atrocities of the old. He refused to abet the schemes of his countrymen, and under their celebrated chief, the jarl Hâsten or Hastings, they retired into Flanders. In 885 they landed in Kent, marched to Rochester, and laid siege to its walls; but the citizens fought bravely, and Ælfred bringing up his army, they fled in hot haste to their ships, abandoning their horses and prisoners. They took refuge in Anglia, but were pursued, overtaken, and captured at the mouth of the Stour.

An interval of two years ensued, which Ælfred spent in

protecting the kingdom with castles and walled towns, and in fortifying the city of London.

In 893 Hastings and his men once more arrived off the mouth of the Thames and the Rother, their whole fleet numbering 330 vessels. Having captured a fortress which the English peasantry were building in the fens, the chief army marched to Appledore; while 80 vessels, under Hastings, sailed up the Thames, landed at Milton, near Sittingbourne, and commenced the construction of a large and formidable entrenchment. The Danish leader's distribution of his forces, as Sharon Turner observes, was eminently judicious. His two armies were but a mile apart, and could therefore act separately, or combine for any joint operation which might be considered desirable. They were secured from any attacks on the right by the vicinity of their countrymen in Essex; on the left they were protected by the sea. The rich meadows and corn-fields of Kent fell to them, therefore, without a blow; and Hastings secured an ample supply and a safe position, which his courage and policy might make the step to a throne (A.D. 893).

Ælfred's difficulties were increased by the death of Guthred, and the consequent defection of the Northumbrian Danes. But in the military constitution of his kingdom he found a more serious obstacle. The *fyrd*, or levée-en-masse—the national militia—could not be compelled to serve for a longer period than about forty days; while it was also needful to provide for the garrisons of the towns, and the cultivation of the country. He therefore divided his forces into divisions, one of which alternately served in the field, or remained at home. Then, endeavouring to secure the neutrality of the East Anglians by fresh oaths and hostages, he took up with his army an impregnable position between the two bodies of the sea-rovers.

In the course of the war, Ælfred's soldiers surprised a fortress at Benfleet, where Hastings had left his wife and children. The noble king sent back the youths and their mother to the sea-rover;[1] but his magnanimity met with no response from the Dane, who, pressing forward into Mercia, endeavoured to strike a blow at the very heart of the kingdom.

Followed in all haste by Æthelred and two other ealdormen, the Danes were surrounded in a disadvantageous position on the banks of the Severn, and were nearly compelled to capitulate by famine. With all the desperate courage of their race, however, they broke through the English army, suffering a terrible slaughter. Ubiquitous, and as incapable of being destroyed as the heads of Hydra, they once more came to a rally in Essex, and entrusting their wives, children, and plunder to the care of their kindred, the East Anglians, crossed the island by forced marches to Chester, whose noble Roman fortifications they proceeded to occupy. They made this city their headquarters, while detachments scoured the country in all directions, carrying off the kine from the stall, and the corn from the garner; and after loading themselves with booty, they recrossed the country as swiftly as before, and sheltered themselves during the winter in Essex and the southern shires. In all these movements they had been hotly followed by the royal army, and in various skirmishes had suffered severe loss; but such was their celerity, that Ælfred could never bring them to stand the hazard of a pitched battle. As soon as his standard appeared in the distance, they mounted their steeds and rode away. Their ravages in the open country were terrible, but they never

---

[1] He sent them back, after baptizing them, with the message, 'that he released them, because he did not make war on women or children.'

succeeded in capturing a walled town, nor did they ever venture within the borders of Ælfred's territory of Wessex.

Early in 896 the restless pirates ventured up the river Lea, which was then deeper than it now is, and at Ware or Hertford, about twenty miles from London, built an entrenched camp. In the summer it was attacked by the citizens, but they were driven back after a desperate contest. This success encouraged the Danes to draw nearer to the great English city, so that, to protect the burghers while they gathered in their harvest, Ælfred surrounded it with his forces. He afterwards proceeded, at no small personal danger, to reconnoitre the Danish position. He found it defended by the Danish fleet, and unassailable, unless the fleet retired or could be rendered useless. For this purpose he raised a fortress on either bank of the river below the Danish camp, and digging three new channels from the Lea to the Thames, so reduced the level of the former that the Danish vessels lay aground. Hastings, on discovering the result of Ælfred's stratagem, quickly abandoned his fleet; and escaping from their camp by night, the Danes dashed across the country, with a speed which outstripped their swiftest pursuers, to Quatbridge (now Quatford), on the Severn. There they entrenched themselves for the winter. The Danish fleet, meanwhile, was seized by the Londoners, who carried down to the city such of the ships as could be got afloat, and burned the others.

Three years had passed away since Hastings landed in England; and what had he effected? He had displayed both courage and military skill, and unequalled tenacity; but the English king was 'like a towering rock, which, unharmed itself, broke and scattered around it the most furious waves that assaulted it.' Foiled in his hopes of conquest, and worn out by the perseverance of his great opponent, the Danish leader quitted England in 897, crossed the Channel, and sailed up the Seine. He troubled the peace of Ælfred no more.

In the same year the Northumbrian pirates, with a fleet of six ships, entered the Solent,—the bright and beautiful strait that separates the garden island of Wight from the green coast of Hampshire. Ælfred despatched nine ships against them. They found the Danes lying near the shore, three stranded on the beach, while their crews were engaged in plunder. The others engaged Ælfred's squadron with their usual desperate ferocity; but two were captured, and the third escaped with only five men. No sooner was this battle over than the crews of the stranded ships returned from their inland foray, and the ebb of the tide left the English vessels aground, with three of them close to the enemy, the others at some distance off. Crossing the sands on foot, the Danes made a fierce attack on the nearest ships, but were beaten off with a loss of one hundred and twenty men. The Danes then contrived to float their galleys, and, with characteristic celerity, to put to sea before the Englishmen. One vessel got clear off, her consorts were wrecked on the Suffolk coast, and by the king's orders their crews were executed as pirates. The same punishment was inflicted on the crews of twenty other Danish vessels, which were captured during the summer.

Some of our historians have been pleased to censure this severity, as at variance with Ælfred's usual humanity. One writer asserts that it was unjustifiable, because the Danes do not seem to have violated 'the law of nations,' as then understood. Another, however, writes in the king's defence, and points out that he always, and very rightly, drew a broad line of demarcation between pirates and warriors. A recent authority more justly observes that it would have been very difficult to draw such a line when all were robbers and pirates alike, and that Ælfred's true principle of action seems to have been—to distinguish between such Danes as attacked him from abroad, and such as attacked him from the Danelagh at home. He could put forward no claim to the allegiance or gratitude of the former; but the men of Northumbria, Norfolk, and Suffolk had, through their chiefs and princes, sworn fealty to him, had received his benefits, and were bound to protect the territories which they harried with fire and sword. From the position they occupied, they could always disturb the tranquillity of the realm; and he may therefore have come to the conclusion that their bad faith deserved to be punished by measures of exceptional rigour.

Thus ended Ælfred's second great struggle with his persistent enemy; and its successful conclusion left him virtual ruler of all the English land. It was followed by a terrible pestilence, engendered by the filthy habits of the Danes, which sacrificed a greater number of lives than the war had done, and among its victims carried off many of the most powerful lords. Otherwise, the remainder of the great king's reign was spent in tranquillity; and Ælfred showed himself as wise in the council as he had been resolute in the field.

Mr. Pearson observes, that it confounds all ordinary notions to know that the desolating wars of so many years had rather affected the civilisation than the wealth of the kingdom. Asser—the native, it is true, of a poor country, Wales—assigns the great riches of the people as a reason why the monastic profession had declined in honour among the Saxons. Still more wonderful is it to hear of Ælfred, with the limited revenue of a Saxon king, initiating and often completing great public works; restoring London, which had been burned down, with a splendour which excited the wonder of his contemporaries; erecting palaces of stone, and enriching their halls with abundant decorations. He despatched costly gifts to Rome, and even, it is said, to the shrine of St. Thomas in India. He treated his friends with equal munificence; Asser, for example, receiving not only two monasteries, but a costly silken pallium, and a porter's load of incense. Of these facts Mr. Pearson offers the following explanation,— that wealth, up to a certain point, was a fixed quantity in the State; consisting not as now of factories, farms, and businesses, which a few years' neglect would ruin, but of plate, and jewels, and wrought fabrics, which a conquest only transferred from one man to another. It may be, too, that the rent of the king's tenants was frequently paid in labour, and that to employ this would be a matter, not of expense, but economy.[1]

The close of Ælfred's reign does not seem to have been marked by any notable events. The great king was occupied in works of peace, less ostentatious, and, to the vulgar mind, less attractive than those of war, but infinitely more glorious and permanent in their consequences. He laboured to establish justice and equity among his subjects, and to ensure a due and orderly administration of the law. During years of strife and hostility a spirit of insubordination had risen among the people, and peace, justice, and religion were regarded with contempt. To arrest these evils Ælfred made no new statutes, but he codified those already in existence upon certain immutable principles. His code has been described as consisting of three parts. The first is an abstract of the Hebrew law,

[1] Pearson, *Early History of England*, pp. 115, 116.

indicating the divine foundations of society, and combining the secular view of offences as injurious to individuals or the State, with the Christian view of them as sins against God. We are told, therefore, that the conception of the State as an ideal commonwealth, which looked upon man's right living as its first object,—a conception afterwards enlarged, and to some extent realized by Cromwell and the Puritans,—is due to Ælfred; and the standard he indicates is one so high that he can hardly have hoped to attain it,—the gradual extinction of slavery, the duty of hospitality, and the Christian law of love.

The second division of his code contained the chief statutes of the kingdom as sanctioned by the Witenagemót. The king was for the first time regarded as the sacred head of the State, and treason punished with death. Loyalty to the great thegns was made equally an essential; and the 'frank-pledge' system, by which every man was bound to give some surety for his good conduct, received a universal extension. The right of feud was limited, and the power of the judicial courts extended.

Thirdly, the ancient laws of Wessex were embodied in the code, with the object, perhaps, of explaining the customs of that province.

The division of England into shires and counties has been long ascribed to Ælfred, but without any foundation; it undoubtedly existed prior to his time. It is equally certain that he did not introduce 'trial by jury,' which cannot be traced farther back than to the thirteenth century. In truth, Ælfred was no innovator, and the troubled time in which he lived was not favourable to innovations. He wisely considered it safer and more prudent to amend the defective laws of his predecessors, than to hazard, by sudden changes, the destruction of the basis of all law,—reverence for established authority.

It is from this point of view the great legislator has been regarded by a modern poet (Lord Houghton):

> 'There rose from out a most discordant age,
> A mind attuned to that slow harmony
> With which the Former of Humanity
> Unfolds His book of will, from page to page.
> War with that generous passion he did wage
> Which was the soul of Christian chivalry;
> But *governing*, his wise humility
> Against high Heaven threw down no venturous gage.
> He knew how steadily moves the spirit of law,
> Even as the dial-shade,—that men with awe
> May recognise the one lawgiving hand;
> And thus the ruler, whom his own proud will
> Urges unbridled, be it for good or ill,
> Brings on himself like shame, and misery on the land.'

That Ælfred was what we have described him,—a *codifier* rather than a *legislator*,—we know from his own words:—' I then, Ælfred the King,' he says,[1] 'these laws together gathered, and had many of them written which our fore-gangers held, those that one liked. And many of them that one not liked I threw aside, with my Wise Men's thought [with the consent of his council], and on other wise bade to hold them. Forwhy I durst not risk of my own much in writ to set, formerly to me unknown was what of them would like those that after us were. But that which I writ, either in Ine my kinsman's days, or in Offa's the King of the Mercians, or in Æthelbehrt's, that erst of English kin baptism underwent, those that to me rightest seemed, those have I herein gathered, and the others passed by. I then, Ælfred, King of the West Saxons, to all my Wise Men these showed, and they then quoth that to them it seemed good all to hold.'

[1] Thorpe's *Laws and Institutes*, i. 58 (Ælfred's Dooms).

The exertions he made to secure a righteous administration of the laws were of the noblest kind. He sat daily to hear the appeals of all classes of his subjects. He reviewed the decisions of his judges, and abrogated them when contrary to equity. If the judge had erred through ignorance, he was suspended until by study he had fitted himself for his office; if through corrupt notions, he was punished with inexorable severity. The ancient author of the *Miroir des Lois* asserts that Ælfred condemned forty-four unjust judges to be hung in one year as murderers. The crimes of several of these offenders are enumerated: one suffered because he had condemned to death a man who was insane; another, for executing a person who had proved his innocence; a third, for inflicting capital punishment on a father for the flight of his son; a fourth, for executing a person under the age of one-and-twenty; a fifth, for condemning a man who was not the party accused; a sixth, for hanging one who had escaped from prison. In reference to Ælfred's punishment of these unjust judges, Mr. Sharon Turner wisely remarks, that human life was the object which they were intended to secure. And surely, he exclaims, to teach judges to discriminate well in their adjudications; to be careful of the life of the accused, and to judge by law, not by arbitrary will or passion, or ignorant caprice; to confine each officer entrusted with power of life and death to his own district, and to give all striking examples, that they are responsible for the just execution of their legal duties,—is at all times a most wise and salutary occupation. In those days of virtue, the security of the subject could not have been maintained without it. The fruits have been, an administration of justice from the time of Ælfred to our own, which, notwithstanding occasional imperfections

"He sat daily to hear the appeals of all classes of his subjects."—LIVES OF OLD ENGLISH WORTHIES, *Page* 50.

where the lessons of Ælfred were forgotten, can be paralleled in no other country for equity, discernment, learning, and integrity.

The success of the king's salutary measures, and of the system of police which he established, is shown by the exaggerated language of the old chronicler. He tells us that, to test the honesty of his subjects, Ælfred caused jewels and golden bracelets to be suspended in the highways, and no one ventured to take them down; a maiden might travel from one end of the kingdom to the other without injury or insult; and if a purse of money were dropped in the road, it would lie for months until recovered by its true owner.

CHAPTER IV.

Asser's Character of Ælfred—His Love of Learning—His Architectural Works—His Piety—His Economy of Time—His Impartiality—His Death.

FOR a very full and detailed view of Ælfred's public and private character, we are indebted to Asser, his friend and biographer; and before we conclude our summary of his remarkable achievements, it seems desirable that the old monk's elaborate statement should be placed before the reader.[1] We begin with his account of Ælfred's marriage and married life:[2]—

His nuptials were celebrated in Mercia with much splendour, among countless multitudes of people of both sexes. But, after continual feasts, both by night and day, he was suddenly seized with an overwhelming pain, whose causes none of his physicians could determine; and, what is worst of all, it has been protracted from the twentieth to the fortieth year of his life.[3] Many thought it arose in the favour and fascination of the people who surrounded him; others, in

---

[1] Asser was Bishop of Sherborne or Exeter in Ælfred's reign. The authenticity of his *Vita Ælfredi* has been vindicated by Dr. Lingard.

[2] In our translation we chiefly follow Dr. Giles.

[3] It seems to have been a kind of chronic gastritis.

some enmity of the devil, who is always jealous of the good; and others, in an unusual kind of fever. He had this sort of disease from his childhood; but once, Divine Providence so willed it, that when he was in Cornwall for the sake of enjoying the chase, and had turned aside to pray in a certain chapel where rests the body of St. Guerir, and now also that of St. Neot,—for King Ælfred was always, from his infancy, a frequent visitor of holy places for the sake of prayer and almsgiving,—he prostrated himself in prayer, and entreated of God's mercy, that, in His boundless clemency, He would exchange the torments of the malady which then afflicted him for some other less severe disease; but with this condition, that the disease should not show itself externally in his body, lest he should become an object of contempt, and less able to benefit mankind; for he greatly dreaded leprosy, blindness, or any similar complaint, which renders men useless when it afflicts them.

After he had finished his devotions, he proceeded on his journey; and in a brief time he felt within him that the Almighty had heard his prayers, and relieved him of his disorder, and that it was entirely eradicated—though it had first befallen him in the flower of his youth—by his devout and pious prayers and supplications to Almighty God. Sad to say, however, it was replaced at his marriage by another, which incessantly tormented him, night and day, from the twentieth to the forty-fourth year of his life. And if ever he was relieved, by God's mercy, from this infirmity for a single day or night, yet the dread of it never left him, but rendered him almost useless, as he thought, for every duty, whether human or divine.

The sons and daughters whom he had by his wife above-mentioned were, Æthelfreda, the eldest; after whom came Eadward; then Æthelgifa, then Æthelswitha, and Æthelwred; besides some who died in their infancy, one of whom was named Eadmund. Æthelfreda, when she arrived at a marriageable age, was united to Æthered, Earl of Mercia; Æthelgifa also was dedicated to God, and submitted to the rules of a monastic life. Æthelwred, the youngest, by the divine counsel and admirable prudence of the king, was consigned to the schools of learning, where, with the children of almost all the nobility of the country, and many also who were not noble, he prospered under the anxious care of his teachers. Books in both languages, Saxon and Latin, were read in the schools. The pupils also learned to write; so that before they were of an age to practise manly arts,— namely, hunting and such pursuits as befit noblemen,—they became studious and well-informed in the liberal sciences. Eadmund and Æthelswitha were bred up in the royal court, and received great attention from their attendants and nurses; nay, they continue there to this day, with the love of all about them, and displaying affability and gentleness towards all, both natives and foreigners, and in complete subjection to their father: nor among their other studies which appertain to this life, and are meet for noble youths, are they suffered to pass their time idly and unprofitably without acquiring the liberal arts; for they have carefully learned the Psalms, and various Saxon works, especially the Saxon poems, and are continually in the habit of making use of books.

Meanwhile, the king, during the frequent wars and other trammels of this present life, such as the invasions of the heathen, and his bodily infirmities, duly administered his government, besides pursuing the chase in all its branches. He also instructed his workers in gold, and artificers of all kinds, his falconers, his hawkers, and dog-keepers; built houses, majestic and admirable, beyond all the precedents of his ancestors, by his new mechanical inventions; ordered his learned men to recite the Saxon books, and especially to learn by heart the Saxon poems, and to make others learn them; and he alone never desisted from studying with all his energy. He attended mass and the other daily services of religion; and was frequent in prayer and psalm-singing, at the hours both of the day and the night. He also repaired to the churches, as we have already said, in the night-time, to pray in secret, and without the knowledge of his courtiers; he bestowed alms and largesses on both natives and foreigners of all countries; to all he was gracious and affable, and curiously eager to investigate things unknown.

Many Franks, Persians, Gauls, Danes, Britons, Scots, and Armoricans, noble and ignoble, voluntarily submitted to his rule; and all of them, according to their race and deserts, were ruled, loved, honoured, and enriched with money and power.

Moreover, the king was wont to hear the Holy Scriptures read by his own countrymen, or, if by any chance it so happened, in company with foreigners, and he attended to the recital with eager solicitude. His bishops, too, and all ecclesiastics, his earls and nobles, ministers and friends, were loved by him with wonderful affection; and their sons, who were bred up in the royal household, were no less dear to him than his own. He caused them to be instructed in all kinds of good morals, and, among other things, never ceased to teach them letters night and day; but as if he had no consolation in all these things, and suffered no other annoyance either from within or without, yet was he harassed by such daily and nightly sorrow, that he complained to God, and to all who were admitted to his familiar love, that Almighty God had made him ignorant of the divine wisdom and of the liberal arts. In this he emulated the pious, the wise, and the wealthy Solomon, King of the Jews, who at first, despising all present glory and riches, asked wisdom of God, and received both wisdom and worldly glory; as it is written, 'Seek first the kingdom of God and His righteousness, and all these things shall be added unto you.'

But God, who is ever the Searcher of the inner thoughts, the Inspirer of all good intentions, and the most plentiful Helper in the formation of noble desires,—for to these He would not incite any man, unless He also amply supplied that which the man justly and properly desires to have,—stimulated the king's mind; as it is written, 'I will hearken what the Lord God will say concerning me.' So that Ælfred availed himself of every opportunity to procure coadjutors in his good designs, and to aid him in his aspirations after wisdom, that he might attain to what he aimed at; and like a wary bird which, rising in the early summer morning from her beloved nest, wings her rapid flight through the trackless plains of ether, to descend on the manifold and varied blossoms of grass, herbs, and shrubs, essaying that which pleases most, for the purpose of bearing it to her home,—even so did the king direct his gaze afar, and seek without that knowledge which he had not within, namely in his own kingdom.

Now God, at that time, as some satisfaction to the king's benevolence, yielded to his petition, and sent certain lights to illuminate him; namely, Werefrith, Bishop of Worcester, a man well-versed in Scripture, who, by the royal command, first turned the books of the *Dialogues of Pope Gregory and Peter his Disciple* from Latin into Saxon, and, while keeping closely to the sense, interpreting them with clearness and elegance. Next to him was Plegmund, a Mercian by birth, Archbishop of Canterbury, a venerable man, and endowed with great wisdom; then came Æthelstane and Werewulf, also Mercians by birth, the royal priests and chaplains, and very learned. These four had been invited from Mercia by King Ælfred, who raised them to much honour and power in the kingdom of the West Saxons, besides the privileges which Archbishop Plegmund and Bishop Werefrith enjoyed in Mercia. Through their wise teaching the king's desires incessantly increased, and were gratified. Night and day, whenever he had leisure, he commanded such men as these to read books to him, for he never suffered himself to be without the company of one of them; wherefore he possessed a knowledge of every book, though of himself he could not yet understand anything of books, for he had not learned to read.

But the king's praiseworthy thirst after knowledge could not be satiated even by this arrangement; wherefore he sent messengers beyond the sea to Gaul in search of teachers, and he invited from thence Gumbold, a venerable priest and excellent singer, most learned in Holy Scripture. He also obtained from thence a priest and monk named John, of most energetic talents, erudite in all kinds of science, and skilled in many arts. By the instruction of these men the king's mind was greatly enlarged, and he enriched and favoured them with great influence.

[Asser then proceeds to narrate the occasion of his own first introduction to the king at 'a vill' called Dene (perhaps East Dene, near Chichester), and the distinction with which he was honoured. Ælfred, he says, gave him the bishopric of Exeter, with all the diocese which belonged to him in Saxony (Wessex), and in Cornwall, besides innumerable presents daily in every kind of worldly wealth, which he fears to recount, lest it should weary the reader. He continues :—]

On a certain day we were both of us sitting in the king's chamber, conversing on all kinds of subjects, as usual, and it happened that I read to him a quotation out of a certain book. He heard it with extreme attentiveness, and addressed me with a thoughtful mind, showing me at the same time a book which he carried in his bosom, wherein the daily services, and psalms, and prayers which he had read in the course of his youth, were written, and he commanded me to inscribe my quotation in the same volume. When I heard this, and comprehended his ingenuousness of disposition, and his devout desire of studying the words of divine wisdom, I gave, though in secret, unbounded thanks to Almighty God, who had implanted so great a love of knowledge in the king's heart. But I could find no empty space in the volume in which to write the quotation, it was so full of various matters; wherefore I made a little pause, to the end that I might stir up the bright intellect of the king to a higher acquaintance with the divine testimonies.

On his urging me to lose no time, but write it with all speed, I said, 'Are you willing that I should inscribe the quotation on some separate leaf? for it is possible we may meet with similar extracts which will please you; and in that case, you will be glad that we have kept them apart.'

'Your plan is excellent,' he replied; and I then made haste to prepare a clean sheet, and at the top of it I wrote what he bade me; and on that same day I wrote therein, as I had anticipated, no less than three other quotations which gratified him; and from that time we conversed together daily, and found out other extracts which interested him, so that the sheet became full, and deservedly so; according as it is written, 'The just man builds upon a moderate foundation, and gradually ascends to higher things.' Thus, like a most productive bee, he flew hither and thither, asking questions as he went, until he had eagerly and unceasingly collected the honey of many various flowers of Holy Scripture, with which he thickly stored the cells of his mind.

Now, when the first quotation was copied, he was eager at once to read, and to interpret in Saxon, and afterwards to teach others; even as we read of that happy thief who recognised his Lord—ay, the Lord of all men—as He hung upon the blessed cross, and, saluting Him with his bodily eyes only, because his hands were pierced with nails, exclaimed, 'Lord, remember me when Thou comest into Thy kingdom!'

It was only towards the end of his life that Ælfred began to learn the rudiments of the Christian faith. Inspired by God, he commenced the study of the Scriptures on the sacred festival of St. Martin (November 11th); and continued to learn the flowers collected by certain masters, and to reduce them into a single volume, nearly as large as the *Psalter*, which he called his *Enchiridion* or *Manual*, because he carefully kept it at hand both day and night, and derived, as he told me, no small consolation from it.

But, as a certain wise man has sagaciously written—

> 'Of vigilant minds are they whose pious care
> It is to govern well;'

and I must be watchful, inasmuch as I just now drew a kind of comparison, which was yet a contrast, between the happy thief and the king; for the cross is hateful to every one, wherever suffering exists. But what can one do if one cannot escape from it? Or by what art can he remain suspended, and improve his condition? Whether he will or no, he must endure his punishment as best he can.

Now Ælfred was pierced with many nails of tribulation, though seated on a royal throne; for from his twentieth year to the present, which is his fortieth (A.D. 888), he has suffered constantly with most severe attacks of an unknown disease, so that he has not a moment's ease either from the pain which it causes, or from the gloom which is cast over him by his dread of its immediate return. Moreover, the constant invasions of foreign nations, by which he was continuously harassed by land and sea, without any interval of peace, were a just cause of disquiet. What shall I say of his repeated expeditions against the pagans, his wars, and incessant cares of government?—of the daily embassies sent to him by foreign nations, from the Tyrrhenian Sea to the farthest end of Iberia?—for we have seen and read letters, accompanied with presents, which were sent to him by Abel, the patriarch of Jerusalem. What shall I say of the cities and towns which he restored, and of others which he built, where none had previously been? —of the royal halls and chambers, wonderfully erected by his command, of timber and stone?—of the royal vills constructed of stone, removed from their ancient site, and handsomely rebuilt by the royal command in more suitable places?

Besides the affliction above-mentioned, he was disturbed by the quarrels of his friends, who would voluntarily endure little or no toil, though it was for the common necessity of the kingdom; but he alone, supported by the divine help, strove, like a skilful pilot, to steer his richly-laden argosy into the safe and much desired harbour of his country, though nearly all his crew were aweary, and yet he suffered them not to faint or hesitate, though sailing amid the manifold waves and eddies of this present life.

For all his bishops, earls, nobles, favourite ministers, and prefects, who, next to God and the king, had the whole government of the kingdom, as was fitting, continually received from him instruction, respect, exhortation, and command. Nay, at last, when they were disobedient, and his long patience was exhausted, he would reprove them severely, and censure at pleasure their vulgar folly and obstinacy; and in this way he directed their attention to the common interests of the kingdom. But, owing to the sluggishness of the people, these admonitions of the king were either not fulfilled, or were not carried out until the hour of need, and so did not end so much as they should have done to the advantage of those who put them into execution; for I will say nothing of the castles which he ordered to be built, but which, being begun late, were never completed, because the enemy broke in upon them by land and sea, and, as frequently happened, they who had thwarted the royal ordinances repented when it was too late, and blushed at their non-fulfilment of his commands. I speak of repentance when it is too late on the testimony of Scripture, whereby numberless persons have had cause for too much sorrow when many insidious evils have been wrought. But though by these means, sad to say, they may be bitterly afflicted, and roused to sorrow by the loss of fathers, wives, children, ministers, servant-men, servant-maids, and furniture and household stuff, what is the use of hateful repentance when their kinsmen are dead, and they cannot aid them, or redeem those who are captive from captivity? for they are unable even to assist those who have escaped, as they have not wherewithal to sustain even their own lives. They repented, therefore, when it was too late, and grieved at their foolish neglect of the royal commands, and they praised the king's wisdom with one voice, and sought to accomplish what they had before despised, namely, the erection of castles, and the execution of other things generally useful to the whole kingdom.

Of his fixed purpose of holy meditation, which in the midst of prosperity and adversity he never neglected, I cannot now with advantage omit to speak. For, whereas he often thought of the necessities of his soul, among the other good deeds to which his thoughts were night and day directed, he ordered that two monasteries should be built, one for monks at Athelney, which is a place surrounded by impassable marshes and rivers, where no one can enter but by boats, or by a bridge laboriously constructed between two other heights; at the western end of which bridge was erected a strong tower, of beautiful work, by command of the aforesaid king; and in this monastery he collected monks of all kinds, from every quarter, and placed them therein.

Another monastery, also, was built by the same king as a residence for nuns, near the eastern gate of Shaftesbury; and his own daughter, Æthelgifa, was placed in it as abbess. With her many other noble ladies, bound by the rules of the monastic life, dwell in that monastery. These two edifices were enriched by the king with much land, as well as personal property.

These things being thus disposed of, the king began, as was his practice, to consider within himself what more he could do to augment and show forth his piety. What he had begun wisely, and thoughtfully conceived for the public benefit, was adhered to with equally beneficial result, for he had heard it out of the book of the law, that the Lord had promised to restore to him tenfold; and he knew that the Lord had kept His promise, and had actually restored to him tenfold. Encouraged by this example, and wishing to exceed the practices of his predecessors, he vowed humbly and faithfully to devote to God half of his services, both day and night, and also half of all his wealth, such as lawfully and justly came into his possession; and this vow, as far as human discretion can perceive and keep, he skilfully and wisely endeavoured to fulfil. But that he might, with his usual caution, avoid that which Scripture warns us against,—'If you offer aright, but do not divide aright, you sin,'—he considered how he might divide aright that which he had vowed to God; and as Solomon had said, 'the heart of the king is in the hand of God,' that is, his counsel, he ordered with wise policy, which could come only from above, that his officers should first divide into two parts the revenues of every year.

This division made, he assigned the first part to worldly uses, and ordered that one-third of it should be paid to his soldiers, and also to his ministers, the nobles who dwelt at court, where they discharged divers duties; for so the king's family was arranged at all times into three classes. The king's attendants were most wisely distributed into three companies, so that the first company should be on duty at the court for one month, night and day, at the end of which they returned to their homes, and were relieved by the second company. At the end of the second month, in the same way, the third company relieved the second, who returned to their homes, where they spent two months, until their services were again wanted. The third company also gave place to the first in the same way, and also spent two months at home. Thus was the threefold division of the companies arranged at all times in the royal household.

To these, therefore, was paid the first of the three portions aforesaid,—to each according to their respective dignities and peculiar services; the second to the operatives, whom he had collected from every nation, and had about him large numbers of men skilled in every kind of construction; the third portion was assigned to foreigners, who resorted to him from every nation far and near; and whether they asked money of him or not, he cheerfully gave to each with wonderful munificence according to their respective merits, according to what is written, 'God loveth a cheerful giver.'

But the second part of all his revenues, which came yearly into his possession, and was included in the receipts of the exchequer, as we have already mentioned, he, with ready devotion, gave to God, ordering his ministers to divide it carefully into four parts, and providing that the first part should be discreetly bestowed on the poor of every nation who came to him; and on this subject he said that, as far as human discretion could guarantee, the advice of Pope St. Gregory should be followed: 'Give not much to whom you should give little, nor little to whom much, nor something to whom nothing, nor nothing to whom something.' The second of the four parts was devoted to the two monasteries which he had founded, and to those therein who had dedicated themselves to the service of God. The third part was assigned to the school he had succeeded in establishing, including many of the nobles of his own nation. The fourth he allowed to the neighbouring monasteries in all Wessex and Mercia; and also, during some years, ultimately, to the churches and servants of God in Wales, Cornwall, Gaul, Armorica, Northumbria, and sometimes also in Ireland. According to his resources, he either gave to them in advance, or afterwards, if life and success should not fail him.

The king having arranged these matters, bethought himself of that sentence of Holy Scripture, 'Whosoever will begin alms, ought to begin from himself,' and wisely began to reflect what he could offer to God from the service of his body and mind; for he proposed to consecrate to God no less out of this than he had done out of things external. Moreover, he vowed, so far as his means and his state of health would allow, that he would give up to God the half of his services, bodily and mental, by night and by day, voluntarily and with all his might; but inasmuch as he could not equally distinguish the length of the hours by night, on account of the darkness, nor, frequently, those by day, on account of storm and cloud, he began to consider by what readiest means, relying on the help of God, he might fulfil until his death the solemn engagement which he had contracted.

After long meditating on the matter, he at length, by an ingenious and useful device, commanded his chaplains to supply a sufficient quantity of wax, which he caused to be weighed in such a manner that a mass was left in the scales equal to the weight of seventy-two *denarii;* and this mass he caused to be worked up into six candles, each of equal length, so that each candle might have twelve divisions (*uncia pollicis*) marked upon it longitudinally. Thus, then, the six candles burned for twenty-four hours (a day and a night) without fail, before the sacred relics of many of God's elect, which always accompanied him wherever he went, except that, sometimes, they would not continue burning a whole day and night till the same hour at which they were lighted on the preceding evening, owing to the violence of the wind, which would blow intermittingly through the doors and windows of the churches, the fissures of the divisions, the plankings, or the walls, or the thin canvas of the tents; and so they were unavoidably extinguished before the appointed time. The king therefore considered by what contrivances he could exclude the wind; and so, with much ingenuity, he ordered a lantern to be beautifully constructed of wood and white ox-horn, which, when skilfully planed till it is thin, is not less transparent than a vessel of glass. Now this lantern was wonderfully made, as we have said, of wood and horn; and by night a candle was put into it, which shone as brightly without as within, for the opening of the lantern was also closed up, according to the king's command, by a door made of horn.

By this means, then, six candles, lighted successively, lasted for four-and-twenty hours, neither more nor less; and when these were extinguished, others were illuminated.

All these things being properly arranged, the king, eager to devote to God the half of his daily service, as he had vowed,—and even more, if his ability on the one hand, and his malady on the other, would allow him,—showed himself a minute investigator of the truth in all his judgments, and this especially for the sake of the poor, to whose interest, day and night, among other duties of his life, he was ever wonderfully attentive. Nor had the poor many protectors besides the king in the entire realm; for all the noble and powerful had directed their thoughts to secular rather than to heavenly matters: each was more bent on the things of the world, to his own profit, than on the public weal.

As far as his royal judgments were concerned, he strove to be impartial towards both the noble and ignoble, who often quarrelled perversely at the meetings of his earls and officers, so that hardly one of them would admit the justice of the decisions of either the earls or magistrates (*præfecti*); and in consequence of this pertinacious and obstinate dissension, all desired to obtain the king's judgment, and both parties hoped to secure each its own desire. But if any person were aware of an injustice on his own side in the cause, though by law and agreement he was compelled, however reluctantly, to appear before the king, yet, with his own good will, he never would consent to go. Well aware was he that in the royal presence no part of his wrongdoing would be concealed; and no marvel, for the king was a searching investigator in passing sentence, as he was in all other things. He revised nearly every judgment pronounced in his absence, throughout his whole dominion, whether it was just or unjust. And if in such judgments he discovered any iniquity, he summoned the judges, either through his own agency, or through that of his loyal servants, and mildly inquired of them, Why had they judged so unjustly? Had they been actuated by ignorance or malevolence? Was it for the love or fear or hatred of any, or through the influence of money? And if the judges acknowledged that they had pronounced such and such decisions because they knew no better, he would discreetly and moderately reprove their inexperience and folly, as thus: 'I wonder truly at your insolence, that whereas, by God's favour and mine, you have held the rank and the office of the wise, you have neglected the studies and labours of the wise. Either, therefore, resign immediately the temporal duties which you hold, or more zealously endeavour to study the lessons of wisdom. Such are my commands.'

At these words the earls and magistrates would tremble, and endeavour to direct all their thoughts to a knowledge of justice, so that—wonderful to say!—almost all his earls, prefects, and officers, though untaught from their cradles, were earnestly bent upon the acquisition of learning, preferring to master a new discipline with slow labour than to resign their functions; but if any one of them, from old age or slowness of talent, was unable to make progress in liberal studies, he commanded his son, if he had one, or one of his kinsmen, or, if there were no other person to be had, his own freedman or servant, whom he had some time before advanced to the office of reader, to recite English books before him, day and night, whenever he had leisure. Then they lamented with deep sighs, in their inmost hearts, that in their youth they had never attended to such pursuits; and they congratulated the young men of our days, who happily could obtain instruction in the refined arts, while they execrated their own lot, that they had not acquired these things when young, since now, being old, they were unable, though they desired, to learn.

Such is the interesting and curiously minute narrative of Asser, presenting us with a portrait of Ælfred which, I think, no one can regard without admiration. It shows us a just, an enlightened, a devout, an equitable, and a resolute prince;

a man far in advance of his contemporaries, and gifted with a natural superiority, which fully accounts for the remarkable influence he exercised. We can add to this portrait a few details from other sources, but they will only enhance the beauty and splendour of its colours.

Ælfred deserves a foremost place among royal authors. He attempted a complete version of the Bible, but his early death prevented him from bringing it to a successful termination. He rendered into English the Chronicle of *Orosius*, which forms a clear and concise history of the world to the fifth century of the Christian era, connecting the events recorded in the Scripture with the earlier annals of the Roman empire. He made considerable additions to the original text; including a geographical description of the people of Germany, and the voyages of Audher towards the North Pole, and of Wulstan in the Baltic, as they were probably recited to our English king by the adventurers themselves.

Not of less importance was the *Ecclesiastical History* of the so-called 'Venerable' Bæda, which Ælfred translated into vigorous old English. We may say with Mr. Hallam,[1] that Bæda (or Bede) surpasses every other name of our ancient literary annals; and that though he was little more than a diligent compiler from older writers, he may perhaps be reckoned superior to any man whom the world (so low had the East sunk like the West) then produced. Ælfred's object in translating it was, evidently, to bring his subjects acquainted with the past of their own country; and he executed his work with equal fidelity and spirit.

Of the *Consolations of Philosophy* by Boethius, which Alfred also placed within the reach of the English, the sagacious and

---
[1] Hallam, *Literary History*, i. 5.

moderate critic already quoted says:—'Few books are more striking from the circumstances of their production. [It was written in prison, shortly before he fell a victim to the jealousy of the Emperor Theodoric, A.D. 524.] 'Last of the classic writers, in style not impure, though displaying too lavishly that poetic exuberance which had distinguished the two or three preceding centuries, in elevation of sentiment equal to any of the philosophers, and mingling a Christian sanctity with their lessons, he speaks from his prison in the sworn-like tones of dying eloquence.'

His translation of Boethius seems to have been with Ælfred a 'labour of love.' First, he rendered the Latin *word for word;* then, having thoroughly mastered the meaning, he paraphrased the text in English, so as to render his version both attractive and intelligible. The narratives borrowed from the Old Mythology—as, for example, the beautiful story of Orpheus and Eurydice—which Boethius intersperses in his *Dialogues*, Ælfred developes into animated tales, such as the minstrels were accustomed to recite during the intervals of their songs. In rendering the poetical effusions of his author, the king ventured on a bolder flight; and his 'imitations'—for they are not translations — contain so much of Ælfred's own thought, and are embellished with so many flowers of English poetry, that they justly deserve to be ranked as original pieces.

A selection of extracts from the *Confessions of St. Augustine,* the *Pastoral Instructions of St. Gregory,* and the same Pope's *Dialogues,* also form a portion of the Latin library translated by Ælfred, and are still extant. His other works have been lost: among these the most interesting would seem to have been his *Apologues*, of 'wonderful sweetness,'—a collection of fables imitated from Phædrus.

Oxford lays claim to Ælfred as the founder of her university; but it must be confessed that the claim is not supported by any satisfactory evidence.

We have had abundant proof of Ælfred's philanthropy, but a still more striking example may yet be adduced. In India, on the Malabar and Coromandel coasts, there lived in those days a race of Syrians, who, though living under the rule of Hindoo rajahs, professed the Christian religion. How, and in what manner, they first arrived on these coasts, is a matter of conjecture. But, at all events, *there* they dwelt; accepting the word of God as their law of life, and preserving their faith unshaken in the very bosom of idolatry.

From one of the many travellers who were always welcomed with eagerness at the court of Ælfred, he learned of the existence of this singular isolated people, and resolved to send Swithelm, the Bishop of Sherburn, to their assistance. It was a long, a toilsome, and a dangerous expedition, but Swithelm accomplished it in safety; and not only carried his king's gifts to India, but returned with those which the Hindoo-Syrians entrusted to his care, for delivery to their benefactor, —gems, and spices of sweet odour.[1]

When we sum up all these excellences of character, and consider how much Ælfred achieved in a comparatively brief reign, we cannot regard as an exaggeration the panegyric pronounced upon this royal worthy by one of his biographers. 'If we think of his wonderful exercises of devotion, we feel as if he could never have forsaken the cloister; it of his wars, we are inclined to believe that he had passed all his days in a camp; if of his learning and writings,

[1] Sir F. Palgrave, *History of England—Anglo-Saxon Period*, i. 185, 186.

that he had spent all his time in academic shades; if of the ordinances he made for the good of his people and the security of his kingdom, that laws had been the special study of his life, and the art of government the sole subject of his meditations.'

Some of his apophthegms and wise maxims have been handed down to us. The following specimens are given in the English version of Sir John Spelman.

> 'Thus quoth Alfred : It behoveth the knight
> Advisedly to look to provide against death and famine,
> And to have care of the military expedition, that the Church
> Have quiet, and the husbandmen be at peace,—
> His sod to sow, his meadows to mow,
> And to follow his ploughing to the behoof of us all.
> This is the duty of a knight, to see that these things go as they should.'

'Thus quoth Ælfred: Without wisdom wealth is worth little. Though a man has a hundred and seventy acres sown with gold, and all grew like corn, yet were all that wealth worth nothing, unless that, of an enemy, one could make it become a friend. For what differs gold from stone but by discreet using it?'

'Thus quoth Ælfred: Worldly wealth at last cometh to the worms, and all the glory of it to dust, and our life is soon gone. And though one had the rule of all this middle world, and of the wealth of it, yet could he keep his life but a short while. All thy happiness would but work thy misery, unless thou couldst purchase Thee, CHRIST. Therefore, when we had our lives as God has taught us, we then best serve ourselves. For then be assured that He will support us; for so said Solomon, that wise man, Well is he that doth good in this world, for at last he cometh where he findeth it.'

'Thus quoth Ælfred:[1]—My dear son, sit thee now beside me, and I will deliver thee true instruction. My son, I feel that my hour is coming. My countenance is wan. My days are almost done. We now must part. I shall go to another world, and thou shalt be left alone in all my wealth. I pray thee (for thou art my dear child), strive to be a father and a lord to thy people; be thou the children's father, and the widow's friend; comfort thou the poor, and shelter thou the weak; and with all thy might, right that which is wrong. And, son, govern thyself by law. Then shall the Lord love thee, and God above all things shall be thy reward. Call upon Him to advise thee in all thy need, and so He shall keep thee, the better to compass that which thou wouldst.'[2]

Ælfred died in the fifty-third year of his age, in A.D. 901, six nights before All-Hallow's Mass-day. He left several children. Eadward, the eldest son, succeeded him. Æthelfreda, the eldest daughter, is praised in the old chronicles as the wisest lady in England. She married Æthelred, Earl of Mercia. Æthelwerd, another son, was educated at Oxford, and gained a high repute for erudition: he died in 923. Æthelgifa, the second daughter, became Abbess of Shaftesbury; and Ælfritha, the youngest, married Baldwin, Count of Flanders.

[1] This saying seems to have been addressed by Ælfred, on his deathbed, to his son and successor Eadward.
[2] Spelman.

Our story of the life and reign of our great king fitly concludes with a poet's 'trumpet song of praise :'[1]—

> 'Behold a pupil of the monkish gown,
> The pious Ælfred, king to justice dear!
> Lord of the harp and liberating spear,
> Mirror of princes! Indigent renown
> Might range the starry ether for a crown
> Equal to *his* deserts, who, like the year,
> Pours forth his bounty,—like the day doth cheer,—
> And awes, like night, with mercy-tempered frown.
> Ease from this noble miser of his time
> No moment steals; pain narrows not his cares.
> Though small his kingdom, as a spark or gem,
> Of Ælfred boasts remote Jerusalem;
> And Christian India, through her wide-spread clime,
> In sacred converse gifts with Ælfred shares.'

---

[1] Wordsworth, *Ecclesiastical Sonnets.*

English Worthies.

BOOK II.—ARCHBISHOP DUNSTAN.

DUNSTAN (*alone*). Kings shall bow down before thee, said my soul,
    And it is even so. . . .
       Cherished by His smile
    My heart is glad within me, and to Him
    Shall testify in works a strenuous joy.
    Methinks that I could be myself that rock
    Whereon the Church is founded,—wind and flood
    Beating against me, boisterous in vain.
    I thank you, gracious powers! supernal host!
    I thank you that on one, though young in years,
    To put the glorious charge to try with fire,
    To winnow and to purge. I hear you call!
    A radiance and a resonance from heaven
    Surrounds me, and my soul is breaking forth
    In strength, as did the new-created sun
    When earth beheld it first on the fourth day.
    God spake not then more plainly to that orb
    Than to my spirit now. I hear the call.
      HENRY TAYLOR, *Edwin the Fair*.

'A strenuous bishop, zealous without dread of person, and, for aught appears, the best of many ages, if he busied not himself too much in secular affairs.'

            JOHN MILTON.

CHRONOLOGICAL LANDMARKS.

FROM THE DEATH OF ÆLFRED THE GREAT TO THE ACCESSION OF EADGAR.

A.D. 901. Eadward, surnamed the Elder, succeeds his father, Ælfred. Æthelwald, a son of Æthelred, claims the crown, and coalesces with the Northumbrian Danes; but is defeated by Eadward, who, powerfully assisted by his sister Æthelflæd, the 'Lady of the Mercians,' recovers all Mercia, East Anglia, and Essex, and builds numerous fortresses.

A.D. 922. Death of Æthelflæd, and annexation of Mercia to Wessex. Eadward's dominion now extends to the Humber; and the princes of Wales, Northumberland, Strathclyde, and Scotland, submit to him of their own will, choosing him 'to father and to lord.'

A.D. 925. Æthelstan, his son, comes to the throne, and makes Northumberland 'an integral portion of the realm.' All the vassal princes renew their homage to him in 926.

A.D. 933. Revolt of the Scotch and Strathclydians, who league themselves with the Northmen.

A.D. 937. Battle of Brunanburh, in which the rebels and the heathens are completely overthrown by Æthelstan and his brother Eadmund. This battle was one of the severest fought in these early times of our history, and is commemorated by a soul-stirring ballad or ode in the *Saxon Chronicle*, which relates how, 'from the morning dawn till God's noble creature, the sun, sank in the western sea, Æthelstan, the king, with his fierce West Saxons and his Mercians, hard in hand-play, clove the shields of the warrior Northmen, and pressed on the hated clans of the weary war-sad Scots, hewing the flyers behind amain with swords well-sharp. Five youthful kings lay on the battle-field, by swords in slumber laid; and seven, too, of Anlaf's earls; and of the army countless, both Northmen and Scots. The Northmen's chieftain was constrained to flee to his ship's prow with a little band. The Northmen, a bloody relic of darts, shamed in mind, fled in their nailed barks over the deep water of the roaring ocean; while the royal brothers, king and ætheling, in fight triumphant, returned to their country, the West Saxons' land. They left behind them, to devour the corses, the sallow kite, the horn-beaked swarthy raven, the dusky "pada," the white-tailed erne, the greedy gos-hawk, and that grey beast—the wolf of the weald. Greater carnage hath not been in this island, of people slain by the edge of the sword, since from the east Angles and Saxons, mighty war-smiths, came over the broad seas to Britain.'[1]

A.D. 940. Death of Æthelstan, and accession of his younger brother, Eadmund 'the Magnificent,'[2] aged eighteen.

A.D. 941. Revolt of the Northumbrians under Anlaf. It is quelled by Eadmund, who recovers Leicester, Lincoln, Nottingham, Stamford, and Derby. Anlaf embraces Christianity.

A.D. 943. Dunstan is made Abbot of Glastonbury.

A.D. 944. Eadmund conquers all Northumberland.

A.D. 945. Eadmund ravages all Cumberland, and 'grants it all to Malcolm, King of the Scots,' on condition that he should be his fellow-worker as well by sea as by land.

A.D. 946. Eadmund is stabbed by Leofa at Pucklechurch on St. Augustine's Day. He is succeeded by his younger brother, Eadred 'the Excellent.'

A.D. 955. On the death of Eadred, the younger sons of Eadmund come to the throne; the elder, Eadwig, reigning in Wessex as superior lord, while the younger, Eadgar, reigned as under-king north of the Thames.

---

[1] *The Saxon Chronicle*, A.D. 937.
[2] So styled by Florence of Worcester.

A.D. 957. Eadgar chosen King of the Mercians.
A.D. 958. Death of Eadwig, and consolidation of all England under Eadgar, surnamed 'the Peaceful.'

CONTEMPORARIES.

Emperors of Germany, . Conrad (911); Henry the Fowler (920); Otho the Great [1] (936-973).
Emperors of the East, . Constantine IX. (911); Constantine and Romanus (915-959).
Kings of France, . . Rodolph (923-936); Louis IV. (936-954); Lothaire (954-986).

---

[1] Otho married one of Eadmund's sisters.

BOOK II.

DUNSTAN, ARCHBISHOP OF CANTERBURY.

A.D. 925 (?)-988.

CHAPTER I.

Birth and Birthplace of Dunstan—His Early Years—Character of his Genius—Struggle between Love and Ambition—Brain Fever—The Married Clergy—A Revolution contemplated—Dunstan's share in it—Becomes Abbot of Glastonbury—Is called to Court.

IT is the misfortune of all men who form decided views of policy, or act upon ideal conceptions of what is right, or bend all their energies to the accomplishment of some great change, to enlist their enthusiastic panegyrists, and their not less enthusiastic detractors, among whose conflicting statements it becomes difficult for impartial observers to gather a clear, just, intelligible view of the real character of these men, or the exact tendencies of their experiments. The man himself is represented by the one party as a great statesman or a Christian reformer, by the other as a fanatic ideologist or wild revolutionist. His career is equally coloured with antagonistic lights and shades;

and what his friends represent as a glorious life-work, entitling him to the admiration of posterity, his enemies picture as a series of nefarious and fraudful achievements, which later ages should reprobate in the bitterest terms. Dunstan, one of the greatest figures of our old English history, has in times past, and in those pleasing fictions which our fathers accepted with such good faith as authentic narratives, been a remarkable object of this alternate eulogy and calumny, of this abuse of the painter's brush, of these frantic pleadings of injudicious friends and obstinate enemies. Let it be *our* humble endeavour, in the narrow limits allowed to us, to show him as what he really was, and to sketch his life with impartiality. We have no right to dress up our English Worthies in the rags and trappings of our fantastic theories. Let us accept them in all the truth and reality of their noble manhood, with their faults as well as their grand qualities, with their admirable actions as well as with their wasted or mistaken work ; and let us never forget to thank God that England's annals show how much, with all their errors, they did for England's welfare.

Dunstan was of noble, or rather, royal lineage. His father's name was Herstan, his mother's Cynedryda. He was born at Glastonbury, in what year is uncertain, but according to one authority, in 925.[1]

If we may believe that a man's birthplace has an influence on his character, that the scenery and associations among which he passes his childhood modify his tastes, stimulate his imagination, and direct his modes of thought, then Dunstan was assuredly fortunate in the scene of his earliest impressions.

[1] There seems reason to believe he was born some years earlier.

As Dean Hook eloquently says,[1] to all the generations of men by whom Britain has been inhabited, Glastonbury has offered attractions, though the interest through which the attraction has arisen has varied greatly in different periods of our history. It was at one time an island, standing in the centre of an estuary, covered with fruit-trees and shrubs, and from the clearness of the waters by which it was surrounded, deriving the name which was given to it by the Britons, *Ynyswytryn*, or the glassy island. The Romans knew it as *Insula Avalonia*. The Saxons called it *Glæstingabyrig*, a word of the same import as that which was adopted by the aborigines. Somewhere in the fated isle of Avalon, the outcast Briton dreamed that his great King Arthur slept in fairy bower, to awake, in due time, as the avenger of his country's wrongs: hither the Irish would come, under the mistaken notion that it was the burial-place of their St. Patrick; Saxon and Norman reverenced the foundation, as they imagined, of Joseph of Arimathea; the modern antiquarian looks with respect upon the ruins of the one venerable fane which was the sole inheritance of the Anglo-Saxon from the British Church; and the laureate almost persuades us to accept the incredible as true, when he transports us to

> 'The island valley of Avilion,
> Where falls not hail, nor rain, nor any snow,
> Nor ever wind blows loudly; but it lies
> Deep-meadowed, happy, fair, with orchard lawns
> And bowery hollows, crowned with summer sea.'[2]

But Dunstan was not only fortunate in his birthplace on account of its sacred associations and the exquisite beauty

[1] Dr. Hook, *Lives of the Archbishops of Canterbury*, i. 382.
[2] Tennyson, *Morte d'Arthur*.

of its landscapes, but because its monastery, as a famous seat of learning, provided him with those means of cultivation his energetic intellect required for its due development. It was occupied at this time by certain scholars from Ireland, who seem to have been no less deeply versed in secular than in sacred literature. They were married men—contrary, we need hardly say, to the great canon of monastic life, which forbids the sweet domestic affections to the tenant of the 'convent cell,' or the priest of the Papal Church; and, to maintain themselves and families, they had established a kind of college or school, whither the young nobility of the surrounding country repaired for education.

Among these pupils Dunstan soon distinguished himself by the superiority of his talents; and not only by his superiority, but by his versatility. In this respect he would have delighted Milton himself. He not only acquired a complete knowledge of the Holy Scriptures, and of the treatises of the early Fathers; he not only addicted himself to the study of arithmetic, astronomy, geometry, and music; he not only cultivated an enthusiastic passion for poetry; he not only excelled in drawing, and displayed great artistic taste as a sculptor,—but he showed himself possessed of a fine mechanical skill; he illuminated missals with exquisite taste, and he wrought in gold and silver, copper and iron.

A youth with so grand a power of work, and such remarkable natural powers, was naturally the object of the admiration of his parents and tutors. They stimulated his imagination by their praises,—they encouraged him in his enthusiastic efforts. His frame, however, was too weak for his spirit, as is often the case with men of a highly sensitive organization; and under the stress laid upon it, it gave way, and he was attacked with a brain fever. In one of its paroxysms, he eluded the watchfulness of his attendants, and springing from his bed, he hurried to the abbey church. It was night, and the doors were shut; but the workmen employed in repairing the roof had built up a scaffold outside, and the young student in his frenzy clambered wildly up its framework, and hurried to and fro about the upper portion of the building. When daylight came, he was found by his friends asleep in the aisle of the church, and wholly uninjured. Nay more, he was relieved of the fever, and free from delirious excitement. Such an occurrence could not be otherwise regarded in the tenth century than as a marvellous interposition of the divine power; and Dunstan himself came to believe — what was evidently a phase of his frenzied dream—that he had been hunted by demons in the shape of wild dogs, and had driven them off by the name of the Lord.[1]

As Dr. Hook very justly remarks,[2] one of the occasional consequences of a brain fever is, that the patient, after recovery, is liable, under any potent stimulus, to a fresh attack; and it occasionally induces a partial insanity upon some one point, without interfering with the acuteness and vigour of the mind in other respects. This, he says, was the case with Dunstan. John Bunyan, the clear-sighted author of the *Pilgrim's Progress*, in an after time, believed that the spirits of darkness were leagued against him, and that he was from time to time brought into direct conflict with Satan and Satanic agencies. The spirit of the age encouraged a similar monomania in Dunstan.

The influence of this monomania we shall frequently have

---

[1] Osbern's *Life of Dunstan*, in *Anglia Sacra*, ii. 92.
[2] Dr. Hook, *Lives of the Archbishops*, i. 386.

occasion to observe, in following up the different stages of Dunstan's career. But the truth is, the great priest's organization was of a specially sensitive character, and in moments of high excitement he was apt to escape from the restraints of self-control. As the poet says,

> 'Great wits to madness nearly are allied,—
> Thin the partition which the two divide.'

And, unquestionably, Dunstan's mind frequently trembled on the narrow border-land which separates a fine and noble intellect from certain forms of insanity. In our judgment of him, we are bound to keep this truth ever present before us.

Some curious incidents of his early life are related by one of his oldest biographers. They have been repeated by Dr. Hook in his agreeable and impartial narrative; and we shall therefore spare our readers the older and clumsier version in favour of the later and more elegant. Dr. Hook says:—

'Change of scene was prescribed when the fever left him, and, with his high connections, he easily obtained admission into the court of Æthelstan. Here his beauty, his engaging manners, and his various accomplishments, soon made him a favourite. But his diminutive form and delicate health made him less fit for the mead-hall than for the bower of the ladies, who knowing his artistic skill, consulted him frequently when engaged in their works of embroidery. The great favour which the young scholar's acquirements secured for him with the ladies, excited the jealousy of the other courtiers, and reports were now spread that he had learned in the Isle of Avalon to practise heathen charms and magic.

'Reckless of consequences, with the rashness and vanity of youth, he took every opportunity of exercising his talents, and of displaying the versatility of his powers. It is maintained by Southey, that among the natural gifts or acquired arts and accomplishments of Dunstan, we are to include the powers of a ventriloquist; and certainly the supposition is confirmed by several events in his life. This power or art had not at that time been vulgarized, nor was it confined, as now, to mimics or impostors of the lowest description. If Dunstan possessed it, he without doubt regarded it as a miraculous gift. Such a gift he would think he might employ to further his own purposes, and these he identified with the cause of God. He would feel as little compunction, in so acting, as that which is experienced by many a modern man of genius, who, with the pen of a ready writer, and with strong party feelings, communicates to the public, under a pseudonym, garbled statements, of which he would be unwilling to acknowledge himself the author. Whether Dunstan called into play this dangerous accomplishment on one occasion when he was in attendance in the bower of the fair lady Ethelwyne, and was superintending her work, as busy with her maidens she was embroidering a clerical vestment; or whether, having invented an Æolian harp, as some writers are pleased to suppose, he hung it against the wall until the wind, entering through the crevices, caused soft and gentle sounds to vibrate from it,—certain it is that the lady and her maidens, instead of being melted into ecstasy, rushed from the apartment, and, declaring that Dunstan knew more than a Christian ought to know, confirmed by their own testimony the suspicions already excited.[1]

[1] Some writers suppose that Dunstan invented an Æolian harp; yet, if so, it is surprising we hear no more of the invention. But even if he did, the wind would not have acted upon it through the chinks of the wall of Æthelwyne's apartment, because all the royal chambers were hung with

'He was now accused formally before the king, and was exiled from the court; but he was not permitted to depart in peace. The cold-water ordeal was that to which witches and wizards were subjected; and there were youngsters at court who were minded to test the truth of their convictions, by seeing whether Dunstan, if immersed in water, would sink or float. When he had mounted his horse, they followed him, dragged him from his seat, threw him into a pond; and when he had managed to crawl to the bank, they set their dogs to chase him, and these of course appeared to the imagination of the poor youth as so many demons let loose upon him from hell.'

At this time Dunstan was deeply in love with a fair lady of the court of Æthelstan. Nor went his love unhappily: the lady was his equal in rank, and returned his affection; her sympathies and tastes, moreover, were congenial with his own. Compelled to leave the royal presence, and, what was much bitterer, the presence of this beauty, he repaired to Winchester, and endeavoured to obtain permission to marry from his kinsman, Bishop Ælphege. In the English Church a considerable laxity had long prevailed upon a point which the Roman Church has always regarded as of strict importance. Monks and priests were allowed to marry, and, as a consequence, their lives were eminent for virtue, tenderness, and piety. In the time of Odo and Dunstan, says Dr. Vaughan,[1] the English, and a great portion of the Continental clergy, were, many of them—we may perhaps say most of them—

tapestry. It is possible, however, that Dunstan, with his subtle intellect, had acquired a more than ordinary knowledge of natural phenomena, and we can well believe that he would not hesitate to employ this knowledge in dazzling the minds of the ignorant.

[1] Dr. Vaughan, *Revolutions of English History*.

married men. Strange as it may seem to modern ears, this was true of the monks as well as of the parochial priesthood. Yet the sentiment of the age and the practice of the Church were undoubtedly hostile to a married clergy. The opposition of the Church it is easy to understand, for it was the great purpose of Rome to create a peculiar caste, debarred from the cultivation of the domestic sympathies, and taught to concentrate all their feelings, wishes, desires, powers, and aspirations on the sole object of extending the authority of the Holy See. The opposition of the age can only have originated in meaner motives, — in a paltry superstition and a narrow creed; in a belief that there was something specially sacred in the cruel repression of man's purest tendencies,— those tendencies which find their centre and focus in a wife's devotion, and the living smiles of happy children.

In England the married priests and monks came to be looked upon as a degraded class; and in the reign of Æthelstan a party of reformers or revolutionists arose, under the leadership of Archbishop Odo and the Chancellor Thurketul, bent upon their removal from the Church, on the compulsory celibacy of the priesthood, and on the introduction of the Benedictine system[1] into the English monasteries. Thus, then, the English Church, at the epoch we are considering, was split into two hostile camps—the Benedictines and the secular clergy—upon the all-important question of marriage or no marriage. If we look below the surface, however, we shall see that the real point at issue was, the amalgamation of the Church with the people, or the elevation of the priesthood into an alien and privileged caste.

[1] The Benedictines took what was called a vow of chastity on entering monastic life.

Ælphege, the Bishop of Winchester, to whom Dunstan had betaken himself for assistance, was one of the leaders of the Benedictine, or pro-celibacy party; and the reader, therefore, will easily conceive that his love-sick young kinsman did not find in him the helper he sought. On the contrary, Ælphege exerted all his influence—all the influence of his sacred character and fanatical enthusiasm—to attach Dunstan to his own side, and induce him to take the vows in a Benedictine monastery.[1] We can imagine what arguments he employed to convince the acute intellect of his young relation. We can imagine how he debated on the glory of subduing fleshly lusts, and conquering worldly desires; on the superior vigour of mind to be acquired by a life lifted above the contact of mean and vulgar passions. We can imagine how he pointed to the examples of apostles, and saints, and martyrs; how he held out the prospect of a crown of sanctity to be won by the exercise of a splendid self-denial. A young man's thoughts are naturally of love and beauty; and Dunstan listened at first with unwilling ears.[2] But at the bottom of his heart glowed the fire of ambition, waiting only for a favourable moment to flame forth with unsuspected intensity; and Ambition, in all times and with all great minds, has ever been stronger than Love. The only avenues to power in Dunstan's age, as none knew better than Dunstan, were through the camp and the cell. For the camp he had no vocation. We can believe that his subtle and passionate genius looked with scorn on the rude soldiers, whose principal, if not only, claim to respect was

---

[1] Osbern, in *Anglia Sacra*, ii. 95, 96.

[2] 'Respondit ille excellentioris gratiæ esse, qui in sæculo consenuit, et tamen quæ monacho digna sunt fecit.'—OSBERN, *Anglia Sacra*, ii. 95.

their rough valour—the virtue of the brute. Conscious of no ordinary mental powers,—conscious of possessing the strong will and the prompt brain which fit men to govern their fellows,—he felt that, as a priest, but in no other capacity, could he attain to the highest places in the State. True it was that priests could marry, but he saw that married priests were treated with contumely and scorn, and that he must ally himself with the Benedictines if he would tread the path that led to power and fame.

Between the conflicting passions of love and ambition,—between the natural dictates of the heart and the reasonings of an aspiring intellect,—he was so tossed and spent that his brain once more gave way, and he fell prostrate for some weeks before a second attack of fever and delirium.

When he recovered, his mind was made up. He crushed out in his heart its warm and tender feelings, and surrendered his whole soul to the voice which he supposed was of heaven, but which really was the voice of an uncontrollable ambition. He abandoned the hope of an earthly bride for 'the spouse of Christ,'—the bright affections and simple joys of home for the austerities of the monastic cell and the anxieties of the statesman's council-chamber. Undoubtedly he believed that, in coming to this decision, he was obeying the dictates of a celestial power; but, alas, we are never in want of excuses for self-deception!

Dunstan, having come to a conclusion so gratifying to Ælphege, was ordained priest, and despatched to Fleury for the purpose of learning the rule of St. Benedict, and the discipline of the strictest monasteries.

A man always led by the impulses of an excited imagination, he returned from Fleury passionately devoted to celibacy and monasticism. The government of Glastonbury was too lax for his new enthusiasm; and instead of entering the monastery, he established himself as an anchorite in a small cell, or reclusorium, attached to the abbey church, and so situated as to command a view of the altar. We are told that its dimensions were five feet in length and ten and a half feet in width, and that its height was not sufficient to allow its occupant to stand upright, unless he could have buried half his body underground. Yet in this living tomb the convert immersed himself, and wrestled manfully with the passions which still animated his warm and imaginative nature.[1]

It was a terrible struggle, like that which John Bunyan underwent before he became a Christian, and while he yet laboured in that valley of the shadow of Death which he afterwards described with so much vigour. Dunstan sought to repress the impulses of the flesh by hard physical toil, working at a forge until his strength was utterly spent,[2]—by fasting, long hours of vigil, and self-inflicted scourgings, which, spite of himself, extorted the shriek of pain; and thus reducing his body, while his mind remained unnaturally stimulated, we need not wonder that he was haunted by visions, or that he sometimes believed he was contending personally with the Evil One. Everybody knows the old and absurd legend which describes him as tempted by Satan under the guise of a beautiful woman. That such frenzies should beset him is no matter for marvel, when we consider the nature of the self-conquest he was bent upon achieving; but matter for marvel it is, that, under all the circumstances, the self-conquest was achieved.

[1] Osbern, in *Anglia Sacra*, ii. 96.
[2] It is said that he cast two large bells for the monastery of Abingdon.

The reputation for sanctity which Dunstan attained by his extraordinary acts of penance, and that other reputation which was due to his supposed possession of supernatural powers, attracted to his cell a noble visitor, destined to recall him, by her influence, to his true position in the outer world. This was Æthelgifa, a widowed lady of royal lineage, who seems to have been greatly benefited by his ghostly counsel, and who, in return, greatly benefited her counsellor by attracting him to her house, where his mental powers were reawakened by conversation with men of distinction. Thus drawn out of his dangerous self-absorption, he was ready to obey the command of the new king, Eadmund, to return to court.

But his place was not yet ready for him. He was not of a nature to brook superiors, and men were hardly prepared to estimate him as he estimated himself. Biding his time, he once more returned to Glastonbury, not, however, as simple monk, but as abbot (A.D. 943).[1]

This, says Charles Knight,[2] was a proud step over the heads of his brethren, who held their easy way, untempted by any friend, and not at all covetous of saintly honour through bodily mortification. But to the new abbot, notwithstanding his power,—'as well in causes known as unknown, in small as in great, and even in those which are above and under the earth, on dry land and on the water, on woods and on plains,'—this step was but one towards the accomplishment of the great work which his mind now meditated—the reform both of Church and State.

In his abbatical capacity he had not lost his faculty of seeing visions. According to one of the chroniclers, when the queen, St. Ælgifa, had borne to Eadmund, the mighty

[1] *Saxon Chronicle, in anno cit.* [2] Knight, *Popular History*, i. 131.

king, a son named Eadgar, St. Dunstan heard voices, as though on high, singing and repeating, 'Peace to the Church of England in the times of the child that is now born, and of our Dunstan.' That in one of the trances produced by excessive mortification the abbot may have ratified to himself this mysterious benediction, is not improbable; that he published it abroad, is a proof of that union of political subtlety with fanatical devotion which, as it seems to us, so eminently distinguished him.

It is essential that the reader should take a right view of the nature of the work which Dunstan set himself to do, and which he succeeded in accomplishing. We must not be led away by the extravagance of his eulogists on the one hand, or of his detractors on the other. We must not be prejudiced against him by the coarse legends attributing to him miraculous powers, which are related by his contemporary biographer, Osbern. That he permitted the dissemination of these stories among the vulgar, and that they exercised a very considerable influence, we cannot doubt; but in Dunstan's age the atrocious doctrine was widely, if not universally, accepted, that the end justifies the means. Dunstan was the first of the great priest-ministers and ecclesiastical statesmen who held such sway in Europe for eight centuries, down to the days of Cardinal Ximenes in Spain, and Cardinal Mazarin in France. But he was also, what Mazarin and Ximenes were not, a bold and a sincere Church reformer. Let us first look at him in that capacity: we shall hereafter have occasion to examine his statecraft.

We have already indicated in general terms the direction in which his reforming—perhaps we should say his revolutionizing—tendencies displayed themselves. But Mr. Pearson has commented on the entire question with so much force and clearness, that we venture to condense his views for the further information of the reader.[1]

Dunstan's intention, as Pearson says, was undoubtedly to reform the monastic rule, which had gone through several phases of prosperity and decline. The first missionaries to the Saxons had been monks; and a central conventual establishment, from which priests went out on circuits to the remote parishes, had formed the nucleus of every diocese.[2] Gradually monasteries had been established on a rule resembling the Benedictine, but modified, as he thought best, by their English founder, Bennet. Unfortunately, the ideas of the eighth century, while they made the alienation of public land for private purposes difficult, favoured it in the interests of religion; and it became usual for the great thegns to obtain grants from the Witán, on condition of founding monasteries or convents, over which they themselves presided, superintending the discipline, but living within the walls with their wives and families. Bæda's evidence is scarcely needed to convince us that such a practice could not but conduce to painful irregularities, especially when convents were frequent resting-places of rich and royal travellers. It was a lesser, yet a serious evil, that the State was thus deprived of its means for maintaining and rewarding soldiers, and the fact may perhaps help to explain the repeated triumphs of invaders.[3]

When England at last recovered itself under Ælfred, the Christian Church had almost to be reconstructed; it was no

---

[1] Pearson, *Early and Middle Ages of England*, pp. 134-136.
[2] See fuller particulars in Kemble's *Saxons in England*, ii. 414, 415.
[3] Bæda, *Ad Ecgbert Antist.*, secs. 11, 12.

question of restoring monasteries, but of providing parish priests and schoolmasters. A liturgical service like that of the missal possesses the great advantage of making no high demands upon intellect; a number of untrained men were hastily ordained to supply vacancies, and, by a breach of the early custom, were allowed to retain their wives. Similarly, but with less reason, the members of the old monasteries transformed themselves into canons, and asserted their right to marry.

The innovation, on the whole, would seem to have been beneficial to public morality; for there is unquestionable evidence, too monstrous to be detailed, that the enforcement of celibacy among men with the passions of savages, and without the restraining influences of civilised life and public opinion, had produced a fearful harvest of crime.

But the change, be it observed, had sprung from circumstances, not from conviction; it had never been sanctioned by the Church; the conscience of the best men of the time was against clerical marriages; and a certain sense of guilt seems accordingly to have demoralized those who accepted the new privilege; they even appear to have availed themselves of the doubtful legality of their marriage contracts, to annul them at pleasure, and take second wives.[1]

Moreover, earnest men complained that the priest no longer thought of enriching the Church, but of providing for his family; and without reference to the questionable duty of endowing the establishment, it is easy to see that the incomes calculated to support single men would leave little margin for charity, when strained to support households. Lastly, the

[1] 'Some priests have two wives and more' (Wolstan, 614, quoted by Lingard in his *Anglo-Saxon Church*, ii. 276).

tendency of those times, on the Continent and in England, was to feudalism: the fiefs, granted in theory for a life's service, in practice became everywhere hereditary. No good man—assuredly no wise man—could desire to see hereditary bishops and abbots enjoying the highest rewards of learning and piety. Merely from a political point of view, to preserve a counterpoise to the State, and an outlet for the intellectual energy of the lower classes, it was of the highest importance that the Church should not be *feudalized*. The most certain means to save it was to hew down the evil, root and branch, to prevent the priest from having a family. Considering all these practical reasons, which no clergyman could then fail to appreciate,—considering, moreover, that in the reaction against the gross vices of the flesh which the polished Roman society had practised, the superstitious purism of the Essenes and Montanists had been taken up into popular Christianity, —we can hardly wonder that Dunstan and the best men of his time should make it the great work of their lives to put down marriage among the clergy. That their very triumph laid the foundation for other forms of evil and misery, is certain. That Dunstan's character was disfigured by little affectations, was impulsive, and wanted quiet strength, was harsh when he thought God's cause in danger, and superstitiously prone to mistake his own views for God's will, may be established from his words and acts. But he belongs none the less to the splendid army of idealists, who risk everything to destroy the habits in which vulgar men find happiness.

As Abbot of Glastonbury, Dunstan put forth all his energy and vigour; and Æthelgifa having at her death bequeathed to him a noble estate, he had ample means to carry out his lofty ideas. He enlarged his monastery by suitable offices, and rebuilt the church on a scale of sufficient splendour. Enforcing the strictest Benedictine rule, he dismissed the monks who refused to embrace it. The married clergy were summarily expelled. He showed himself, as might be expected, a great patron of letters; and the monastery school, supplied with able and erudite teachers, became the great public institution of England, to which the sons of the wealthy and noble flocked from every quarter. His activity restored him to bodily and mental health; and the visions which he still continued to see, appeared no longer under the form of demons and evil spirits, but of angels and ministers of grace.

He did not long pursue this tranquil though active life at Glastonbury. The affairs of the kingdom were in a deplorable state of disorganization, and a strong hand and resolute brain were needed at the helm. The Danes having revolted, had defeated King Eadmund at Tamworth; had compelled him to surrender to Anlaf, their leader, the provinces north of Watling Street; and to promise him the monarchy of all England if he survived Eadmund.

Anlaf, however, died in the following year. By the advice of Thurketul, Dunstan was recalled to court as one of the royal counsellors; and Eadmund, guided by their policy, speedily retrieved his past losses. He expelled the inhabitants of the five Danish burghs,—Leicester, Derby, Nottingham, Lincoln, and Stamford,—and replaced them by Englishmen. Anlaf the younger and Reginald, the two princes of the north, did homage and embraced Christianity. The Cumbrian dynasty was reduced, and the alliance of Scotland secured.

DEATH OF EADMUND.

But in the year 946, says the chronicler,[1] Eadmund, the mighty King of the English, on the day of the feast of St. Augustine, while at a town which in English is called Pucklecirce [Pucklechurch], he was attempting to rescue his sewer from the hands of a most vile robber (Leofa), for fear lest he should be killed, was slain by the same man, and being taken to Glastonbury, was there interred by St. Dunstan, the abbot.

[1] Roger de Hoveden, A.D. 946 (p. 66).

CHAPTER II.

Accession of Eadred—His Character—Dunstan's Influence—A Legend—Accession of Eadwig—Scene at his Coronation—Banishment of Dunstan—His Recall—Accession of Eadgar—Dunstan as a Statesman—His Policy—What he accomplished—Eadgar's Vices—A Penance—The Story of Ælfrida.

EADRED, the brother of Eadmund, succeeded him on the throne. At first his counsels were greatly influenced by Thurketul; but when the latter withdrew from public life, and became Abbot of Croyland, Dunstan enjoyed an undivided authority over the young king. Eadred and he were, in truth, united by more than political ties,—by the bonds of friendship; and owing to the severe disease which afflicted the king, and prevented him for a time from taking solid food, he was greatly in need of the support of a resolute and loyal adviser. Such he found in the Abbot of Glastonbury, who acted as chief director of the affairs of the realm, superintended the management of his finances, planned his campaigns against the Danes, and finally subjugated Northumbria,—was, in fact, what his biographer calls him, *Rex, et Regis Imperator* (king, and general of the king). When the bishopric of Winchester was pressed upon him, through Eadred's mother, he refused it on account of his affection towards her son: 'While thy son liveth,' said he, 'the episcopal mitre shall never cover my brows.' It is true, —and his enemies have turned the fact to every advantage,— it is true that he honestly made one exception, and said that if the throne of Canterbury were vacant, he might venture to accept it. But, as Dean Hook remarks, his conduct is perfectly intelligible to those who can, by a stretch of the imagination, suppose a great man to be influenced by high motives. He had a mighty work to accomplish; and so long as Odo was crowned with the mitre of Canterbury, he was contented with the reality of power. Odo treated him as a father might treat a son of brilliant genius, and was wholly governed by him. Under such circumstances, Dunstan could gain nothing by leaving the court, and he was too conscientious to undertake the office, and not fulfil the duties, of the episcopate. On the other hand, in case of Odo's death, he was willing to ascend the primate's throne, to prevent it being filled, perhaps, by some individual hostile to his interests, and opposed to his principles of policy. Whether abbot, bishop, or archbishop, he knew that he could still be only Dunstan; that is to say, the greatest administrator in the kingdom, and its ablest reformer.

To the hagiographers, who had to account for every action of the sainted founder of English monachism, this particular action became, at a later period, the source of much anxiety. It was easy to represent his refusal of the see of Winchester as a proof of the grandest self-denial; but then how explain his willingness to accept a higher dignity? Incapable of comprehending the true object and real character of a man like Dunstan, they resorted to a clumsy legend in their endeavour to 'whitewash' their hero's reputation. They declared that his apparently worldly preference for Canterbury arose from the influence of a dream, in which Saints Peter, Paul, and Andrew had made their appearance, and inflicted upon him a severe whipping for refusing Winchester, promising a repetition of the undignified punishment if he should decline the archiepiscopal mitre whenever it might be placed at his disposal.[1]

In 956 Eadred died, and the Witán called to the throne Eadred's nephew Eadwig, surnamed, on account of the beauty of his person, 'the Fair.' He was between seventeen and eighteen years of age, and, according to royalist writers, of a very lovable disposition and engaging manners; according to the monastic, he was profligate, treacherous, and unstable. He had previously espoused the cause of the secular or married clergy, and an antagonism between him and Dunstan was therefore of immediate growth. His coronation followed soon after his accession. It proved a stormy scene. After having received the allegiance of the Witán, and sworn, in his turn, to be faithful to his subjects, he repaired to the banquet. He soon wearied of it, and retired to his private chamber to enjoy the company of his fair wife Ælgifa, whom he had but recently married, and her mother Æthelgifa. Meanwhile, many of the thegns at the banquet murmured at the absence of their sovereign; and Dunstan, apparently looking upon it as a special insult to himself and his party, went forth with the Bishop of Lichfield, and breaking in upon the royal retirement, requested Eadwig to return to his proper place at the head of the feast.

Eadwig refused. Dunstan, inflamed beyond all control, then pressed the crown upon Eadwig's head, and, with the

[1] Osbern, *Anglia Sacra*, ii. 104.

Bishop of Lichfield's assistance, dragged him back into the hall, and forcibly seated him upon his throne.[1]

The cause of this outburst on Dunstan's part has been very variously stated. Some authorities account for it as an intentional defiance of the royal power, intended to strike the multitude with awe, and to confirm them in their belief of the great minister's supreme authority. Others regard it as an act of violence, originating in the abbot's anger at the tacit reproach implied by the king's quick retirement from a scene of riot. The youthful sovereign withdrew disgusted; the great ecclesiastics remained to countenance the disorder. But surely we may be content with a more simple interpretation. The powerful minister was indignant at the king's abrupt departure, because, in all probability, he regarded it as a personal insult. Hastening to bring him back, he found him in the company of a woman whom the king, indeed, had married, but who, on account of her consanguinity, Dunstan refused to recognise as his wife. At the sight he lost all self-control, and gave way to the violence we have already narrated.

Whatever the cause, sufficient to know that the event resulted in open war between Eadwig and Dunstan. The former threw himself into the arms of the seculars, and called upon his great antagonist to furnish an account of the treasures entrusted to his charge by the late king. Dunstan recognised the force of the gathering storm, and fled to the Continent.[2] He was then deprived of his abbacy. Carrying

---

[1] Osbern, *Anglia Sacra*, ii. 105.
[2] It is said that the queen employed some mercenaries to surprise Dunstan and put out his eyes. However, he escaped to Flanders, where the abbey of St. Peter (in Ghent) was allotted to him as a residence by the Count Arnulf.

on the war against the Benedictine party, Eadwig sequestrated all their newly founded establishments, and also dispossessed his grandmother Ælgifa, a patroness of the Benedictines, of some property which she had long claimed. The populace now took part with Dunstan and his followers. A general revolt broke out in Northumbria and Mercia (A.D. 957), whose inhabitants proclaimed Eadgar the ætheling as their king. Wessex also shared in the insurrection; and Eadwig would have been stripped of his kingdom had he not submitted to the Benedictine leaders. As it was, Eadgar was raised to the throne as joint king, with the northern provinces for his share. He immediately recalled Dunstan, and made him Bishop of Worcester (A.D. 957).

Odo signalized his victory by ordering Eadwig and Ælgifa to be divorced. The king at first rebelled. Then, in a spirit of savage fanaticism, the primate despatched his retainers to drive the queen from the palace. They went further; for with a red-hot iron they branded the face of the youthful beauty, in the hope that her scars would render her an object of disgust in the king's eyes. Afterwards she was banished to Ireland. Her husband besought her to return to him, and this she undertook to do when healed of her wounds. But on her way back she fell into the hands of Odo's retainers at Gloucester. To prevent her from again making her escape, they severed the sinews of her legs. She baffled them, nevertheless, for in a few days death released her from her sufferings; and not long afterwards Eadwig was found dead in the same place, but of what or how he died, no authority tells us (A.D. 958).

Before his death, Odo, his bitterest enemy, had passed away, and one Elfsin, a learned but violent man, was appointed to the primacy. He repaired to Rome to secure the pallium, but perished in a snow-storm among the Alps.

Brithelm, Bishop of Wells, was then appointed to the see, but he was of too weak a mind to withstand the overmastering influence of Dunstan; and on the death of Eadwig, Eadgar compelled him to retire to his own diocese, while Dunstan became primate and patriarch of the mother Church of the English; by whom, remarks Hoveden,[1] by whom and other prudent men, Eadgar, the King of the English, being becomingly instructed, he everywhere checked the wicked; reduced the rebellious under the yoke of correction; cherished the virtuous and modest; restored and enriched the churches of God that had been laid waste; and having removed all corruptions from the monasteries of the secular clergy, gathered together multitudes of monks and nuns for the praise of the mighty Creator, and ordered more than forty monasteries to be erected for them. All these he honoured as brethren, and cherished as most beloved sons, admonishing by his example the pastors he had set over them, to exhort them to live regularly and without reproach, to the end that they might please Christ and His saints in all things.

The actual government of England was thenceforth in Dunstan's hands, and to Dunstan belongs the praise which the chronicler lavishes upon a cruel and profligate king. Eadgar's true merits were, brute courage, and implicit obedience to his great minister's advice. The latter wisely contented himself with the substance, and allowed all the show to Eadgar. Apparently he shrank into the background, but not the less did he securely pull the strings by which the royal puppet moved. Yet the reality and fulness of his power were so generally

[1] Roger de Hoveden, A.D. 859.

known, that a contemporary says, 'No one in the whole realm of the English, without his order, would stir hand or foot.'[1]

In nothing was the minister's skill more signally shown than in the way in which he made the best use of Eadgar's few virtues. Eadgar was fond of pomp. Dunstan, says Dr. Hook, encouraged those progresses through the land, which not only brought the king into contact with his people, but afforded to the people the advantages arising from a speedy administration of justice, the king's court being the high court of appeal. Eadgar was also partial to nautical display, and Dunstan ministered to his taste by organizing splendid naval reviews, which contributed to the efficiency of the royal fleet.

If we sum up the progress made by England in Eadgar's reign, we shall recognise a magnificent testimony to his minister's far-seeing and all-comprehending genius, and be forced to own that, as a statesman, he is entitled to be ranked with the greatest this realm has produced. Under his firm and liberal rule, trade flourished, commerce developed, population increased. Justice was equitably administered to all classes; disorder was sternly repressed; copies of the Bible were freely placed in the churches, for the edification of the people; Northumbria was reduced and divided into dependent earldoms; the supremacy of the English king over the Scots was confirmed; piracy was checked and punished; standard measures were made and deposited at Winchester; drunkenness was to some extent arrested: nothing escaped the vigilant eye, the long-reaching arm of Dunstan. He may have been a zealot, but he was assuredly a great man.[2]

[1] Osbern, *Anglia Sacra*, ii. 107.

[2] It is necessary to remind the reader that by a certain class of historians Dunstan has been painted in much darker colours, and that in the pages

Probably his most difficult task was how to deal with Eadgar's vices. Eadgar was steeped in lust. No woman was safe from his insolence. His debauchery was so open, that Dunstan could not but be aware of it; and it must have been scarcely less distasteful to the statesman than to the priest. Yet he durst not separate himself from it,—the king was too necessary to his projects. Once only do we find him acting with characteristic decision. This king, of whom the Saxon chronicler writes that 'he reared up God's honour, loved God's law, preserved the people's peace, and was the best of all kings that had lived in the memory of man,'—this king, on a visit to the monastery at Wilton, fell in love with a beautiful nun named Wielfrida; and when she spurned his invitations, dragged her from 'the cloister shade' to become his mistress. In deal-

of those who import religious differences into matters of critical inquiry, no justice is done to his evident enthusaism or magnificent genius. He was a Roman Catholic priest and prelate: this seems sufficient to cloud the eyes and warp the judgment of writers who otherwise can be tolerably impartial. But even a poet can fall into the same extreme, as is shown by the following sonnet of Wordsworth's:—

> 'Urged by Ambition, who with subtlest skill
> Changes her means, the Enthusaist as a dupe
> Shall soar, and as a hypocrite can stoop,
> And turn the instruments of good to ill,
> Moulding the credulous people to his will.
> Such DUNSTAN:—from its Benedictine coop
> Issues the master Mind, at whose fell swoop
> The chaste affections tremble to fulfil
> Their purposes. Behold, pre-signified,
> The Might of spiritual sway!—his thoughts, his dreams,
> Do in the supernatural world abide.
> So vaunt a throng of followers, filled with pride
> In what they see of virtues pushed to extremes,
> And sorceries of talent misapplied.'

Ecclesiastical Sonnets, xxviii.

ing with a crime so foul as this, Dunstan knew himself to be supported by public opinion; and when he next repaired to court, he refused the king's proffered hand, exclaiming that he would no longer remain the friend of one who had made Almighty God his foe.[1]

Eadgar was in no condition to brave the anger of the Church or its representative; and expressing great contrition for his offence, he offered to perform whatsoever penance the archbishop might enjoin. Dunstan, aiming at his vanity a blow which he knew would be deeply felt, enjoined that the king should not wear his crown in public or private for seven years;[2] that he should promulgate a code of laws for the better administration of justice, and undergo certain severe fasts.

In reference to the last portion of the royal penance, Dean Hook quotes what he calls 'an ample provision for evasion' of it from the penitential canons published by the archbishop himself. His quotations are interesting, and therefore we subjoin them; but we must confess that there appears no ground for supposing that in Eadgar's case the evasion was allowed.

'When the man fasts [this applies to a wealthy man], let him distribute to all God's poor all the entertainment which he himself should have enjoyed, and let him lay aside all worldly business for the three days of fasting, and frequent the church night and day, as oft as possible, and watch there with almslight, and call on God, and pray earnestly for forgiveness, with weeping and wailing, and often kneel before the sign of the cross; and sometimes in an erect posture, sometimes prostrating himself on the ground. And let the great man diligently

---

[1] Osbern, *Anglia Sacra*, ii. 111.

[2] When the seven years were at an end, the king seems to have been virtually re-crowned. The ceremony was performed by Dunstan at Bath.

learn to shed tears from his eyes, and to weep for his sins; and let him feed as many poor as possible for these three days, and on the fourth day let him bathe them all, and distribute provisions and money; and in his own person make satisfaction for his sins by washing of their feet. And let masses be said for him this day, as many as can possibly be procured; and at the time of the masses let absolution be given him, and then let him go to housel, unless he be yet involved in so much guilt as that he ought not to receive it; at least let him promise that he will always from that time forth do the will of God, and desist from the contrary, by the divine help, in the best manner that he ever can; that he will retain Christianity, and wholly abandon all heathenism; and rectify mind and manners, word and work, with all diligence; that he will advance all that is right, and destroy all that is wrong, through the help of God, as earnestly as he can. And he who performs what he promises to God, does it to the best advantage in his own person.

'This is that softening of penance which belongs to wealthy men, and such as abound in friends; but one in a lower condition cannot make such dispatch; but, therefore, he must pursue it in his own person with the greater earnestness. And it is most righteous, that every one revenge his own crimes on himself by diligent satisfaction; for it is written, "Every one shall bear his own burden."'

It is stated in the same code, adds Dean Hook, that inferior men may redeem their fasting; and it is shown how this may be done:—

'One day's fasting may be redeemed with a penny, or with two hundred psalms. A year's fasting may be redeemed with thirty shillings, or with freeing a slave that is worth that money. A man, for one day's fasting, may sing *Beati* six times, and six times *Pater Noster*. And for one day's fasting let a man bow down to the ground with *Pater Noster* sixty times. And a man may redeem one day's fasting, if he will prostrate himself on all his limbs to God in prayer, and, with sincere grief and sound faith, sing fifteen times *Miserere mei Deus*, and fifteen times *Pater Noster;* and then his penance for the whole day is forgiven him.

'A man may complete seven years' fasting in twelve months, if he sing every day a psalter of psalms, and another in the night, and fifty in the evening; with one mass, twelve days' fasting may be redeemed; and with ten masses, four months' fasting may be redeemed; and with thirty masses, twelve months' fasting [may be redeemed], if a man will intercede for himself, and confess his sins to the shrift (with a sincere love of God), and make satisfaction as He directs, and diligently cease from them for ever.'[1]

Dunstan's administration must be judged by its results; and these, as we have said, indicate that he was possessed of no ordinary genius as a statesman. We are entitled to praise as a successful ruler the man who calls order out of chaos, and substitutes peace and wellbeing for a state of war and confusion. In the reign of Eadgar, to recapitulate his achievements, a uniform coinage was established throughout the kingdom;[2] the laws of police and trade were strictly enforced; drunkenness was made the object of severe legislation; agriculture was encouraged; private feuds were denounced and punished; the Danes were awed or conciliated

---

[1] Johnson, *English Laws and Canons*, i. 445-447, cit. by Dr. Hook.

[2] Standard measures were also made and deposited at Winchester.

into tranquillity; justice was administered by judges who went on regular circuits; piracy was almost annihilated; and the English coast protected by a powerful navy. The ecclesiastical reformer will set against these successes, as a counterbalance, the universal power claimed and secured by the clergy, and the enforcement of celibacy on priests and monks. But the augmented jurisdiction and widening influence of the Church was not altogether an evil in an age when the common people needed some protection against the oppression of the great landholders; and at all events it must be owned, that while the errors of Dunstan's policy were the errors of his time, its excellences were far in advance of it.

In his warfare against the married clergy, Dunstan did not succeed without the interposition of a supposed miracle. The question was being discussed in a synod held at Colne, in Wiltshire, in 978. Dunstan was opposed, on behalf of the pro-matrimonial party, by Bishop Burnhelm, the 'Scotorum Pontifex,'[1] who appears to have conducted his argument with much eloquence and ingenuity, and who was supported by his clients with an overpowering clamour. Dunstan, unable to resist either the eloquence or the noise, declared that he referred his cause to God's judgment. As he spoke, the building, which was filled with a surging and excited crowd, suddenly gave way: hundreds were killed or wounded in the crash, while Dunstan and his friends escaped, owing to their being seated on the only beam which remained solid.

The nature of this incident has been much disputed. Dunstan's apologists, such as Palgrave and Lappenberg, think it was accidental; his enemies ascribe it to a secret application of his mechanical skill. But it is difficult to

[1] Sir F. Palgrave, *History of England*, ch. xiii.

see how it could have been effected by mechanical means without discovery; or how, supposing all the beams but one had been sawn through, their crash could have been so opportunely contrived. It seems more reasonable to suppose that it was one of those lucky strokes which are observable in every great man's career. At all events it was deemed miraculous by Dunstan's followers, and was held to have settled the question of celibacy or non-celibacy in his favour.[1]

We have outrun, however, the chronological sequence of events. Eadgar the Pacific died in 975, and the succession of his eldest son Eadward was strongly opposed by a powerful party, under Ælfere, the ealdorman of Mercia, who wished to place an anti-Dunstanite king on the throne in the person of Æthelred, son of Eadgar and Ælfrida. Both the claimants were minors; but while Eadward was naturally under the influence of his father's minister, Æthelred was equally under the influence of that minister's enemy. On Dunstan's part, therefore, the struggle was a life-and-death one. He acted with his usual decision; convoked the divan; eloquently defended the legitimate rights of Eadward; proclaimed him king, and anointed him on the spot.

During Eadward's reign Dunstan continued to enjoy the supreme authority. But a powerful faction, as we have seen, was formed against him; and their plots might have resulted in his overthrow, but for an act which was as iniquitous as it was impolitic. They resolved to surprise the young king. At Corfe, one of the royal manors, Ælfthryth, better known as Ælfrida, was residing with her son Æthelred. Eadward

[1] This miracle procured the archbishop's peace, on the score of the canons.—WILLIAM OF MALMESBURY.

had been hunting in the neighbourhood of Wareham, and in the heat of the chase had outstripped all his retinue. From the leafy depths of the forest suddenly emerged a dwarf, who undertook to guide his prince to a place where he might obtain rest and refreshment. He led him to Corfe, where he was received by Ælfthryth with a treacherous kiss. She brought to him a bowl of wine; but as, sitting on his horse, he held it to his parched lips, he was suddenly stabbed in the back. Immediately perceiving the treachery which had entangled him, he struck his spurs into his horse's flanks, and rode away with all speed. But growing faint with loss of blood, he fell from his seat, was dragged in the stirrups, and tracking his course with blood, was hurried and hurled along until nothing was left of the bright and blithesome sovereign but a disfigured and lifeless body (979).

The horror excited by this deed of atrocious cruelty has found expression in the metrical lament of the Saxon chronicler:[1]—

> 'There has not been 'mid Angles
> A worse deed done
> Than this was,
> Since they first
> Britain-land sought.
> Men him murdered,
> But God him glorified.
> He was in life
> An earthly king :
> He is now after death
> A heavenly saint.
> Him would not his earthly
> Kinsmen avenge,
> But him hath his heavenly Father
> Greatly avenged.

---

[1] *Anglo-Saxon Chronicle*, A.D. 979.

> The earthly murderers
> Would his memory
> On earth blot out,
> But the lofty Avenger
> Hath his memory
> In the heavens
> And on earth wide spread.
> They who would not erewhile
> To his living
> Body bow down,
> They now humbly
> On knees bend
> To his dead body.'

Æthelred was shortly afterwards crowned king. It fell to Dunstan, as primate, to place the crown on the head of the fratricide. The stern old man accompanied the reluctant action with a terrible curse:[1]—' Even as by the death of thy brother thou didst aspire to the kingdom, hear the decree of Heaven. The sin of thy wicked mother, and of her accomplices, shall rest upon thy head; and such evils shall fall upon the English as they have never before endured, from the day when they first came into the land of Britain even until the present time.'

[1] William of Malmesbury.

CHAPTER III.

Æthelred the Unready—A Shameful Reign—Writings of Dunstan—His Canons of Canterbury—His Death—His Burial—His Tomb re-opened by Archbishop Warham.

THE English historian turns with shame and humiliation from the annals of the reign of Æthelred the Unready. He feels that at no epoch of its history, before or since, has his country played so poor a part. And all the darker and more dreary seems the period from its contrast with the brilliancy of Eadgar's reign. But the contrast is due, in the main, to the presence in the one case, to the absence in the other, of a man of genius. The first years of Æthelred were free from any severe disaster, because Dunstan still held the reins of power in his steady hand. It was after the death of the great minister that those troubles began which have thrown so dark a shade on our English chronicles. So long as Dunstan lived, or at least so long as his influence prevailed in the councils of the State, the country still enjoyed domestic peace, and comparative freedom from the attacks of external enemies. It is true that 'coming events cast their shadows before;' and Dunstan, with a statesman's sagacity, foresaw in what peril his country was soon to be involved.

It was with difficulty he maintained his ascendency over the young king, as the latter advanced towards manhood. In a quarrel which broke out between him and the citizens of Rochester, Æthelred, in defiance of the primate, ravaged the Church lands; and though Dunstan threatened him with Saint Andrew's vengeance, he could only pacify the king by the payment of a sum of money. He accompanied it with a prophetic denunciation: 'The evils,' he said, 'which God has pronounced, will shortly come upon you; but they will not come while I live, for this also hath God spoken.' The ships of the Northmen had already reappeared on the English coast; and as Æthelred was incapable of any vigorous and determined policy, and equally incapable of listening to the counsel of a wise adviser, Dunstan might well predict the approach of unutterable woes.

Finding himself thwarted and flouted by the king's unworthy favourites, Dunstan seems to have retired to Canterbury, to have weaned himself from political affairs, and have devoted his energies to the performance of archiepiscopal duties. It is said that he preached with great eloquence, and that he was very active in the erection of new churches.

Not only as priest, and statesman, and ecclesiastical reformer did Dunstan win and deserve distinction, but also as an author. His printed works, according to Wright, are: *Regularis Concordia Anglicæ Nationis Monachorum Sanctimonialiumque* (included in Rymer's *Apostolatus Benedictinorum in Anglia*); and *Tractatus maximi Domini Dunstani Archiepiscopi Cantuariensis vere Philosophi de lapide Philosophorum* (included in Ripley's *Chemical Works*). The following are ascribed to him by the bibliographers Bale and Pitts: *Ordinationes Cleri*, lib. i.; *Leges Decimarum*, lib. i.; *Contra Sacerdotes malos ad Papam*, lib. i.; *Solutiones Dubiorum Eucharistiæ*, lib. i.; *Epistolæ ad Dirasos*, lib. i.; *Epistolarum contra Edwinum*, lib. i.; and *Benedictionarium Archiepiscopale*, lib. i.[1]

The reader may desire to see a specimen of Dunstan's ability as a writer, and we therefore quote the canons which he published after his appointment to the see of Canterbury. They are not only characteristic of the man, but of the age; and though they form an extract of some length, I trust the young student will not find them uninteresting:[2]—

'We charge that God's servants diligently perform their service and ministry to God, and intercede for all Christian folk, and that they be all faithful and obedient to their superiors, and all unanimous for their common benefit, and that they all be helpful and obedient to each other, both in relation to God and the world, and that they be faithful and true to their worldly lords. And that they all honour each other, and that the inferiors obey the superiors with diligence, and that the superiors love and instruct diligently their inferiors. And that at every synod, every year, they have their books and vestments for divine ministrations, as also ink and parchment for [writing down] their instructions, and three days' provision. And that every priest have his clerk to the synod, and an orderly man for his servant,—none that is indiscreet or loves foolery; and let all proceed in order, and in the grace of Almighty God. And that every priest give information in synod, if anything aggrieve him, and if any man hath highly abused him; and [let them be] for him all in one, as if it had

---

[1] Dr. Hook refers to a MS. in the Bodleian Library, which contains a picture of Dunstan on his knees, worshipping our blessed Lord; and this is stated, in a very ancient note, to have been executed by his own hand, as well as the writing, which is certainly of his age.

[2] They are printed by Johnson in his *English Canons*, vol. i. pp. 412-425. The appended notes are also from Johnson.

been done to themselves; and let them so assist him, that the man may do satisfaction, as the bishop directs.

'And that every priest give information in synod, if he know any man in his district that is contumacious against God, or fallen into mortal crimes, whom he cannot reduce to satisfaction, or dare not by reason of secular men. And that no suit between priests be commenced before secular men, but that their equals be arbitrators and umpires; or let them lay their cause before the bishop, if there be a necessity. And that no priest do of his own accord desert the Church to which he has been blessed and married. And that no priest interfere with another in anything that concerns his minister, or his parish, or his guildship, or in any of the things which belong to him. And that no priest receive a scholar without the leave of the other by whom he was formally retained.[1] And that every priest do moreover teach manual arts with diligence. And that no learned priest do reproach him that is half learned; but mend him, if he know how. [Excellent counsel!] And that no noble-born priest despise one of less noble birth: *if it be rightly considered, all men are of one origin.*

'And that every priest do justly state his own accounts, and be not an unrighteous clergyman, a covetous merchant. And that every priest give baptism as soon as it is desired; and that he give it in charge to his district, that every child be baptized within thirty-seven nights, and that no one remain too long unbishoped. And that every priest industriously

---

[1] 'Clergymen were educated in this age, by putting children into the family of a bishop or a priest, or into a monastery, where they were instructed in the books which contained their religious offices; and so soon as they could read and write, they received the first tonsure, that is, they were made *ostiaries*, though in after ages there was a difference of time between their being shaved and receiving the first order.'

advance Christianity, and extinguish heathenism; and forbid the worship of fountains,[1] and necromancy, and auguries, and enchantments, and soothsaying, and false worship, and legerdemain, which carry men into various impostures; and to groves, and altars, and also many trees of divers sorts, and stones.[2] And many do exercise themselves in variety of whimsies to such a degree as they by no means ought to do.

'And that every Christian man diligently win his child to Christianity, and teach him the Lord's Prayer and the Creed.

'And that men abstain on the Sunday from markets and courts of law. And that men abstain from fabulous readings and absurd fashions, and from scandalous shavings of the hair.[3]

'And that every man learn to be expert in saying the Lord's Prayer and the Creed, as he desires to be in holy ground, or to be esteemed worthy of the *housel*;[4] for he who refuseth to learn that, is not a good Christian; and he cannot of right undertake for others at baptism, nor at the bishop's hands. Let him who knows it not, first learn it.

'And that there be no violent strife between men on festival

---

[1] This heathen custom, however, prevailed long after Dunstan's time.

[2] In his fine historical romance of *Harold*, Lord Lytton has vividly depicted the influence still exercised in England by the superstitions of the North.

[3] 'It is well known that the several modes of cutting or shaving the hair were, among the heathen, tokens of men's being devoted to one idol or another. The Danes being heathens, or half Christians, had introduced these fashions here in England.'

[4] The 'housel' is the Eucharist, or sacrament of the Lord's Supper, administered to the dying man. The reader will remember the line in *Hamlet*:

'Unhouselled, unanointed, unanelled;'

that is, not having received the sacrament and extreme unction.

or fasting days. And that on festival and fasting days, oaths and ordeal be forborne. And that priests keep their churches with all honour for divine ministrations and pure services, and to no other purpose; and that they allow of no indecent thing, either in or next it, nor of any idle word or work, nor of indecent drinking. Nor let any dog or swine come within the verge of the church, so far as man can govern. And that nothing be lodged in the church that is not befitting it.

'And that men be very temperate at church-wakes, and pray earnestly, and practise nothing unbecoming there. And let no man be buried in a church, unless it be known that he in his lifetime have so pleased God, that men on that account allow him to be worthy of such a burying-place.

'And that no priest celebrate mass in any house but a hallowed church, except on account of some man's extreme sickness. And that the priest never celebrate mass at least without a hallowed altar. And that a priest never celebrate mass without book; but let the canon be before his eyes to see to if he will, lest he mistake. And that every priest have a *corporus* [a white linen cloth in which to lay the consecrated elements] when he celebrates mass, and a subumblum [a kind of vest or cassock] under his alb, and every mass vestment decently put on. And that every priest take care to have a good book, at least a true [or orthodox] one. And that no priest celebrate mass alone, without one to make responses to him. And that no man take the housel after he hath broke his fast, except it be on account of extreme sickness. And that no priest celebrate mass more than thrice at most in one day.

'And that the priest have the housel always in readiness for them that may want it, and that he keep it with diligence and purity, and take care that it does not grow stale : if it be kept so long that it cannot be received, then let it be burnt in a clear fire, and let the ashes be put under the altar; and let him who was guilty of the neglect, diligently make satisfaction to God.

'And let a priest never presume to celebrate mass, unless he hath all things appertaining to the housel, viz. a pure oblation, pure wine, and pure water. Woe be to him that begins to celebrate, unless he have all these; and woe be to him that puts any foul thing thereto, as the Jews did, when they mingled vinegar and gall together, and then invited Christ to it, by way of reproach to Him.

'And let it never be that a priest celebrate mass, and do not eat the housel himself, or hallow again that which was hallowed before. And that every chalice in which the housel is hallowed be molten; and that no man hallow it in a wooden chalice.[1] And that all things near the altar or belonging to the church be very cleanly and decently ordered; and let what is holy be laid up with reverence, and let nothing come near it; and let a light be always burning in the church when mass is sung. And that no hallowed thing be neglected, as holy water, salt, frankincense, bread, or any thing that is holy. *And that no woman come near the altar while mass is celebrating.*

'And that the hours be timely notified by ringing, and that every priest then look out his tide-song in the church, and that prayers be there diligently made in the fear of God, and intercessions for all people. And that no mass priest or minister priest ever come within the church door or into his stall without a stole; at least that he do not minister at the altar without his vestment.

'And that no ecclesiastic cover his tonsure, nor permit

[1] Because the molten or metal chalice could be more easily cleansed.

himself to be mis-shorn, nor his beard to grow for any long time, if he will have God's blessing, and St. Peter's, and ours.

'That all priests be uniform as to the feasts and fasts, and all bid them in the same manner, that they may not misinform the people.

'And that all fasts be made meritorious by alms; that is, that every one give alms in devotion to God, then is his fasting more acceptable to God.

'And that all priests use the same practice in relation to the service of the Church, and keep an equal pace in the service of the Church through the course of the year.

'And that the priest diligently instruct the youth, and dispose them to trades, that they may have a support to the Church. And that priests preach to the people every Sunday, and always give them a good example.

'And that no Christian taste blood of any kind.

'And that the priests remind the people of their duty to God, to be just in tithing and other matters: first, the plough alms fifteen nights after Easter; and the tithes of young animals by Pentecost; and the fruits of the earth by All Saints; the Rome-fee at Peter-mass: and church-scot at Martin's-mass. And that priests so distribute the people's alms as both to render God propitious, and to dispose the people to almsgiving. And that priests sing psalms while they distribute alms, and earnestly charge the poor to intercede for the people.

'And that priests guard themselves against over-drinking, and teach the same to other men. And that no priest be a common rhymer, nor play on the music by himself or with other men, but be wise and reverend, as becomes his order.

'And that priests guard themselves against oaths, and

that they earnestly forbid them. And that no priest too much love the company of women, but love his lawful wife, that is, his church. And that no priest be concerned in false witness, nor be complice with a thief. And that a priest ever decline ordeal, not an oath. And that a priest do not make his purgation against a thane, without the thane's fore-oath. And that no priest be a hunter, or hawker, or player at dice, but divert himself with his book, as becometh his order.

'And that every priest teach them who confess to him penance and satisfaction, and help them in doing it, and that they housel sick men when there is a necessity, and also anoint them if they desire it, and after their departure diligently cover them, and not permit any indecency towards the corpse, but discreetly bury in the fear of God.

'And that every priest have both oil for baptism and for the anointing the sick, and be ready [in ministering] of rites to the people, and earnestly promote Christianity in every respect, and both teach them well, and give them a good example: then will Almighty God reward him in the manner most desirable to Himself. And that every priest know how to make answer when he fetches the chrism, as to what he has done in relation to the prayers for the king and the bishop.'[1]

In 988 the great archbishop began to grow very feeble; his constitution having been weakened by austerity and excessive labour. It was evident that his end was near.

---

[1] The young reader is advised to study these canons carefully, as they afford vivid glimpses of the manners and customs of England in Dunstan's age.

He himself knew it, and awaited death with a calm composure. He preached his last sermon on Ascension Day, but not without much difficulty; pausing occasionally, and once retiring from the pulpit, though he returned and concluded his discourse. He spoke with pathetic eloquence of the great work wrought by our Lord in redeeming mankind, and holding out to all believers the joys of heaven; he besought those who listened to rise to that blessed place, whither their Saviour had already ascended, on the wings of prayer; and, finally, he bade them cherish a remembrance of him who was addressing them, as he felt, for the last time. After attending the usual feast in the public hall, he revisited the church, and pointed out the spot where he wished his body to be interred. Then he returned to his palace, and in his private chamber performed various acts of devotion, and calmly conversed with his most intimate friends. On the following Saturday he lay on the bed of death, and received the holy sacrament from the hands of his chaplains; after which, with failing voice, he gave utterance to the following prayer:—

'Glory to Thee, Almighty Father, who hast provided for them that love Thee the Bread of Life, that we may be now mindful of Thy wonderful mercy in sending to us Thine only begotten son, born of the Virgin Mary. Glory to Thee, O Heavenly Father; for when we were not, Thou didst give unto us existence; and when we were sinners, Thou didst grant unto us a Saviour. Glory to Thee, through the same, Thy Son our Lord and God, who with Thee and the Holy Ghost doth govern all things, world without end.'[1]

These were the last words of the great statesman-priest of

---

[1] Osbern, *Anglia Sacra*, ii. 118, 119.

the tenth century. On the Sunday after Ascension Day he was buried in the cathedral of Canterbury, near the high altar.

The historian of that glorious cathedral relates, on Osbern's evidence, that at one time his monument was conspicuous both from the altar and the choir; but, according to Gervase, he was buried in the undercroft, deep in the ground, with a pyramid over him, and at his head the matin altar. When Conrad's choir was rebuilt, after the great fire which destroyed so much of the ancient cathedral, the monks, at night, before entering the choir, removed the primate's body, clothed it anew (for the vestments were decayed), bound it about with a linen girdle, and placed it in a wooden coffin, which they enclosed in one of massive lead and iron. Then they transferred it to a stone tomb on the south side of the high altar.

Five hundred years after this translation, the tomb was opened by order of Archbishop Warham (*temp.* Henry VII.), under circumstances which the primate describes in a letter to the Abbot of Glastonbury:[1]—

'After due search,' says Warham, 'we found a certain small wooden chest, upright, like a tomb, girt with iron, preserved uninjured, on the south side of the high altar, where it is most evident that the body of St. Dunstan lies honourably buried. This small chest we caused to be opened with due reverence : . . . we found within it a certain leaden cist, and underneath, inside, a single small piece of lead a foot long, on which was engraved, "*Hic requiescit Sanctus*

---

[1] The Glastonbury monks pretended that Dunstan lay interred in their abbey church; and even after Archbishop Warham's letter, claimed to hold possession of some of his bones.

Dunstanus, Archiepiscopus." Then within the same cist were found pieces of linen, very white, redolent, as it were, with the odour of balsam: these being unrolled, we discovered the skull of the said saint, entire, and the different bones of his body, with many other similar relics.'

English Worthies.

BOOK III.—HAROLD II.

'The sage, ne'ertheless,
The realm committed
To a highly-born man :
Harold's self,
The noble earl.'
The Saxon Chronicle.

'In brief, no man was more prudent in the land, more valiant in arms, in the law more sagacious, in all probity more accomplished.'
Vita Haroldi, in *Chron. Ang. Norm.*

'HAROLD INFELIX.'
Inscription on a Tomb in Waltham Abbey.

CHRONOLOGICAL LANDMARKS.

FROM THE DEATH OF DUNSTAN TO THE ACCESSION OF EADWARD THE CONFESSOR.

A.D. 988. Attempts at Danish settlement under the Dane-king Swegen, and Olaf Tryggwisson, King of Norway.

A.D. 988. Battle at Watchet, in Somersetshire; the Danes defeated.

A.D. 991. Norwegian invasion: Essex ravaged, and Ipswich plundered. Battle of Maldon, in which the ealdorman Brihtnorth is killed. Æthelred for the first time attempts to buy off the Danes. 'The year which beheld the fight of Maldon, beheld also, for the first time, peace bought by the lord of all Britain from a few ship-crews of heathen pirates. This was the beginning of that senseless and fatal system of looking to gold to do the work of steel, of trusting to barbarians who never kept their promises, and who naturally, as soon as they had spent one instalment of tribute, came back again to extort more. But this obvious lesson was one which Æthelred and his advisers seemed never able to learn. The spirit of the nation was thus quenched, and its energy frittered away.'[1]

A.D. 992. The English fleet gain a great victory over the Danes, and save London, now rapidly growing in importance, from destruction.

---

[1] Freeman, *History of the Norman Conquest*, i. 304.

A.D. 993. The Northmen commit terrible ravages on the coast of Yorkshire and Northumberland, capturing Bamborough,

    'King Ida's fortress, stern and square.'

A.D. 994. A regular intercourse with Normandy was about this time established.

    Combined expedition against England of Kings Olaf and Swegen, who with a fleet of ninety-four ships sail up the Thames, and attack London, but are beaten off by its inhabitants. The enemy then betake themselves to the south-eastern counties, which they harry with fire and sword. Æthelred again resorts to the dishonourable expedient of buying them off, laying a tax on all England to raise the sum of £16,000. Soon afterwards Olaf was induced to conclude peace with Æthelred, whom he visited at Andover ; and this peace he faithfully observed.

A.D. 997. The Danish ravages are resumed ; the southern counties suffer severely.

A.D. 998. The Danes establish themselves in the Isle of Wight.

A.D. 999. They extend their desolation to Kent, and sail up the Medway to Rochester.

A.D. 1000. Æthelred the Unready wages war against his vassal, King of Cumberland, and almost simultaneously quarrels with the Duke of the Normans (Richard the Good). An English force invades Normandy, and is slaughtered in the peninsula of Coutances, only one man escaping to tell the tale. Such, at least, is the romance fabricated by the old Norman chroniclers ; but as the Norman duke soon afterwards marries his sister Emma (Ælfgifu) to the English king, there is good reason to doubt its credibility.

    This marriage of Æthelred and Emma (1002) is to be noted as one of the landmarks of English history, inasmuch as it was the first stage in the Norman conquest of England. It led to the 'settlement of the Normans in England, their admission to English offices and estates, and their general influence in English affairs. Through Emma came that fatal kindred and friendship between her English son and her Norman great-nephew, which suggested and rendered possible the enterprise which seated her great-nephew on the throne of England.'—(FREEMAN.)

A.D. 1001. The Danes invade Sussex and Hampshire, and push their inroads into Devonshire ; when they attack Exeter, but are driven off by the citizens. They are finally bribed to quit the country, with a sum of £24,000.

A.D. 1002. The connection between Normandy and England alarms the Danes, who in irregular array are scattered up and down the country. They resolve to anticipate, by the murder of the king and Witán, any league which may be formed against them. Information of their designs reaching the king, he, with consent of the Witenagemót, orders a general massacre of the Danes on the next St. Bride's day, November 13. 'The people who had seen their wives and daughters insulted, their houses occupied, and their stores consumed by the invaders in time of peace, executed their commission with fearful secrecy, sparing none, however exalted, and sometimes torturing their victims. When all excuses have been exhausted, it remains certain that the crime revolted the public feeling of the times : "it was such wickedness as the heathen themselves knew not of ;" the Sicilian vespers and the Irish massacre are its appropriate parallels. But the extent of the slaughter must not be overrated : it was probably confined to the counties south and west of Watling Street ; and it certainly only aimed at the invading soldiery, for names that indicate a Danish origin are still to be found, as before, in the charters of the Witán. The Danes vowed revenge, and for the next four years kept their vow terribly.'[1]

A.D. 1003-4. Invasion of England by the Danish king Swegen : he captures Exeter, Wilton, Salisbury, Norwich, and Thetford ; fights an indecisive battle with Ulfcytel, Earl of the East Angles.

A.D. 1005. A terrible famine in England.

A.D. 1006. Scottish Invasion. King Malcolm besieges Durham, but is defeated by the English. The Danes ravage Kent and Sussex, and make the Isle of Wight their headquarters.

---

[1] Pearson, *Early and Middle Ages of England*, p. 148.

In the winter they desolate Hampshire and Berkshire. A tribute of £36,000 is paid to them.

A.D. 1009. Æthelred collects a great fleet to defend the English coast, but its leaders, Brihtric and Wulfnoth, quarrel: the latter retires with twenty ships,—is pursued by Brihtric; but a terrible storm breaking forth, the whole fleet is irretrievably dispersed. The Danes again invade England, and make an unsuccessful attempt on London.

A.D. 1010. The whole kingdom is harassed with fire and sword.

A.D. 1011–12. Canterbury besieged and captured, and the archbishop Ælfheah murdered. Tribute-money (£48,000) again paid to the Danes, whose leader, Thurkill, enters the English service.

A.D. 1013. Last invasion of England by Swegen: he captures Oxford and Winchester, but is repulsed in an attack upon London. The West Saxons, however, submit to his arms, and Swegen is crowned King of England. Æthelred seeks refuge on board Thurkill's fleet, and Emma and her sons repair to Normandy. Thither, in January 1014, they are followed by Æthelred.

A.D. 1014. Swegen dies at Gainsborough (February 1014). The Danes elect Cnut (or Canute) to the throne, but the Saxon Witán decree the restoration of Æthelred, if he will promise to follow good counsel, and reign righteously. He marches against Cnut, and expels him from Lindesey. The ætheling Eadmund marries Ealdgyth, widow of a powerful Danish thegn.

A.D. 1015. Cnut invades England, and ravages the shires of Somerset, Dorset, and Wilts. Wessex submits to him. He prepares to attack London.

A.D. 1016. Death of Æthelred (April 23). He is succeeded by his son Eadmund, though the English Witán elect Cnut. Eadmund breaking out of London, is joined by a powerful force, whom he concentrates at the Pens, on the edge of the Forest of Selwood: there he is attacked by Cnut, whom he defeats. Collecting fresh levies, he marches eastward, and again gives battle to the Danes at Sherstone. The fight is long contested, but indecisive. In a third battle he raises the siege of London, and wins a fourth at Brentford. He then returns to Wessex to recruit his army, while Cnut again invests London, and again without success. The Danes then march on a plundering expedition; are hotly pursued by Eadmund, and overtaken at Oxford, where they are totally defeated. The Danish army is saved from total destruction by the treachery of Eadric, one of Eadmund's nobles. A fifth army is now collected by the indefatigable king, who follows the invaders into Essex, and pursues them along the high ground south of the river Crouch. He overtakes and engages them at Assandun (now Assington). 'He began the battle,' says Mr. Freeman, 'with a furious assault upon the Danes; he even forsook the royal post, and charging, sword in hand, in the front rank, burst like a thunderbolt upon the thickest of the enemy. The Danes resisted manfully, and the fight was kept up with equal valour, and with terrible slaughter, on all sides; but, on the whole, the Danes had the worst, and they were beginning to give way, when Eadric again betrayed his lord and king, and all the people of English kin. He was in command of the men of Herefordshire, and of the forces of some other parts of his old earldom: at the head of these troops he took to flight.' The result of his treachery is the victory of the Danes. Eadmund returns into Gloucestershire, and begins levying a new army; but Cnut offering terms of peace, a conference takes place between the two kings, and it is agreed that Cnut shall rule north of the Thames, and Eadmund south; the latter, however, receiving also East Anglia, Essex, and London. This arrangement lasts but a short time, Eadmund Ironside dying in November 30, 1016.

A.D. 1017. The reign of Cnut is thus summed up by Mr. Pearson:—'To a certain degree he restored the lustre of the British crown, and commanded the respect of the German emperor, who granted free entrance and protection to the English pilgrims to Rome. But the type of the man was low: he had the cunning of a fox, the passions of a child, the vindictive memory of a savage; he murdered the friend who had saved his life, for using a few bitter words, and for beating him at chess. He might have anticipated the union of

England and Normandy by a great Scandinavian federation, of which England should be the nucleus: he contented himself with assigning a sort of patriarchate to the English Church over Denmark, and with giving a few foreign bishoprics to Englishmen; but so ordered his viceroyalties, that after his death his three sons were able severally to seize the countries they governed. He established order and peace in England, and freed the country from the presence of the Danish army. Though a heavy sum was paid for their departure, the benefit was incalculable; and Canute (Cnut) deserved the gratitude which rewarded him. But he had not the power of organization which William the Conqueror possessed; he left the country as he found it, parcelled it into little sovereignties, with no common name or system which might blend together the hostile nationalities. To have made the immediate feudatories of the crown fourteen hundred instead of three, would have been a work that might have compensated the bloodshed of Æthelred's reign and the murders of his own accession. Cnut continued to govern by dukes; and by one of his great peers the Anglo-Danish dynasty was overthrown.'[1]

A.D. 1026. Cnut makes a pilgrimage to Rome.

A.D. 1035. Death of Cnut. Harold Harefoot is chosen king by the men of London, Mercia, and Northumberland; the West Saxons, led by the famous Earl Godwine, are in favour of his brother Harthacnut. A division of the kingdom takes place; Harold reigning north, and Harthacnut south of the Thames. But as the latter remains in Denmark, the West Saxons are virtually governed by Earl Godwine and Queen Emma.

A.D. 1036. Ælfred, the son of Æthelred and Emma, attempts to secure the crown; is received by Godwine, and lodged at Guildford, where he is seized by the emissaries of Harold, carried to Ely, blinded, and put to death. This act, however, is by some authorities described as the act of

---

[1] A much higher estimate of Cnut is given by some historians, and especially by Mr. Freeman.

Earl Godwine; and that he had some degree of complicity in it, seems probable, when the evidence is impartially considered. Probably, however, his share in the matter amounted to this: he left Ælfred without guards, and allowed him to be seized by Harold's emissaries, on condition that his life should not be endangered.

A.D. 1037. Harold now becomes king over all England; he banishes Queen Emma.

A.D. 1039. Inroad of the Welsh.

A.D. 1040. Duncan, King of Scotland, lays siege to Durham, but is put to flight with great slaughter. Harold dies at Oxford, March 17. Harthacnut is unanimously chosen king. His conduct, however, is that of 'a conqueror in a hostile land.' He imposes a tax on the English for the benefit of his Danish fleet; orders the disinterment of his brother's corpse, which is treated with great indignity, and flung into the Thames.

A.D. 1041. Godwine is tried for the murder of Ælfred; and having asserted his innocence upon oath, is declared 'not guilty.' A heavy tax of about £33,000 is levied on the English. Godwine secures the favour of Harthacnut by the present of a splendid war-ship, fully armed and manned. An insurrection takes place at Worcester, which is put down by Harthacnut's 'house carls,' or bodyguard, with terrible severity. The king recalls Eadward, the surviving son of Æthelred and Emma, from Normandy, and treats him with much honour.

A.D. 1042. Death of Harthacnut, June 8, at the marriage feast of Tofig the Proud, a great Danish thegn, with Gytha, the daughter of Osgod Clapa. Eadward is immediately chosen King of England.

[Here we may pause to review the prospects of our country at this important epoch, as indicated in Mr. Freeman's graphic language:—

'The accession of Eadward,' he says, 'at once brings us among the events which immediately led to the Conquest, or rather we may look upon his accession as the first stage of the Conquest itself. Swend and Cnut had shown that it was possible for a foreign power to overcome England by force of arms. The misgovernment of the sons of Cnut hindered the formation of a lasting Danish dynasty in England : the throne of England was again filled by a son of Woden ; but there can be no doubt that the shock given to the country by the Danish conquest, especially the way in which the ancient nobility was cut off in the long struggle with Swend and Cnut, directly opened the way for the coming of the Norman. Eadward did his best, wittingly or unwittingly, to make his path still easier. This he did by accustoming Englishmen to the sight of strangers,—not national kinsmen like Cnut's Danes, but Frenchmen, men of utterly alien speech and manners,—enjoying every available place of honour or profit in the country. The great national reaction under Godwine and Harold made England once more England for a few years. But this change, happy as it was, could not altogether do away with the effects of the French predilection of Eadward. With Eadward, then, the Norman Conquest really begins : the men of the generation before the Conquest, the men whose eyes were not to behold the event itself, but who were to do all they could do to advance or to retard it, are now in the full maturity of life, in the full possession of power. Eadward is on the throne of England ; Godwin, Leofric, and Siward[1] divide among them the administration of the realm. The next generation, the warriors of Stamford Bridge and Senlac, of York and Ely, are fast growing into maturity. Harold Hardrada [of Norway] is already pursuing his wild career of knight-errantry in distant lands, and is astonishing the world by his exploits in Russia and Sicily, at Constantinople, and at Jerusalem. Swend Estrithson [of Denmark] is also a wanderer,—not startling men by wonders of powers like Harold, but schooling himself and gathering his forces for the day when he could establish a permanent dynasty in his native land. In our own country the younger warriors of the Conquest, Eadwine, and Morkere, and Waltheof, and Hereward,[2] were probably born ; but they must still have been in their cradles, or in their mothers' arms. But among the leaders of Church and State, Ealdred, who lived to place the crown on the head both of Harold and of William, is already a great prelate, Abbot of the great house of Tewkesbury, soon to succeed to the see of Worcester. Stigand, climbing to greatness by slower steps, is already the chosen counsellor of Queen Emma, a candidate for whatever amount of dignity and influence such a

---

[1] Godwine as Earl of the West Saxons, Leofric as Earl of Mercia, Siward as Earl of Northumbria.

[2] The *Last of the Saxons*, whose story forms the subject of an eloquent historical romance by the Rev. Canon Kingsley.

post may open to him. Wulfston, destined to survive them all, has begun that career of quiet holiness, neither seeking for, nor shrinking from, responsibility in temporal matters, which distinguishes him among the political and military prelates of that age. In the house of Godwine that group of sons and daughters were springing up who for a moment promised to become the royal line of England. Eadgyth was growing into those charms of mind and person which won for her the hearts of all save that of the king who called her his wife. Gyrth and Leofwine must have been children; Tostig must have been on the verge of manhood; Sweyen and Harold were already men, bold and vigorous, ready to march at their father's bidding, and before long, to affect the destiny of their country for evil and for good. Beyond the sea, William, still a boy in years, but a man in conduct and counsel, is holding his own among the storms of a troubled minority, and learning those arts of the statesman and warrior which fitted him to become the wisest ruler of Normandy, the last and greatest conqueror of England. The actors in the great drama are ready for their parts; the ground is gradually clearing for the scene of their performance.'

I am now called upon to treat, in the life of Harold, of the great struggle in which he and William of Normandy were the 'worthy rivals for the noblest of prizes;' the great struggle which in its issue exercised so mighty an influence upon the fortunes of England; the great struggle which closed so dramatically on the memorable field of Hastings. The theme is one which has been fitly set forth by some of our ablest writers, and by none more graphically or more fully than by Mr. Freeman. In the following pages I must be greatly indebted to *them* and to *him* for much of their most stirring information; and I trust I shall be able, with the help of such authorities, to tell the story in a spirit that will impress, and with a fulness that will instruct, my younger readers.]

AUTHORITIES.

[The *authorities* for the leading events of Harold's life and reign are very numerous. Among the moderns I have chiefly resorted to Freeman, Pearson, Palgrave, and Thierry; among the earlier historians and chroniclers, to the *Saxon Chronicle*, the *Roman de Rou* (edit. Taylor); William of Poitou; Roger de Hoveden; *Vita Heraldi* (in the *Chron. Angl. Norm.*); Ordericus Vitalis; Matthew of Westminster; Florence of Worcester; Robert of Gloucester; the *Chronicle of the Abbey of Battle;* the *Carmen de Bello Hastingensi* (said to be by Guy, Bishop of Amiens);

Wright's edition of Gaimar's *History of the English;* and Snorro Sturleson's *Heims-Kringla* (edit. by Laing). I have also referred to the *Surrey Archæological Collections,* and M. A. Lower's *Contributions to Literature.*]

CONTEMPORARY SOVEREIGNS.
[1042-1066.]

Emperors of the West,   Henry III. (1039); Henry IV. (1056).

Emperors of the East,   Empress Zoe and Theodora (1042); Michael VI. (1056); Isaac Comnenus (1057); Constantine IX. (1059).

Kings of France,   .   Henry I. (1031); Philip I. (1060).

Kings of Scotland,   .   Macbeda (or Macbeth) (1039); Malcolm (1056).

Duke of Normandy,   .   William, son of Duke Robert and Arlette (1035).

Kings of Norway,   .   Magnus I. (?) (1039); Harold Hardrada (?).

BOOK III.

HAROLD, THE 'LAST OF THE SAXON KINGS.'

A.D. 1023 (?)–1066.

CHAPTER I.

His early Years and Parentage—A Portrait—His first Appearance on the historic Stage—Becomes Earl of the East Angles—His Brother Swegen—An atrocious Act—Harold's Influence—The Normans in England—Eustace of Bretagne—The Affray at Dover—King Eadward's Anger—Godwine refuses to interfere—He is charged with Rebellion, and, through Norman Influence, he and his Sons are banished—Temporary Downfall of the House of Godwine.

AT the accession of Eadward to the English throne, the most powerful man in the kingdom was Earl Godwine; and, indeed, it was through his influence that Eadward obtained the vacant seat of Harthacnut. His wealth was immense; he ruled with almost sovereign sway over lands which in themselves formed a small province; and the strength of his character, his inflexible will, his resolute purpose, and robust intellect, secured him a foremost place in the national councils. His earldom comprised Sussex, Kent, and the greater part of the south of Wessex. His son Harold governed, as viceroy, East Anglia, and the counties of

Huntingdon, Cambridge, and Essex; another son, Swegen, the counties of Oxford, Gloucester, Hereford, Somerset, and Berks;—that is to say, if we draw a line from the Wash to the Severn, Godwine and his family were the virtual rulers of all England south of that line. Eadward was a mere phantom king—a pageant, and not a power—occupying with respect to Godwine much the same relation as the Merovingian kings of France occupied to their 'mayors of the palace.'

To render his position still more unassailable, Godwine had married his beautiful daughter Eadgitha to the king. Her beauty, her intellectual gifts, and her purity of character, are admitted by even the bitterest enemies and calumniators of her father;[1] and the only person in England who was insensible to her merits was her husband. Like many another marriage of policy, this proved unhappy in its result, and by no means contributed to the object Godwine had in view. Eadward—a monk at heart—never lived with her as his wife. He treated her with the shamefulest neglect; and when an opportunity offered, was mean enough, and vile enough, to throw her into prison.

The character of Eadward cannot be painted in any favourable light by the impartial historian. He was English by birth, but no Englishman at heart; and though his reign was free from any great national calamities, his weakness and dishonesty prepared the way for that crowning disaster—the battle of Hastings. He was a slave to superstition,—to the superstition which springs from the ignorance of a weak but devout mind; his chief passion was for relics; he loved the company of priests and monks; and, bred in the Norman

---

[1] 'Sicut spina rosam genuit, Godwinus Egitham,' says Ingulphus; 'as the thorn begets the rose, so Godwine begat Eadgitha.'

court, he selected Normans as his favourites, encouraged the introduction of Norman customs, and promoted Normans to every office of importance in Church and State. One of the first acts of his reign was to place a Norman monk, Robert of Jumièges, in the see of London (1044). Owing to the mental weakness of Eadsiga, Archbishop of Canterbury, Bishop Robert became *de facto* primate of England. So high, says an old writer, did he stand in the king's estimation, that if he had said a black crow was a white one, the king would sooner have believed the bishop's word than his own eyes. Of this royal favour, and of his influential position, Robert of Jumièges skilfully availed himself 'to lay the foundation of the future conquest, by establishing a Norman party in England.'

Eadward's reign, therefore, presents itself to our study as a long-continued struggle between the Norman faction,—supported and encouraged by the royal influence,—and the English popular party, led by Godwine and his great son Harold, and backed by the great body of the English people. We now proceed to trace the leading events of that struggle, as they were developed during the illustrious career of Harold, and to witness its dark conclusion, after the death of Eadward, on the field of Senlac.

Harold was the second son of Earl Godwine and of his wife Gytha. The date and place of his birth are unknown, and few and obscure are the traditions which relate to his early years. He was born before the era of industrious biographers, and he grew up from childhood to youth, and youth to manhood, without any one to record the industry with which he applied himself to the pursuit of letters, or the grace and address he displayed in every kind of manly exercises.

We may well believe, however, from our knowledge of his after career, that he disdained no accomplishment, mental or physical, which would make him worthy of the high fortunes of Godwine's favourite son. It is certain that at an early age he showed himself possessed of no ordinary intellectual powers; that he was gifted with that rarest of all gifts, the faculty of influencing, persuading, and commanding his fellows; that he was an accomplished knight and a dauntless soldier; that he wielded the battle-axe with a mighty arm, yet was sage and calm in council; that he loved the society of clerks and scholars; and was eminently fitted, by natural disposition and careful training, to become the representative and leader of his countrymen.

In stature he was slightly above the ordinary standard; his figure was robust and well knit; his countenance was frank and handsome. A living novelist has painted his portrait with much vividness of colouring; and though he may have drawn to some extent on the resources of his imagination, and may plead in excuse the licence of the romancer, I think it is true enough in the main to justify its insertion in my own more sober pages:—

His port, says Lord Lytton,[1] was that of majesty, and his brow that of mild command. His countenance, though habitually not without a certain melancholy, was wonderfully imposing, from its calm and sweetness. There, no devouring passions had left the cloud, or ploughed the line; but all the smooth loveliness of youth took dignity from the conscious resolve of man. The long hair, of a fair brown, with a slight tinge of gold, as the last sunbeams shot through its luxuriance, was parted from the temples, and fell in large waves half-way

[1] Lytton, *Harold*, Book ii. ch. iv.

to the shoulder. The eyebrows, darker in hue, arched and finely traced; the straight features, not less manly than the Norman, but less strongly marked; the cheek, hardy with exercise and exposure, yet still retaining somewhat of youthful bloom, under the pale bronze of its sunburnt surface; the form tall, not gigantic, and vigorous rather from perfect proportion and athletic habits[1] than from breadth and bulk,—were all singularly characteristic of the Saxon beauty in its highest and purest type. But what chiefly distinguished him was that peculiar dignity, so simple, so sedate, which no pomp seems to dazzle, no danger to disturb, and which perhaps arises from a strong sense of self-dependence, and is connected with self-respect;—a dignity common to the Indian and the Arab, and rare, except in that state of society in which each man is a power in himself. The Latin tragic poet touches close upon that sentiment in the fine lines:

> ' Rex est qui metuit nihil;
> Hoc regnum sibi quisque dat.'

Such, then, we may imagine Harold to have been at the date when his true history really begins; at the date, that is, when we first meet with him as foremost among the leaders of his nation.

His character as a man and a ruler has been sketched by Mr. Freeman from the records left by contemporary chroniclers, especially from the glowing eulogium pronounced by the author of the *Vita Eadwardi*, which is devoted to the praise of Godwine and his family. We shall place Mr. Freeman's summary before the reader in a slightly abridged form :—

---

[1] In the Bayeux tapestry he is represented as lifting a Norman soldier with the greatest ease,—a striking illustration of the repute in which he was held for bodily strength.

In hunger and watchfulness, in the wearing labours of a campaign no less than in the passing excitement of the day of battle, he stood forth as the leader and the model of the English people. Alike ready and vigorous in action, he knew when to strike and how to strike; he knew how to measure himself against enemies of every kind, and to adapt his tactics to every position in which the accidents of warfare might place him. 'He knew how to chase the light-armed Briton from fastness to fastness,—how to charge, axe in hand, on the bristling lines of his Norwegian namesake,—and how to bear up, hour after hour, against the repeated onslaughts of the Norman horsemen, and the more terrible thunder-shower of the Norman arrows. It is plain that in him, no less than in his more successful, and therefore more famous rival, we have to admire, not only the mere animal courage of the soldier, but that true skill of the leader of armies, which would have placed both Harold and William high among the captains of any age.'[1]

Harold, however, was something more than soldier or general,—he was eloquent in speech, wise in council, apt to govern, and an administrator of energy and ability. He was not, indeed, that perfect monster which the world ne'er saw, and in some of the actions of his earlier life we see the influence of that spirit of violence unhappily characteristic of his age. 'But,' as Mr. Freeman remarks, 'from the time when he appears in his full maturity as the acknowledged chief of the English nation, the most prominent feature in his character is his singular gentleness and mercy. Never, either in warfare or in civil strife, do we find Harold bearing hardly upon an enemy. From the time of his advancement to the practical

[1] Freeman, *History of the Norman Conquest*, ii. 38, 39.

government of the kingdom, there is not a single harsh or cruel action with which he can be charged. His policy was ever a policy of conciliation. His panegyrist, indeed, confines his readiness to forgive, his unwillingness to avenge, to his dealings with his own countrymen only.' But he displayed the same spirit of magnanimity towards the enemies whom he subdued, whether they were enemies of himself or his country. As a ruler, he was prompt to punish the evil-doer, but swift to reward the doer of good. As an Englishman, he was ever loyal, true, and honest; and he gave to the State his best service, ungrudgingly and without stint. He set his face as resolutely against Norman favourites at court, as against Norman soldiers on the plain of Senlac.

As to his personal demeanour, it seems evident that he was frank, generous, and courteous,—always affable to his inferiors, always dignified in his bearing towards his king and his brother thegns. His hand was open as the day, and his liberality was not the offspring of policy, but of his natural disposition. He was endowed with that great gift, so valuable to a ruler of men,—the gift of ready and eloquent speech; but he knew how, at times, to conceal the subtle thought beneath the apparently candid thought. He was brave even to rashness, but his presence of mind and promptitude of resource always delivered him from the danger in which his headlong courage sometimes involved him. Finally, it must be owned that he was too easily beguiled in his youth by a fair face; and his unlawful connection with Eadgyth Swanneshals, or Edith the Swan-necked, is one of the most pathetic romances in his romantic career.

At the age of twenty-three or twenty-four Harold was

raised to the dignity of Earl of the East Angles (A.D. 1045).[1] His duties in this illustrious position seem to have prevented him from appearing frequently at court, where Robert of Jumièges was steadily increasing the Norman influence by a variety of artful measures. In the following year his possessions were largely increased. His brother Swegen had sinned with Eadgifa, Abbess of Leominster; but when in reparation of his crime he would have married, the Church prohibited him. In a fury of disappointment he threw up his earldom, and retired, first to Flanders, and thence to Denmark, while his confiscated lordships were divided between his cousin Beorn and his brother Harold. By this circumstance the wealth and influence of the latter must have been considerably increased, though doubtlessly to his regret.

In 1048, after a long interval of peace, the Raven of the Northmen again descended on the English coast, and a body of sea-rovers, under Lothen and Yrling, plundered the Isle of Wight, and Thanet, and Essex. Eadward summoned Earls Godwine and Harold to his side.[2] A fleet was hastily collected, but before it could appear upon the scene, the enemy had sailed for Flanders to dispose of his booty.

In the following year, the self-banished Swegen, in alliance with Osgod Clafa,—the Danish thegn at whose daughter's marriage King Harthacnut had been stricken dead,—appeared at sea, Swegen with seven, and Osgod with thirty-nine ships. Swegen sailed to Bosham, one of the possessions of his house, and anchoring there his squadron, he landed, and betook himself to the king at Sandwich, proffering submission and

---

[1] In this year King Eadward was married to Eadgyth; an event which marks the culminating point of Godwine's power.

[2] *Saxon Chronicle*, A.D. 1048.

soliciting pardon. Pardon he was likely to have obtained, if the old chronicler[1] may be credited, and to the restitution of his earldom, but for the hostility of Harold and Beorn, who refused to restore any part of the lands they had received from the king. Swegen's petition was therefore disallowed, and he was ordered to quit the country in four days. In sore discomfiture he returned to Bosham, and from thence repaired to Pevensey, where he met with his father Godwine, and his offending cousin Beorn. By some means of persuasion which we are ignorant of, he induced Beorn to undertake to plead his cause before the king; and the two rode away to the royal court at Sandwich.

But, on the road, Swegen prevailed over Beorn to diverge with him as far as Bosham, alleging as an excuse that the crews of his ships would desert him, unless confirmed in their fealty by the presence of Beorn. Having arrived at Bosham, he solicited the latter to go on board one of his vessels; and when he refused, caused him to be bound, flung into a boat, carried on board to his own ship, and kept a prisoner. Then he made all sail for Dartmouth, where the unfortunate Beorn was put to death, his body carried ashore, and buried in the church. As soon as the intelligence of this cruel deed spread abroad, Earl Harold, with some of Beorn's friends, and a body of mariners from London, hastened to Dartmouth, took up the body, removed it to Winchester, and interred it in the cathedral, by the side of Beorn's uncle, the royal Cnut.

For this atrocious action, Swegen was publicly proclaimed to be *Nithing*, or *Niddering*, the most shameful epithet in the

---

[1] *Chron. Petrib.* A.D. 1046. But Florence of Worcester does not mention this supposed hostility on the part of Harold and Beorn.

old English language, implying that the man who bore it was a coward and a knave,—an epithet which burned into the bearer's soul, if any sense of honour remained to him, like the red-hot iron into the deserter's flesh. His ships deserted from him—all except two, whose crews, perhaps, were the accomplices of his crime. These were pursued by the men of Hastings, overtaken and captured, and delivered up to the king. Swegen effected his escape, though by what means we know not, and retiring to Flanders, spent the winter at the court of its sovereign. We are equally at a loss to conjecture what influence—unless it was Harold's—he employed to obtain from Eadward, in the following year, a reversal of his sentence of outlawry, and permission to return to England (1050). It is certain, however, that he became sincerely remorseful for his deed of blood and treachery; and I suppose that it was his penitence which eventually induced Bishop Ealdred to act as mediator between him and his sovereign. At all events, Swegen was restored to his earldom, and for the remainder of his life lived like a true and honourable man.

Harold does not appear prominently in our history again until 1051, although we can believe that the events which daily transpired were observed by him with anxiety and impatience.

These events were all indicative of the rapid increase of Norman influence at the court of Eadward, and were regarded by the English with ill-concealed discontent. The popular indignation reached its height, when to the archiepiscopal throne of Canterbury, the sacred seat of Augustine, a foreigner was appointed, and that foreigner the crafty and subtle Robert of Jumièges. The chapter had elected Ælric, 'a person against whom no objection could be urged,—a man of business habits, very acute in worldly matters, respected and beloved by the whole fraternity of Canterbury. The monks of St. Augustine,' continues Dr. Hook, 'were, on this occasion, prepared to countenance and assist the chapter in their proceedings, and entreated the Earl Godwine to support the election. The conduct of the chapter was the more marked and offensive to the king and his courtiers, from the circumstance of Ælric being a near kinsman of Earl Godwine; and it was regarded as a protest against the foreigners. Godwine repaired to the court, and urged the king to sanction the election. But the powerful earl could not prevail against the sinister influence of the royal favourite; and, by a charter from the king, Robert was translated from the diocese of London to the metropolitan see,—an act of despotism on the part of the Crown, which excited the just indignation of the Church, and alarmed the country.'[1]

As a further insult to the national feeling, a foreigner was appointed to the vacant see of London,—one William the Priest; and all the leading offices in Church and State were filled with Normans.

Archbishop Robert hastened to Rome to receive his pall from Pope Leo IX. On his return, he showed no disposition to conciliate those whom his appointment had offended, but quietly involved himself in a quarrel with Godwine respecting some Church lands which adjoined the powerful earl's estates. He conducted himself with the utmost insolence, evidently with the view of provoking Godwine into open anger; but the cautious earl, says the chronicler,[2] bore with the archbishop

---

[1] Dean Hook, *Lives of the Archbishops*, i. 497, 498.
[2] *Vita Eadwardi*, p. 400, A.D. 1051.

patiently, either out of respect to the king, or from the natural temperament of his race, which was not wont to do things rashly or precipitately, but knowing how many things are brought to nought through undue haste, designedly waited his time.

That time was near at hand, though at first the stars in their courses fought against the house of Godwine. The struggle which had so long been impending between the national party and the foreign party came at length to an issue, and, at the outset, the former was defeated. In September 1051 a new visitor came to the court of Eadward,—the cruel and rapacious Eustace, Count of Boulogne, who had married Godgifa, the daughter of Æthelred and Emma, and was, therefore, brother-in-law to the king. He sojourned at the English court for some time, and whatever he asked for, he obtained.[1] On every side he heard the familiar accents of his own Norman tongue; wherever he went, he was followed by Norman attendants; around the king's person were gathered men of foreign birth, so that he may almost be forgiven, if at last he came to look upon England as a conquered country, where the Norman might act as best pleased him. On his way to the coast, to embark for France, he rested at Canterbury; and having duly refreshed himself and his men, proceeded towards Dover. As he was traversing the territory which owned Earl Godwine as lord, he took the precaution of clothing himself and followers in their coats of mail, and quitting his travelling palfrey, he mounted his destrier, which one of his men led in his right hand. Thus accoutred, they rode through the valley of the Dour, and entered the town of Dover.

There they paraded the streets, in insolent defiance of the

[1] William of Malmesbury, lib. ii. 81.

feelings of the citizens, marking out the best houses for their quarters during the night, and taking rude possession of them. But there was one stout Englishman who objected to this forcible entry. He stopped on the threshold the Norman adventurer; and when the latter wounded him with his sword, he hastily armed himself and his household, attacked and killed the intruder.[1] Count Eustace immediately mounted his horse, and with his armed troop besieged the house of the gallant Englishman, whom they murdered, says the Saxon chronicler, before his own hearth. Then they rode through the town, sword in hand, cutting down men and women, and crushing children and infants under their horses' hoofs.[2] The citizens flew to arms, and with wild shouts hastened to the place of combat: a fierce struggle took place, and twenty of the Normans were slain. The count fled with the remainder, and rode in hot haste, across valley and plain, to Eadward's court at Gloucester, where he besought the king to deal out his heaviest punishments on the insolent citizens who had dared to defend the privacy of their own houses.

Eadward waxed furious as the count told his tale. He sent for Earl Godwine, within whose jurisdiction the town of Dover necessarily lay, and bade him hasten thither, and inflict on the offenders all the severity of a military execution.[3] Godwine demurred at punishing men before they had been proved guilty of the offences imputed to them, and suggested that before the whole town was indiscriminately chastised, its magistrates should be summoned to defend themselves before

---

[1] Such is the story told by most of the chroniclers: Roger de Hoveden relates it somewhat differently.

[2] Roger de Hoveden, A.D. 1051.

[3] Mid unfritha—*Saxon Chronicle*, A.D. 1051.

the king and his judges. If they were successful in their exculpation, let them depart unharmed; if they failed, let them, in their bodies and estates, satisfy the king, whose peace they had broken, and the count whom they had injured; but it is unjust, he exclaimed, to condemn, unheard, those whom it is our duty to protect.[1]

Having thus boldly enunciated the true principles of justice, the great earl went his way.

But it was against Godwine the king now turned his wrath, and the archbishop did not fail to increase it by artful representations. Godwine was charged with disobedience and rebellion, and summoned to appear before a Witán convoked at Gloucester. At first he treated the accusation with indifference, in the belief that the royal anger would soon pass away, or, at all events, that the great earls and thegns would do their countrymen justice. But he did not fully comprehend the nature of the influences which were conspiring against him, and we can understand that it must have been with almost incredulous astonishment he learned, that an English Witán had been so corrupted as to be ready to pronounce against himself and his sons a sentence of banishment. He immediately prepared for the struggle, resolving to oppose his popularity with his countrymen against Norman intrigues, while studiously disclaiming any intention of trespassing on the prerogative of Eadward, his king.

He began by levying troops in his earldom south of the Thames, while Swegen summoned all who could bear arms to his standard in Oxfordshire, Gloucestershire, Herefordshire, Somersetshire, and Berkshire; and Harold in East Anglia, Essex, Huntingdon, and Cambridge. The three leaders con-

[1] William of Malmesbury, ii. 119.

centrated their forces at Beverstone, near Gloucester, and sent messengers to the king, demanding that Count Eustace and his followers, with some other Normans then at the royal court, should be delivered up to the judgment of the nation. To this demand Eadward made no reply, but hastily summoned to his assistance the two great northern earls, Siward of Northumbria, and Leofric of Mercia. The men of Northumbria and Mercia armed at the bidding of their chiefs, but armed reluctantly; and were heard to murmur that no blood should be shed by them in support of the Norman interest, or the king's foreign favourites.[1]

Meanwhile Godwine and his sons, seeing no hope but in an appeal to arms, made ready for battle, and resolved to march upon Gloucester.

From the heights of the Cotswolds, on which they had been gathered—says Mr. Freeman, with much picturesque force[2]—they descended the hill-side which overlooks the fairest and most fertile of English valleys. The broad Severn wound through the plain beneath them; beyond its sandy flood, rose, range after range, the hills which guarded the land of the still unconquered Briton. Far away, like a glimpse of another world, opened the deep vale of the Welsh Axe (the Usk), the mountain land of Brecheinoig, where, in the farthest distance, the giant Beacons soar, vast and dim—the mightiest natural fortress of the southern Cymry. Even then some glimpses of days to come may have kindled the soul of Harold, as he looked forth on the land which was before many years to ring with his renown, and to see his name engraved as conqueror on the trophies of so many battle-fields. They

[1] *Saxon Chronicle*, Fragm. p. 164.
[2] Freeman, *History of the Norman Conquest*, ii. 145.

passed by relics of unrecorded antiquity, by fortresses and tombs reared by the hands of men who had been forgotten before the days of Ceawlin, some perhaps even before the days of Cæsar. They passed by the vast hill-fort of Uleybury, where the Briton had bid defiance to the Roman invader. They passed by the huge mound, the Giants' Chamber of the Dead, covering the remains of men whose name and race had passed away, perhaps before even the Briton had fixed himself in the islands of the west. Straight in their path rose the towers—in that day, no doubt, tall and slender—of the great minster of the city which was their goal, where their king sat a willing captive in the hands of the enemies of his people. And still, far beyond, rose other hills, the heights of Herefordshire and Shropshire, the blue range of Malvern, and the far distant Tithestone, bringing the host, as it were, into the actual presence of the evil deeds with which the stranger was defiling that lovely region. Godwine had kept his watch on the heights of Beverstone, as Thrasybulus had kept his on the heights of Phylê:

> 'Spirit of Freedom, when, on Phylê's brow,
> Thou sat'st with Thrasybulus and his train.'
>
> BYRON.

And he now came down with the truest sons of England at his bidding, ready, as need might be, to strive for her freedom either in the debates of the Witán, or in the actual storm of battle.

The battle, however, took place. Leofric of Mercia, though no friend or ally of Godwine, stood forward at this crisis as a mediator between him and the king: he saw that for Englishmen to contend with Englishmen, was simply to surrender the land into the greedy hands of foreigners; and he therefore proposed an armistice between the king and Godwine, and that their dispute should be referred to a meeting of the Witán in London. To this proposal Eadward reluctantly, and Godwine willingly, assented; and on one side and the other, says the *Saxon Chronicle*, they swore the peace of God and perfect friendship.

No sooner, however, was the king relieved from imminent danger, than he hastened to break the agreement into which he had entered. He levied, by royal decree, the whole military force of Northumbria and Mercia, as well as his housecarls and the retainers of his immediate thegns; so that he was soon at the head of the largest army which England had seen for many years. Meantime Godwine and his sons, relying on the royal word, had dismissed their volunteer forces, and now saw themselves out-manœuvred by the king and his Norman advisers.

Eadward fixed his headquarters at Westminster, evidently with the view of overawing the deliberations of the Witán. Godwine, with so much of his army as still held together, repaired to his own house at Southwark. He and his son Harold were then required to dismiss their attendants, and to appear before the Witán without escort, and unarmed. Before obeying the royal summons, the two earls naturally demanded the king's safe-conduct, and hostages to guarantee their personal security both going and coming.[1] Twice they repeated this demand, which under the circumstances was only reasonable, and twice was it refused. They were then summoned to appear without delay, attended by compurgators, to affirm their innocence on oath; and when they still refused to appear, were pronounced contumacious, and ordered to quit

[1] *Saxon Chronicle*, p. 164.

England within five days. The refusal was communicated to Godwine by his friend Bishop Stigand. The great earl, instantly aware of his danger, sprang to his feet, overthrew his table, mounted his horse, and, accompanied by his sons, rode for his life through the darkness of the night. On reaching the coast, he, with his sons Swegen, Tostig, and Gyrth, his wife Gytha, and Judith, the newly married wife of Tostig, embarked for Flanders; while Harold, with his brother Leofwine, travelled westward to Bristol, whence they crossed the Irish Channel to Dublin, bent upon raising forces to avenge the injuries they had sustained.

So far the Norman faction had triumphed. The powerful leaders of the national party had been driven ignominiously into exile; their estates were seized and confiscated; the Lady Eadgifa, though the king's wife, shared the misfortunes of her family, and was deprived of all her possessions in land, chattels, and money. It was not fitting, said Eadward's courtiers ironically, that she should sleep upon a bed of down, while her kinsmen were undergoing the evils of banishment.[1] Into every office of power or dignity Normans were shamelessly thrust. Saxon prelates and abbots were deposed, to make way for Norman monks, and Norman knights were placed in charge of the fortresses and armies of the kingdom.

Such is the story of the fall of Godwine as told by the ancient chronicles; but the reader cannot fail to see that it is characterized by some strange inconsistencies. At Gloucester we see the earl surrounded by a powerful force, virtually dictating terms to his king and his king's favourites; at London we find him stripped of his array, and compelled to submit

[1] William of Malmesbury, p. 82.

in silence to a decree of banishment. If Godwine were the popular champion and the leader of the English nation, how was it that no one rallied to his standard in the hour of his peril? What had become of the men of East Anglia and Wessex? Either his influence was not so powerful over them as some historians have represented, or else he was deceived by the clever machinations of his enemies,—a supposition not very favourable to his sagacity as a politician. Yet it would seem to be the truth. Godwine and his sons repaired, as they supposed, to a peaceful meeting of the Witán: they found themselves surrounded by sword and battle-axe. The array against them was overpowering: resistance was impossible. Before the men of Wessex could have been called into the field, the royal army must have crushed the house of Godwine in the dust. He had no choice but to bend before the unexpected storm, and to seek safety in flight, assured that no long interval would elapse before he would be recalled by the unanimous voice of the nation.

And yet, even if we accept this supposition, a certain singularity and dubiousness attend the details of the story. There is something amazing, as Mr. Freeman remarks,[1] in so sudden and so complete a fall, not only from the general exaltation of himself and his family, but from the proud and threatening position which he had so lately held at Beverstone and Gloucester. In September the equal of his king, in October as impotent as the humblest thegn! Such a catastrophe, so abrupt and terrible a change, could not but deeply impress the minds of the men of his own age. The chronicler of the *Life of Eadward* calls upon his muse to celebrate the sufferings of the innocent, and likens the outlawed earl to Susanna,

[1] Freeman, *History of the Norman Conquest*, ii. 159.

Joseph, and other ancient victims of calumny. And the chronicler of Worcester exclaims: 'That would have seemed wonderful to ilk man that in England was, if any man had previously said that so it should be. For before he was thus upheaven, he wielded power over the king and all England; and his sons were earls and the king's darlings, and his daughter to the king was wedded and married.'[1]

[1] *Chron Wig.* A.D. 1052.

CHAPTER II.

William the Norman visits the English Court — Eadward's Promise — Gradual Rise of a Patriotic Spirit — Harold raises an Army in Ireland, and crosses to England — Godwine raises a Fleet — Harold and Godwine sail up the Thames, and are warmly welcomed by their Countrymen — King Eadward is forced to submit — A great Witán is held — Godwine and his Sons restored to their Estates — Exodus of the Normans — Death of Godwine — The Truth and the Fiction — Godwine's Character — Harold becomes Earl of the West Saxons — He repels a Welsh Invasion.

THE extent to which the influence of the Norman party had increased in England may be estimated from the fact that William, the great Duke of the Normans, was now invited to visit his royal cousin. Visits from foreign princes were not at that time usual or popular in England; and from the hatred with which the Normans were regarded, the visit of this powerful sovereign, whose ambition and genius were already celebrated, was assuredly most unwelcome to the English people.

The invitation was given, however, and accepted; and, as the *Worcester Chronicle* tells us, 'William came from beyond sea with a meikle company of Frenchmen, and the king him received, and as many of his comrades as to him seemed good, and let him go again.'

There can be no question that this visit first suggested to the aspiring brain of the Norman the hope of succeeding to his childless cousin's crown. And he might be pardoned for cherishing such a design, when he found the country already subjected to Norman control. The fleet at Dover was officered by Normans; the garrison of the fortress at Canterbury consisted of Norman soldiers; Norman prelates ruled over the English bishoprics; Norman captains commanded the English levies; and at Eadward's court prevailed the Norman dress, language, and manners. He was received by the king with open arms, and loaded with presents of costly arms, horses, dogs, and falcons. Nay more, he was promised the succession to the English throne, so far as Eadward, by his recommendation, could guarantee that succession. That such a promise was given, no historian can deny; and that this was the only time at which it *could* be given, I think all credible evidence proves. Consider the opportune condition of things which prevailed at the epoch of William's visit: Godwine and Harold, and all the leaders of the national party, were absent; Eadward was wholly given up to Norman influences. Here, in his chamber, and ever at his side, was the Norman duke, whose subtle eloquence was well adapted to bias so impressionable a temperament as Eadward's. Foremost in his council was the primate, Robert of Jumièges, who would not fail to advocate the cause of his national sovereign. It is impossible to doubt that at this time the king undertook to favour the succession of William to the English crown.

The historical evidence on this point has been carefully examined by Mr. Freeman; and to his elaborate pages we refer the reader for his cogent reasons in support of the above opinion. He shows that only during William's visit did circumstances combine to support and encourage his ambition;

that every later court, and every later change of circumstances, tended in favour of the succession of any one rather than of William.

'Before another year had passed,' he remarks, 'the cause of England had once more triumphed: Eadward had Englishmen around him; he gradually learned to attach himself to men of his own race, and to give to the sons of Godwine that confidence and affection which he never gave to Godwine himself. He either forgot his promise to William, or else he allowed himself to be convinced that such a promise was unlawful to make, and impossible to fulfil. But,' says Mr. Freeman, '*William never forgot it.* We may be sure that, from that time, the crown of England was the great object of all his hopes, all his thoughts, all his policy. Even in his marriage it may not have been left quite out of sight. The marriage of William and Matilda was undoubtedly a marriage of the truest affection; but it was no less undoubtedly a marriage which was prompted by many considerations of policy. And among other inducements, William may well have remembered that his intended bride sprung by direct, if only by female, descent from the stock of the great Ælfred. His children, therefore, would have the blood of ancient English royalty in their veins. Such a descent would, of course, give neither William nor Matilda, nor their children, any real claim; but it was a pretension one degree less absurd than a pretension grounded on the fact that Eadward's mother was William's great-aunt. And William knew as well as any man, that in politics a chain is not always of the strength only of its weakest link. He knew that a skilful combination of fallacious arguments often has more practical effect on men's minds than a single con-

L

clusive argument. He contrived, in the end, by skilfully weaving together a mass of assertions, not one of which really proved his point, to persuade a large part of Europe that he was the true heir of Eadward, kept out of his inheritance by a perjured usurper. That all these schemes and pretensions date from the time of William's visit to Eadward, that the Norman duke left the English court invested in his own eyes and in those of his followers with the lawful heirship of the English crown, is a fact which seems to admit of as little doubt as any fact which cannot be proved by direct evidence.'

It may sound a paradox,—but paradoxes in history are often great truths,—it may sound a paradox, yet it is certain that if anything were wanted to secure Godwine's power, it was the very circumstance which seemed to have shattered it. His banishment showed how nobly he had withstood the rapacity of the foreigner and the alien, and proved to every Englishman that he had been his best and truest friend. So long as he had sway in England, men were sure of obtaining redress for their wrongs; the great earl was ever ready to shelter them from the oppression of the royal favourites. But now that he was absent, the Normans behaved like the lords of a conquered land, and nothing could satisfy their immeasurable rapacity. The heart of the country, therefore, went forth after the banished earl, and many there were who preferred to live in exile and under his protection, than in their native land, exposed to the most shameless oppression. Messages were sent to the Flemish court, inviting him to return, and assuring him of a hearty welcome; and men openly pledged themselves to draw the sword in his cause, if he would but deliver England from the thraldom under which it laboured.

Eadward and his advisers could not be ignorant of the general spirit of disaffection; and, afraid that Godwine might at any time appear to profit by it, they got ready forty ships, and stationed them at Sandwich, under the command of Earl Ralph, the king's nephew, and of Odda, the recently appointed earl of the west.

But while thus preparing to meet with armed force a man who, with all his faults, had been a loyal subject, and was a true patriot, no measures were taken to guard the counties along the western border, though they were menaced with an invasion by the Welsh. And in 1052 the storm broke. Gruffydd, or Griffith, the Prince of North Wales, poured his wild warriors into Herefordshire, encountered a mixed array of English and Normans, hastily levied, near Leominster, won a signal victory, and returned to his mountain fastnesses, loaded with plunder.[1] His sudden and successful raid filled the minds of men with terror, and led them to fix their thoughts still more earnestly on the banished earls, who alone were capable of keeping the peace of the land.

Fully apprised of the feeling of his countrymen, Godwine resolved on his return to England. And first he addressed several respectful messages to Eadward, soliciting a reconciliation, and offering to appear in the royal presence, to purge himself on oath of all the charges brought against him. His prayer was supported by Count Baldwin of Flanders and the King of the French. It was never allowed to reach the royal ear, or if it did, was counterbalanced by the representations

[1] *Chronicle of Worcester* A.D. 1052.

of the Norman priests and courtiers. Under these circumstances Godwine appealed to the sword;—not, indeed, to make war against his king, but to deliver him from the influence of false counsellors; not to depose or discrown that king, but to render his throne more secure in the affections of all honest Englishmen.

Meanwhile Harold, less cool and cautious than his father, had from the first determined on regaining his earldom by force, and had employed all the winter in preparing for an expedition. In the summer of 1052 his fleet was ready, and, accompanied by his brother Leofwine, he entered the British Channel, and landed at Porlock, on the confines of Devon and Somerset. His object in landing there, at so great a distance from that part of England where the real strength of the house of Godwine lay, was probably to obtain a supply of provisions. He found the inhabitants, who were mostly of Celtic race, ill-disposed towards him. They mustered in considerable numbers, and attacked the invader; but, after a fierce fight, were defeated with great slaughter, and Harold was left at liberty to carry away what booty he would. He then sailed to the south-west, and along the English Channel, to meet his father, who, with several vessels, sailed from Bruges on the 22d of June, and bore towards Pevensey.

As soon as the Norman commanders of the royal fleet were informed of his movements, they hastened in pursuit of him; but a terrible storm dispersed both armaments, and while the Normans put back to Sandwich,[1] Godwine withdrew to Flanders. The royal fleet was then ordered to return to London, that Eadward might inquire into the supposed misconduct of its chiefs. It sailed up the Thames,

[1] Roger de Hoveden, p. 119.

and soon afterwards the crews abandoned the service, and returned every man to his own home.

Godwine immediately sailed again for the English coast, and having effected a junction with the fleet of Harold and Leofwine off the chalky cliffs of Portland, he made a triumphal procession along the South Saxon coast, receiving accessions of men and ships from every seaport. Wherever his banner was seen, the mighty shout went up, 'We will live and die with Earl Godwine.' At Pevensey, at Hythe, at Folkestone, at Dover, at Sandwich, supplies of provisions were obtained, and hostages were received. Swollen into a mighty armada, the fleet doubled the North Foreland, entered the mouth of the Thames, and sailed up the river to London. The waves, we are told, laboured under the burden of so many keels; the armour of the warriors on board shone resplendent in the sunlight. On the second day of the week they dropped anchor before Godwine's palace at Southwark, and here, while waiting for the tide, he sent messages to the citizens of London. 'Nearly all of them,' says the chronicler emphatically,[1] 'nearly all of them wished entirely as he would have them.' Almost unanimously they declared against the foreigners, and espoused the cause of the champions of English freedom.

Assured of a peaceful reception, Godwine and Harold, as soon as the flood-tide was come, weighed their anchors, and moved in terrible array up the river, close to the southern bank; and their land forces simultaneously accompanied the magnificent procession, fronting the royal army which was drawn up on the north bank, and daring them to the battle. The king had also got together some fifty ships,

[1] Roger de Hoveden, p. 119.

but neither his soldiers nor his seamen were animated with a spirit of loyalty. How could they, as Englishmen, feel any sympathy with a cause which was the cause of the foreigner and the oppressor? What interest had they in riveting the chains for their own limbs? Greatly, says the conqueror, greatly did almost all the English abhor fighting against their own fellow-countrymen and kindred.

It was obvious that, under such circumstances, Godwine's success was certain; and as he was at all times in his career averse to shedding blood, he sent a peaceful message to the king, praying that he and his sons might be restored to all that had been unjustly taken from them.

At first Eadward hesitated; then he refused. The wrath of Godwine's men flamed into fury, and it was with difficulty that he restrained them from an immediate attack on the royal forces. But the latter, on their part, were unwilling to contend with their own countrymen in a cause with which they could have no sympathy, on behalf of the Normans, whom they themselves hated with a righteous hatred.[1] Eadward's counsellors would have had him draw the sword, but he had the sagacity to perceive that he could only do so to his own peril. He therefore authorized Bishop Stigand to act as mediator between earl and king, and it was agreed that hostages should be exchanged, and Godwine's claim referred to a Gemót to be holden on the following day. Thereupon Godwine and Harold landed, and betook themselves, amid the cheers of the multitude, to their house at Southwark.[2]

What would be the result of the morrow's council, the Normans who had gathered about Eadward rightly con-

---

[1] Roger de Hoveden, p. 442.
[2] See *Chronicles of Abingdon and of Peterborough*, under this date.

jectured. They knew it would terminate in the triumphant restoration of Godwine and his sons to their estates and honours, and in their own ignominious expulsion from the land they had plundered. They were wise in time. They prepared for instant flight. And all that night there was mounting in hot haste, of priest, and monk, and captain; and a motley train of palfrey, mule, and war-horse wended its way through the streets of London, headed by the Archbishop of Canterbury and the Bishop of London. And as they went, they fell in with detachments of Saxon troops, who drew up at every point of vantage, with the Saxon cry of 'Down with the outland men.' In this hour of disaster the old Norman heroism was not wanting: prelate and knight charged, sword in hand, and cut their way by sheer force through the ranks of their opponents. Once clear of the city streets, they separated, for better precaution, into various parties. Some crossed the country to Herefordshire; some went north to Robert's Castle; the prelates rode as fast as their steeds could carry them to Walton-on-the-Naze, where they found an open fishing-boat, and, with a few attendants, crossed the Channel to the shore of France. And thus, in 1052, was accomplished the strange hegira of the Norman favourites of King Eadward.

In the following day the great Witán met,—met in the open air,—with the king seated in their midst, the officers of his household about him, the clerks of the chapel and the king's confessor at his side. Foremost in rank sat the lords of the Church, and immediately behind them the great earls, —Siward, and Leofric, and Rolf,—with the Saxon earls, and that higher order of thegns called the king's thegns. Near to these sat the chief citizens of London, and in the same division were the thegn-landowners girt with their swords, and all of varying birth, fortune, and connection. There sate—if we may adopt Lord Lytton's ideal picture—half a yeoman, the Saxon thegn of Berkshire or Dorset, proud of his five hides of land; there, half an ealdorman, the Danish thegn of Norfolk or Ely, discontented with his forty: some were there in virtue of the small offices they held under the crown; some, traders and sons of traders, because they had crossed the high seas three times at their own risk; some traced back their ancestry to Offa and Egbert; some could count only three generations between themselves and the ploughman or neat-herd whose industry or fortune had founded a family; some were Saxons, and some were Danes; a few were Britons, from the western shires, though ignorant, perhaps, of their original race. Further down still stood the ceorls themselves,—a vast but not powerless body; not called upon to vote, or speak, or act, but only to shout 'Yea, yea,' when the judgment of the Witán was announced;—yet not altogether powerless, for they represented in the eleventh century that moving yet silent force which in the nineteenth we call Public Opinion.[1]

Earl Godwine stood forth: he laid his axe at the foot of the throne, and knelt in homage before the king. Then he implored him, in the name of Christ, whose emblem, the cross, he wore upon his crown, that he would permit him to clear himself of the crimes which had been laid to his charge, and when he had cleared himself, would restore him to his royal favour. The demand was granted; and Godwine, with the manly eloquence of which he was a consummate master, addressed the sympathizing Witán. He was followed by

[1] Palgrave, *History of England.* See also Lord Lytton's *Harold.*

his sons, each of whom effectually refuted the accusations of their enemies.

With one accord the Witán revoked the sentence of banishment, and decreed their restoration to their estates and dignities. By another unanimous sentence, they banished all the Normans from England, as enemies of the public peace, favourers of discord, and calumniators of his English subjects before the king. As hostages for the peace, Godwine placed his youngest son Wulfnoth, and one of the sons of Swegen, in Eadward's hands. Godwine's daughter was recalled from her convent to reside in the royal palace; and all the members of his family resumed their earldoms and possessions, except Swegen, who, deeply remorseful for the sins of his early life, voluntarily renounced his honours, and commenced a pilgrimage, barefooted, to Jerusalem. He accomplished the painful task, but soon afterwards died.

Bishop Stigand, who had presided over the Witán held for this great national act of reconciliation, was promoted to the see of Canterbury, vacated by the Norman Robert. The Normans, Hugh and Osbern Pentecoste, surrendered the castles which they held, and obtained safe-conducts to leave England. Of all the Norman host which had settled, like a cloud of locusts, on the fair lands of England, only a few were suffered to remain, the immediate attendants of the king, and those who had not involved themselves in the struggle against Godwine. William, Bishop of London, the most popular of the Norman prelates,[1] was also recalled from banishment, and reinstated in his episcopal dignity. This concession was made to the weakness of the king, but after events showed its impolicy.

[1] Florence of Worcester, A.D. 1052.

Throughout this strange history the moderation of Godwine shines conspicuously. The king was completely in his power, yet he treated him with deference, and consulted his wishes. He might probably have placed the crown on his own brow, but he contented himself with regaining the honours and estates that undoubtedly belonged to his family. Whether, after this time, a *sincere* friendship really sprang up between him and the king, it is difficult to say. At all events, friendship, in a courtly atmosphere, is a plant of slow growth; and so far as Godwine was concerned, a brief period only was allowed for its cultivation.[1]

The next great assembly of the Witán took place at Eastertide 1053. The king kept high festival at Winchester; and among those admitted to the royal table on the Monday of the holiday week, were Earl Godwine, and his sons Harold, Tostig, and Gyrth. The earl had been for some time ailing, and during the banquet he fell from his seat, was raised in the arms of Tostig and Gyrth, and carried to the king's own room, where, on the Thursday following, he died. In such a death we should now-a-days see nothing wonderful, but should ascribe it to an apoplectic or paralytic seizure; but Godwine had many enemies, and these enemies seized upon it as an admirable theme for calumny. They asserted that it was a stroke of the divine vengeance,—a signal chastisement of the man whom, in defiance of all evidence, they persisted in calling the murderer of the youthful Ælfred. And, by degrees, they adorned the incident with fictitious details, until, in the pages of the Norman chroniclers, it assumes the following form:—

One of Godwine's servants, while pouring him out a cup of wine, stumbled with one foot, but quickly recovered himself with the other. 'Sir,' said Godwine to the king, smiling, 'the

[1] Thierry, *Norman Conquest*, i. 139.

"He put the bread into his mouth and fell back suffocated." — LIVES OF OLD ENGLISH WORTHIES, *Page* 171

brother has come to the brother's assistance.' Eadward answered significantly: 'Ay, brother needs brother, and would to God that mine still lived!' 'O king,' exclaimed Godwine, 'wherefore is it that, on the slightest allusion to your brother, you always look so angrily upon me? If I had any share, directly or indirectly, in his death, may the God of heaven grant that this piece of bread may choke me!' He put the bread into his mouth, and fell back suffocated.

Such is the fable related by the later chroniclers.[1] By contemporary writers no such circumstances are recorded. We are simply told that Godwine, who had been for some time ailing, fell down in a fit at the king's table, and three days afterwards expired.[2]

Godwine was buried in the old minster at Winchester with great pomp, and amidst the general lamentation of the English people; and both at the national instance, and out of the affection of the Countess Gytha, rich gifts of lands and ornaments were made to the famous abbey, in honour of the illustrious dead.

We have already been indebted to Mr. Freeman for some striking passages woven into the woof of our plainer narrative. We shall here include his admirable character of Godwine, which we hold to be in the main both just and accurate, though slightly tinged, perhaps, with a not unnatural partiality for the great Saxon earl.

To know what Godwine was, he says, we have but to cast

[1] *The Chron. Abingdon*, A.D. 1052 and 1053. See Florence of Worcester, A.D. 1053.
[2] See William of Malmesbury, Bk. ii., and Henry of Huntingdon, Bk. vi.

away the fables of later days, to turn to the records of his own time, to see how he looked in the eyes of men who had seen and heard him, of men who had felt the blessings of his rule, and whose hearts had been stirred by the voice of his mighty eloquence. No man ever deserved a higher or more lasting place in national gratitude than the first man who, being neither king nor priest, stands forth in English history as endowed with all the highest attributes of the statesman. In him, in these distant times, we can revere the great minister, the unrivalled parliamentary leader, the man who could sway councils and assemblies at his will, and whose voice, during five and thirty years of political life, was never raised in any cause but that of the welfare of England. Side by side with all that is worthiest in our latest history,—side by side with his counterpart two ages afterwards, the second deliverer from the yoke of the stranger, the victor of Lewes, the martyr of Evesham,—side by side with all who, from his day to ours, have, in the field or in the senate, struggled or suffered in the cause of English freedom,—side by side with the worthies of the thirteenth and the worthies of the seventeenth centuries,—will the voice of truthful history, rising above the calumnies of age, place the name of the great deliverer of the Church, the earl of happy memory—'dux felicis memoriæ'—whose greatness was ever the greatness of England, whose life was one long offering to her welfare, and whose death came fittingly as the crown of that glorious life, when he had once more given peace and freedom to the land which he loved so well.[1]

---

[1] We think Mr. Freeman is unjust to the 'Victor of Lewes' in placing him side by side with Godwine, great as we admit the latter to be. But Simon de Montfort was a man of far higher political sagacity, of greater administrative ability, and superior military genius.

On the death of Godwine, Harold was chosen to succeed him in the government of the West Saxons,—a post which was virtually equal to the viceroyalty of the kingdom. When he thus became the foremost man in all England, he was about two or three and thirty years of age. He had already gained, in a remarkable degree, the love and confidence of his countrymen; and when he was appointed to his father's earldom, a universal sentiment of satisfaction spread through the land. Up to this point, indeed, his career had not been altogether stainless; but his genius was of a progressive character, and every year had seen him maturing in sagacity and self-control.

The government of the East Angles, which Harold had previously held, was bestowed upon Ælfgar, the son of Leofric of Mercia, who almost immediately revolted, and was thereupon banished. That of Northumbria, soon rendered vacant by the death of stout old Siward—'Siward Digr,' or the Strong—passed into the hands of Harold's brother Tostig (1055), for whom the king seems to have felt a warm personal affection. The organization of the kingdom thus completed, Harold directed his attention to its external relations.

The Welsh, encouraged by the incompetency of Ralph the Frenchman and the king's nephew, who commanded at Hereford, had crossed the English border under Gruffydd, their prince, and committed terrible ravages. The banished earl Ælfgar, with a force of Danes and Irishmen, had landed in Wales, concluded terms of alliance with Gruffydd, and united with him. The combined army, plundering and burning as they advanced, struck into the southern districts of Herefordshire, meeting with no opposition until they arrived within two miles of Hereford. Here Ralph had concentrated a considerable force, composed of his own Northmen and of the Saxon militia. The latter he insisted on mounting upon horses, though they had always been accustomed to fight on foot; and accordingly they lost heart. They fought indeed with something of their old spirit, until Ralph and his Normans fled before the impetuous onset of the Cymry; and then they joined in the retreat, which soon became a rout. Four to five hundred were slain in the *melée*, but not a man, it is said, was lost by the Welsh. On the same day Gruffydd and Ælfgar entered Hereford without resistance, sacked every house, and burned its beautiful cathedral church.[1]

To meet this danger, Harold alone was the one man capable. He levied an army with the utmost promptitude; crossed England to the scene of the war; and adapting his tactics to those of the enemy, caused his soldiers to adopt a free and loose array, as well as lighter weapons and armour. The Welsh did not care to try the issue of battle with so formidable an opponent. They retreated hastily into their mountain fastnesses, whither Harold found it was vain to pursue them. He therefore dismissed the greater part of his army, bidding them hold themselves prepared to meet their impetuous foe, if need should arise; and with the remainder of his troops, probably his West Saxon levies, he repaired to Hereford, which he proceeded to fortify with a ditch and a strong wall. The great leader's strategy seems for a time to have overawed the Welsh, and both Gruffydd and Ælfgar sued for peace. A conference took place at Billingsley, in Shropshire, where Gruffydd promised to keep within his own borders; and Ælfgar, soliciting the king's pardon, was restored to his forfeited earldom.

[1] Florence of Worcester, A.D. 1055.

But the restless Welsh chieftain observed a treaty only so long as it suited him. In the following year he again crossed the border, and was encountered on this occasion by a priestly warrior, Leofgar, the Bishop of Hereford. The latter, however, was killed (June 16th), and the Welsh ravages continued unchecked. It was obviously necessary that some protection should be secured for the unfortunate inhabitants of the western counties; and negotiations took place between Gruffydd on the one hand, and Ealdred, who had succeeded to the see of Hereford, Harold, and Earl Leofric, on the other.[1] Gruffydd was induced to pay homage to his over-lord, and to forfeit a small portion of his territory. Then for a few months the land was at peace with the Cymry.

[1] Florence of Worcester, A.D. 1056.

CHAPTER III.

Death of the Ætheling Eadward—Harold recognised as future King—Magnificent Position of the House of Godwine—Ancestry of Godwine—Harold's Pilgrimage to Rome—He founds the Minster at Waltham—Invasion of the Welsh under Gruffydd—Harold's great Campaign—Death of Gruffydd, and Subjugation of the Welsh—The Northumbrian Revolt against Earl Tostig—It is put down through Harold's prudent Policy—Eadward's Illness—His last Hours—His prophetic Visions—Nominates Harold as his Successor—His Death and Burial—His Character.

In 1057 the ætheling Eadward, the last surviving son of Edmund Ironside, and heir male of the royal line—the king's heir presumptive, as we should now designate him—visited England, and was received with a hearty welcome by all who desired to see the succession to the throne preserved to the dynasty of Ælfred. But almost immediately after his arrival in London,[1] he fell sick and died; and was buried with his grandfather Æthelred in the cathedral church of St. Paul's.

It may be reasonably conjectured that after this event—after the death of the last direct heir to the crown—Harold may have allowed himself to cherish an ambitious hope of one day securing it for his own brow. He must have been conscious that no other living Englishman had so great a title to it; that no other living Englishman so fully enjoyed the

[1] Florence of Worcester, A.D. 1057.

love and confidence of his fellow-subjects; that no other living Englishman was his superior in the council or on the battle-field. Some such vision may have crossed his mind before, as I think it had crossed the mind of his father Godwine; but now that circumstances tended so directly towards its realization, I can well believe that Harold entertained it with more serious consideration.

This same year was marked by the death of Earl Leofric of Mercia,—an event which necessitated a new apportionment of the great English earldoms. Earl Ralph, who had ruled so incompetently on the Welsh borders, also died. Herefordshire, and apparently Gloucestershire also, was now added to Harold's earldom, who thus became the ruler of nearly all England from the Thames to the Severn,—an increase of power which could not but encourage his ambitious hopes. Mercia was given to Ælfgar, who about this time married, or had already married, Ealdgyth, his beautiful daughter, to the Welsh prince Gruffydd. The East Anglican earldom was bestowed on Harold's youngest brother Gyrth; while another brother, Leofwine, received the lordship of south-eastern England, of Kent and Essex, Hertford and Surrey. 'The whole east of England was thus placed under the rule of the two younger sons of Godwine. But the evidence of the writs seems to show that Harold retained a general superintendence over their governments, whether simply as their elder brother, or in any more exalted character.'[1]

The position of the house of Godwine at this epoch was as unique as it was magnificent. In all its relations and conse-

[1] Freeman, *History of the Norman Conquest*, ii. 415-419.

quences it has been carefully examined by the historian of the period, who is justified in exclaiming that, whatever the origin of the family, they had now won for themselves a position such as no English family ever won before,—such as no English family has ever won since.

Four brothers, sons of a father who, whether earl or churl by birth,[1] had risen to greatness by his own valour and counsel,

---

[1] In reference to Godwine's ancestry, a very clear statement is embodied in one of Lord Lytton's admirable notes to his historical romance of *Harold*. We quote it *in extenso*, as it embodies a host of details in a lucid and comprehensive form :—

'Sharon Turner quotes from the *Kyntlinga Saga* what he calls "an explanation of Godwine's career or parentage, which no other document affords,"—viz. "that Ulf, a Danish chief, after the battle of Skorstein, between Cnut and Eadmund Ironside, pursued the English fugitives into a wood, lost his way, met on the morning a Saxon youth driving cattle to their pasture, asked him to direct him in safety to Cnut's ships, and offered him the bribe of a gold ring for his guidance. The young herdsman refused the bribe, but sheltered the Dane in the cottage of his father (who is represented as a mere peasant), and conducted him the next morning to the Danish camp ; previously to which, the youth's father had represented to Ulf, that his son Godwine could never, after aiding a Dane to escape, rest in safety with his countrymen ; and besought him to befriend his son's fortune with Cnut." The Dane promised, and kept his word : hence Godwine's rise. Thierry, in his *History of the Norman Conquest*, tells the same story, on the authority of Torfœus, *Hist. Nov. Norweg.* Now I need not say to any scholar in our early history, that the Norse chronicles, abounding with romance and legend, are never to be received as authorities *counter* to our own records, though occasionally valuable to supply omissions in the latter ; and, unfortunately for this pretty story, we have *against* it, the direct statements of the very best authorities we possess—viz. the *Saxon Chronicle*, and Florence of Worcester. The *Saxon Chronicle* expressly tells us that Godwine's father was Childe of Sussex (Florence calls him Minister or Thegn of Sussex) ; and that Wolnoth was nephew to Eadric, the all-powerful Earl or Duke of Mercia. Florence confirms this statement, and gives the pedigree, which may be deduced as follows :—

divided by far the greater part of England among them. The whole kingdom, save a few shires in the centre, was in their hands. And three at least out of the four showed that they well deserved their greatness. To the eldest among the four there evidently belonged a more marked pre-eminence still. Two of his brothers—those most recently appointed to earl-

Eadric married Eadgyth, daughter of Æthelred II.	Ægelric, surnamed Leofwine.
	Ægelmar.
	Wolnoth, Childe or Thegn of Sussex.
	Godwine.

'Thus this "old peasant," as the North chronicles call Wolnoth, was, according to our most unquestionable authorities, a thegn of one of the most important divisions in England, and a member of the most powerful family in the kingdom! Now, if our Saxon authorities needed any aid from probabilities, it is scarcely worth asking which is the more probable, that the son of a Saxon herdsman should in a few years rise to such power as to marry the sister of the royal Danish conqueror,—or that that honour should be conferred on the most able member of a house already allied to Saxon royalty, and which evidently retained its power after the fall of its head, the treacherous Eadric Streone! Even after the Conquest, one of Streone's nephews, Eadinus Sylvaticus, is mentioned (Simon Dunelm.) as a "very powerful thegn." Upon the whole, the account given of Godwine's rise in the text of this work appears the most correct that conjectures, based on our scanty historical information, will allow.

'In 1009 A.D., Wolnoth, the Childe or Thegn of Sussex, defeats the fleets of Æthelred under his uncle Brihtric, and goes therefore into rebellion. Thus when, in 1014 (five years afterwards), Cnut is chosen king by all the fleet, it is probable that Wolnoth, and Godwine his son, espoused his cause; and that Godwine, subsequently presented to Cnut as a young noble of great promise, was favoured by that sagacious king, and ultimately honoured with the hand, first of his sister, secondly of his niece, as a mode of conciliating the Saxon thegns.'

doms—were clearly little more than Harold's lieutenants. And a prospect of still higher greatness now lay open to him and his house. The royal line was dying out. No adult male descendant of Æthelred remained; no adult male descendant of any kind remained in the kingdom. The only survivors of the late royal stock were the son and daughters of the ætheling, children born in a foreign land. The time was clearly coming when Englishmen might choose for themselves a king from among their brethren, unfettered by any traditional reverence for the blood of Ælfred, Cerdric, and Woden. And when that day should come, on whom should the choice of England fall, save on the worthiest man of the worthiest house within the realm? We cannot doubt that from the year when the three deaths of Eadward, Leofric, and Ralph seemed to sweep away all hindrances from his path, Harold looked forward to a day when he and his might rise to a rank yet loftier than that of earl. It was no longer wholly beyond hope that he might himself ascend the imperial throne of Britain, and that the earldoms of Britain might be held by his brothers as æthelings of the house of Godwine. The event proves that such were the hopes of Harold,—that such, we may add, were the hopes of England.[1]

Mr. Freeman goes on to add, that it is difficult to determine whether Harold's succession, at this or at any other time, was guaranteed by Eadward, with or without the assent of the Witán. Was any formal promise made? It is certain that Eadward exercised in Harold's favour whatever influence an English king *could* exercise in the nomination of his successor, and that Eadward's nomination was finally and formally made

[1] Freeman, *History of the Norman Conquest*, ii. 421, 422.

upon his deathbed. But such a nomination does not necessarily render improbable or impossible a promise of the same kind at an earlier date. And there do seem to be some reasons for believing that Harold was *generally* recognised as Eadward's heir presumptive after the death of the ætheling, —as, in fact, the future king of England. Thus his name in public documents is coupled with that of Eadward in an unusual and very significant manner. Next, we find vassal princes vowing allegiance to the king and the earl as if they were senior and junior colleagues in one common office,—like the Augustus and the Cæsar of the Roman Empire. We also find Harold appearing in the eyes of foreigners as 'Dux Anglorum,' or Duke of the English. That no such title was borne by him at home we may rest assured, but it would seem to show that his position was princely in its powers and privileges. Lastly, in the chronicle of Florence of Worcester we find him distinctly called by a title, 'sub-regulus,' which is the customary designation of vassal princes, but is nowhere applied to a subject. Taking these things together, are we not justified in concluding that Earl Harold's position was that of a viceroy, publicly destined to succeed to the throne on the death of its present occupant?

In 1058 peace prevailed in the land, and Harold availed himself of the opportunity to make a pilgrimage to the holy shrines at Rome.[1] On his way he passed through France, examining its military condition, and visiting, in all probability, the courts both of Rouen and Paris. At Rome, the individual then in possession of the Papal throne was probably Benedict

[1] The exact date of this journey is unknown, but it is difficult to appropriate to it any other date than the one in the text.

II., afterwards deposed and branded as anti-pope; and as it was Benedict who granted the archiepiscopal pallium to Stigand, the English primate, after a long delay, we may conjecture that Harold was presented to him, and that in granting the pallium he was influenced by a desire to gratify the great English earl.

How long Harold stayed at Rome we know not, but it would seem that he returned to England within the twelvemonth.

Passing over the year 1059, which makes a blank in English history, we pause at the completion and consecration of the minster of Waltham, as the most memorable incident in this part of Harold's career. He established here a dean and twelve secular canons, in enlargement of Tofig's original foundation, whose celebrity was derived from its possession of a wonder-working crucifix, found at Lutegarsbury. He rebuilt the church on a scale of unaccustomed magnificence, and enriched it with relics from Rome, and many precious gifts. He also endowed the canons with lands, and provided them with a schoolmaster or lecturer,—one Adelard of Lüttich.

The church or minster at Waltham was consecrated on the 3d of May 1060, by Cynesige, Archbishop of York, in the presence of King Eadward and the Lady Eadgyth, and all the leading thegns and prelates of the land.

From these peaceful occupations we turn again to the battlefield,—to the sounds and stratagems of war.

In 1062 Gruffydd, the Welsh prince, renewed his incursions into Herefordshire, and swept in a storm of fire and sword along the English border. When the news reached Harold, he determined to deal summarily with this disturber of the kingdom. With a small force of mounted warriors, he rode across country to Rhuddlan, on the north-east frontier of Wales; a place of considerable strength, where Gruffydd had his royal residence. The Welsh prince heard of Harold's approach just in time to gallop headlong to the coast, and escape by sea. The English, on their arrival, found that their prey had escaped; and as they were neither strong enough in numbers, nor sufficiently provided, for a long winter warfare in the deep valleys and wild mountain-passes of Wales, they burned Rhuddlan, and Gruffydd's palace, and all the vessels in port, and then returned to Gloucester.

The winter was spent by Harold in planning a campaign which should finally relieve the country of its old and terrible enemy. He made his preparations with consummate skill, —with a skill which was fully appreciated by the chroniclers of even a century later, whether English or Norman; and in May 1063, accompanied by his brother Tostig, he invaded Wales. He knew that he had to contend with a foe who was formidable chiefly from the celerity of his movements,—a foe who fought no pitched battles, and wasted no time in besieging massive fortresses. To cope with the Welsh tactics, he caused his men to carry but little armour, to fight with the sword and javelin, to march swiftly, to climb intrepidly, and to be patient under the most intolerable hardships. What he required of others, he did himself, and his men, animated by so noble an example, pursued the Cymry into their fortresses. Step by step the Cymry were driven back into their farthest valleys and obscurest glens; their chiefs were slain; and such an ominous belt of sword and spear and axe was drawn around them, that they were glad to yield an unconditional submission. They pledged themselves by solemn oath never again to trespass beyond their frontiers, and agreed that every Welshman taken prisoner on English ground should have his right hand cut off. And they gave hostages to the king and the earl that they would be faithful in all things, and everywhere ready for them, by sea and by land, and render such tribute from the land as had been yielded before to any other king.

So broken was the spirit of the Welsh, that they put to death their prince and leader, Gruffydd, the son of Lewelyn, and sent his head to Harold; so complete was their subjugation, that from that time forth they were unable to oppose a successful resistance to English power. Harold conducted the war in the spirit in which Cromwell, at a later period, warred against the Irish. He resolved to subdue or exterminate, and to strike a blow which should be final. He gave no quarter. Every male who resisted was put to the sword. He fought no pitched battles, but he entangled the Welsh in ambuscades, and engaged them in sudden and unexpected skirmishes; and he marked his victorious progress by trophies of stone, which bore the proud inscription, 'Here Harold conquered.'

The war over, Harold returned to Winchester with the memorials of his victory—the head of Gruffydd, and the beak of his ship. These he presented to King Eadward. He retained for himself a more precious memorial, in the person of Ealdgyth, the widow of Gruffydd, and the daughter of Earl Ælfgar, whom he now took to wife (A.D. 1064). It has been suggested that the marriage was a political one, and that Harold hoped to secure by it some Mercian votes in the Gemót, which would be called to decide on the election of a king; but it is at least as probable that Harold, like many another hero, was sensible of the influence of beauty, and that he wedded Ealdgyth, first because he admired her, and second, because, as future king, he desired to be the father of a legitimate heir.

It should be noted as a signal proof of the complete pacification of Wales, that in the following year Harold began the erection of a hunting-seat at Porth-iscoed, or Portskewet, within what had once been Welsh territory. This hunting-seat was not intended for his own delectation, but for that of his sovereign. The chase was one of the few pleasures which Eadward the monk king permitted himself; and as he grew old, his attachment to it grew stronger.

But from this occupation he was summoned to a new field of warfare. By a long course of oppression, Earl Tostig, his brother, had so harassed and angered his Northumbrian subjects, that at length they broke out into open rebellion (October 1065), and besieged the gates of York, where Tostig had fixed his residence. The earl made his escape, but a fierce slaughter took place among his officers and attendants. They then held a Witán, which voted the deposition of Tostig, declared him an outlaw, and elected in his stead Morkere, or Morcar, the younger son of Ælfgar of Mercia, and brother of the ambitious and treacherous Eadwine.

Morkere, by his activity, showed himself not unworthy of his elevation, if that elevation had been confirmed by the sovereign and Witán of England. Gathering the men of Lincoln, Nottingham, and Derby, he penetrated southwards to Northampton, ravaging all the surrounding country, carrying off corn and cattle, and several hundred prisoners. Harold was immediately despatched to the scene of action. In the name of King Eadward he commanded the rebels to lay down their arms, and whatever grievances they had against their earl, to submit them to the decision of the English Witán. But, as Roger de Hoveden significantly says, they would listen to no arrangement which seemed to imply that Tostig was still their ruler. 'They all with one voice refused, and pronounced him an outlaw, together with all those who had encouraged him to enact unjust laws.' As born freemen, they would not submit to the ferocity of any earl, and would only return to their allegiance, on condition that Eadward confirmed their choice of Morkere.

A Witán was held at Bretford, near Salisbury, to consider the demands of the Northumbrians. Harold in vain endeavoured to obtain a modification of these demands, and to support the claims of his brother Tostig. But when he found that reconciliation was impossible, he, like a true patriot, preferred the interests of his country to those of his family, and advised the king to accede to the wishes of the Northumbrians. At this act of patriotism and self-denial, Tostig waxed furiously wroth, and openly charged his brother with having stimulated the rebellion, so that the latter was compelled to deny his complicity upon oath. The king was anxious to support his favourite by arms, to call to the royal standard the whole levies of England, and, with fire and sword, punish his disobedient Northumbrian subjects. But his wisest counsellors shrank from a course so full of danger. A winter campaign is ever unpopular with voluntary forces, and, moreover, it was doubtful whether these would muster in any considerable numbers to wage war against their own countrymen. So Eadward was overruled, though not convinced. The levies were not summoned; and the king, chafing at his inaction and his disappointment, fell into a sickness which eventually proved mortal.

Under these circumstances, feeling that a resort to armed force was difficult, if not impossible,—that no reconciliation could be effected between the Northumbrians and Tostig,—that it was for the interest of the country to maintain peace within its borders,—and that the humiliation of the great Mercian house was for obvious reasons impolitic, Harold resolved on yielding to the demands of the insurgents. By a Witán held at York, Tostig's deposition and Morkere's election were confirmed, and the former was banished from the kingdom. He fled to the court of his wife's father, the Count of Flanders, and thenceforth busied himself in conspiring against his brother and his native land.

These events were quickly followed by the last illness and death of Eadward, accelerated, it is probable, by his keen sense of the misfortunes that awaited his realm from the ambition of his Norman cousin. He could not conceal from himself, as the approach of death quickened his intellectual foresight, that he had prepared great peril for his country, by his inordinate partiality for foreign favourites. He endeavoured, by constant religious exercises, to dispel these thoughts, and quench the remorse which they awakened. But it was in vain. His last hours were haunted by gloomy visions, which the ministrations of his priests and chaplains could not exorcise. In his fanatical ecstasies, wild memories of prophetic denunciations would cross his mind, and in a loud tone, and with flashing eyes, he would exclaim, 'The Lord hath bent His bow! The Lord hath bared His sword!

He brandisheth it to and fro like a warrior! He boweth the mountains, and cometh down, and the darkness is under His feet! By fire and sword will He manifest His wrath!'[1]

The thegns and prelates in attendance upon him listened and trembled, as if it was the voice of one of the old Hebrew prophets that rung through the darkened chamber. Stigand alone, the astute and somewhat worldly Archbishop of Canterbury, ridiculed, with a smile of contempt, what he regarded as a dotard's fancies;[2] and, thinking more of present duties than of future terrors, he solicited the dying king, after the old English custom, to nominate a successor. He named, without hesitation, as the only man worthy to rule, Harold the Earl. The choice was manifestly a patriotic one; for if selfish considerations had influenced him, he would have chosen Eadgar the Ætheling, a grandson of Eadmund Ironside. But with the clearness of vision a deathbed often gives, he saw that the kingdom needed the firm hand and cool brain of a loyal patriot, of a wise statesman, of an experienced soldier; and he remembered that Eadgar was but a youth of Hungarian birth and foreign training,—weak, timorous, imbecile,—wholly unworthy of so great and so solemn a trust.

On the 5th of January 1066, and at the palace of Westminster, King Eadward died, and he was buried in the great abbey which his pious munificence had founded.

It is difficult, says Mr. Pearson, to do justice to Eadward's character; and yet it seems to us that its principal features are strongly marked. He was one of those men who shine best in private positions, who are unfitted, by temperament and intel-

---

[1] Ailred, *Vita Eadwardi* (*Hist. Angl. Script.*), i. 400.

[2] Ailred, *Vita Eadwardi* (*Hist. Angl. Script.*), i. 400; Robert of Gloucester, p. 350.

lect, for the burthen of any great responsibilities. In the cloister he would have made an excellent monk, for he was devout after the fashion of his time, and strict in the performance of every religious exercise. He wanted the liberal sympathies, the breadth of view, and the decision of will, which are requisite in the man who would successfully govern men; and had he not been supported at one time by the shrewd and sagacious Godwine, and at the other by the chivalrous Harold, his reign would probably have been a record of disasters. As it was, England, on the whole, enjoyed under his rule a considerable measure of tranquillity; and hence, when at a later period, men, smarting under Norman tyranny, looked back to these comparatively halcyon days, they were naturally led to invest the king with a wholly fictitious character. He became in their eyes a just and merciful sovereign, a pure and peaceful saint. But the truth is, that it was only his weakness which prevented him from being a tyrant, and that not one of his predecessors inflicted by his exactions so terrible a blow on the fortunes of England, as Eadward, surnamed the Confessor, inflicted by his neglect of true English interests, and his criminal partiality for Norman favourites.

CHAPTER IV.

Election of Harold as King—An Episode in his Life—His Visit to Normandy—How he was received by Duke William—A Crafty Plot—Harold's Oath and the Sacred Relics—Harold's Coronation—His Popularity—How the Tidings were received in Normandy—A Striking Scene—William and his Barons—Preparations for the Invasion of England.

IMMEDIATELY on the death and burial of Eadward, the Witán met 'in solemn conclave,' and chose Harold to be their king. These events are narrated with much picturesque force by the annalist in the *Saxon Chronicle*:—

Here Eadward King,
Of Angles lord,
Sent his stedfast
Soul to Christ,
In God's protection, [a]
Spirit holy.
He in the world here
Dwelt awhile
In royal majesty,
Mighty in council—
Four and twenty—
Lordly ruler!—
Of winters numbered,
He wealth dispensed;
And he á prosperous time—
Ruler of
In distinction governed

Welsh and Scots,
And Britons also—
He, son of Æthelred—
And Angles and Saxons,
Chieftains bold.
Wherever embrace
The cold sea waves,
There all to Eadward,
The noble king!—
All the warrior-men
Gave faithful obedience.
Aye was blithe-minded,
The harmless king,
Though he long erst—
Of land bereaved—
In exile dwelt
Wide o'er the earth,

Since Cnut o'ercame
The race of Æthelred,
And Dane-kings wielded
The beloved nation
Of Angle-land,
And for eight and twenty
Of winters numbered
Wealth dispensed.
After forth came,
In vestments princely,
King with the chosen good,
Chaste and mild,
Eadward the noble.
The nation he guarded,
Both land and people,
Until suddenly came
Death the bitter,
And so dear an one seized.
This noble, stedfast soul
From earth angels carried
Into heaven's light.
And the sage [the Witán, or
  Wise], ne'ertheless,
The realm committed
To a highly-born man,
Harold's self,
The noble earl!
He in all time
Had faithfully obeyed
His rightful lord
By words and deeds;
Nor aught neglected
Which needful was
To his sovereign king.[1]

Before, however, we commence our narrative of Harold's memorable reign, we must deal with the most vexed and the obscurest episode in his life; an episode, moreover, of the utmost importance, from the fatal influence which it unquestionably exercised.

In all our early English history, no more romantic incident occurs than the visit of Harold to his rival, Duke William, and the oath which he took of allegiance to him. The year in which this visit was made is not certainly known, and a certain degree of obscurity rests about some of its details; but we are inclined to believe that it was made in 1064, and that its object was to obtain the restoration of his brother and nephew, Wulfnoth and Hakon. The reader will remember that, on the occasion of Godwine's reconciliation with King Eadward (see p. 169), Wulfnoth and Hakon were placed in the hands of the

---

[1] The *Saxon Chronicle*, A.D. 1061.

latter as securities for the earl's fidelity; and the general statement is, that Eadward sent them to be educated at the court of William. It is true that Mr. Freeman, whose authority on all matters connected with this period of our history is not to be neglected, is disinclined to believe the circumstance of the hostageship, and that he ascribes Harold's visit as the result of his being wrecked, during a pleasure voyage, on the coast of Ponthieu; but we venture to think that pleasure voyages were not among the pastimes of the Saxon nobles, and that the almost unanimous testimony of historians leads to a different conclusion.

Under some circumstances or other, it is, however, certain that Harold visited the court of William of Normandy.

The common account runs: that Harold, as the heart of Eadward grew more inclined towards his English counsellors, besought him to restore to their family the two hostages, his brother Wulfnoth and his nephew Hakon, placed in his hands of old as a guarantee for Godwine's fidelity, and who had for ten years been detained at the Norman court. The king voluntarily consented to their return; but when Harold prepared to cross the seas and claim them in person, he displayed a strong disinclination:—'I will not gainsay thee,' he said; 'but if thou goest, it will be against my desire, for I foresee that thy journey will bring some dread misfortune upon England and upon thyself. I know Count William, and his subtleness of soul, and that he hates thee, and will yield nothing to thee, unless it brings some advantage to himself. The better way would be to send some trusty person in thy behalf.' But Harold is described by the chronicler as ever alive very keenly to the claims of family; and, moreover, it is not improbable that he may have wished to measure himself with the man whom he could not but regard as his future competitor for the crown of England.

By constant pressure he obtained the king's consent, and then set forth on his journey as on a pleasant adventure,—his falcon on his wrist, and his greyhounds running before him.[1] He knew how ardent a lover was Duke William of hawking and the chase, and prepared to join in his favourite pastimes.

In three vessels he and his suite embarked from a point near the Sussex port of Bosham; after having first paid their devotions in that venerable church, which still remains as a memorial of the remote past. Overtaken by a storm, they were driven towards the mouth of the Somme, where the coast belonged to a barbarous freebooter, Guy, Count of Ponthieu, one of Duke William's vassals. It was the custom of that maritime country, and of many others, as Thierry remarks, to imprison every stranger unfortunately wrecked upon its shores, instead of treating him with humane consideration, and to set a ransom upon his head. Harold and his attendants were treated in accordance with this cruel practice,—were stripped of almost all their baggage, and flung into prison, perhaps into chains, in the inland fortress of Belrem (now Beaurain), near Montreuil.

It is said, however, that one of the English effected his escape, entrusted with a message from King Harold, and made his way to Duke William at Rouen. The illustrious Norman was not less indignant at the base action of his vassal, than delighted at an accident which had thrown his rival into his hands. He demanded Harold's release. His demand was immediately complied with, and Count Guy conducted

---

[1] He is thus represented in one of the interesting pictures of the Bayeux tapestry.

the English earl to Eu, whither William repaired to meet him. Guy received a large sum of money, and a gift of land on the banks of the Eaulne; Harold was most cordially and courteously greeted, and invited to become the duke's guest at Rouen. As the old chronicler writes:

> 'Tot droit à Roun la cité
> L'en amena li Dux od sei.'

At Rouen he was entertained with great splendour, with feats of arms, with costly pageants, and magnificent banquets:

> 'A maint rice torneiment
> Le fit aler mult noblement.'[1]

Harold and his train were admitted into the Brotherhood of Warriors, which the duke had instituted; and, finally, were induced—we might almost say compelled—to accompany him on an expedition against the Bretons. In crossing the dangerous stream of the Coconow, Harold saved the lives of several Normans, who would otherwise have perished in the quicksands. On their return, William and Harold rode side by side, sat at the same table, and shared the same tent. On one occasion William spoke of his early intimacy with Eadward the Confessor. 'When we lived together like brothers,' said he, 'under one roof, the good king promised that if he ever attained the throne of England, its heritage should be mine. And now, Harold, I hope that thou wilt assist me in realizing Eadward's promise; and if by thy assistance I gain the kingdom, I will grant to thee whatever thou shalt demand.'[2]

We can believe that Harold's wrath was great, but he knew

---

[1] *Roman de Rou*, lines 10810, 10811.
[2] Eadmeri, *Hist. Nova*, p. 5.

himself to be in the power of an unscrupulous adversary, and out of compulsion muttered some indefinite promise.[1]

'Since, then, I have thy consent,' resumed the duke, 'I will tell thee what thou must do. Thou must fortify the Castle of Dover, and hold it for me until my coming. Thy sister Thyra thou shalt give in marriage to one of my most powerful nobles, and my daughter Adeliza thou thyself shalt wed. Moreover, when thou departest home, I would have thee leave one of the hostages whom thou claimest, and when I am king of England, I will restore him to thee.'

That he had been ungenerously entrapped into a fatal snare, it is probable enough that Harold now perceived; though, of course, he could not anticipate all its terrible and most grievous consequences. He seems, however, to have met fraud by dissimulation, and, for the sake of his personal freedom, to have allowed William to believe that he had gained his end. And yet he had not formed a true conception of his rival's far-reaching and subtle duplicity.

A few days passed, and a great council of nobles was summoned to meet at Bayeux. The duke had previously caused to be brought together, from every church and convent in Normandy, the bones and relics of the most famous saints; and this 'holy spoil,' enclosed in a large casket, and covered with cloth of gold, was placed in the council-chamber. Surrounded by his barons and principal officers, with his crown on his brow, and his sword of state in his hand, he took his seat. Four *reliquaries*, or small caskets of relics,—or, as some say, a missal,—were laid upon the cloth of gold. Then spake the duke.

'Approach, Earl Harold, and in the presence of this famous

[1] *Roman de Rou*, ii. 11114.

assembly, confirm by oath the promises which thou hast made me; namely, that on the death of my cousin Eadward, thou wilt assist me to obtain the crown of England; that thou wilt wed my daughter Adeliza, and send thy sister hither to be given in marriage to one of my barons.'

Confused, surprised, and shaken with a wrath which he durst not reveal, Harold approached, laid his hands upon the sacred reliquaries, and vowed to execute his agreement. 'If I live,' he muttered, 'and if God help me!' And all the Norman barons repeated, 'Ke Dex li dont!' (May God help him!)

Then Odo, Bishop of Bayeux, and William's half-brother, suddenly drew aside the cloth of gold; and Harold perceived, with a shudder and a pale countenance—

> 'Heraut forment s'espoanta
> Des relikes k'il li monstra,'[1]—

the awful relics of the sainted dead, on which, unwittingly, he had taken his oath. He felt instinctively that the act he had done would in later years bring forth evil fruit.

In reference to this story we have only to add, that though many of its details may be the fictitious additions of sensation-loving chroniclers, its general truth cannot be questioned; and Harold's oath, when the fortunes of England came to be decided by the sword, proved a powerful weapon in the hand of her great enemy.[2]

One point in this transaction, says Pearson, is remarkable. There were at this time several exiles in Normandy,—Normans

---

[1] Compare Eadmer, pp. 5, 6; William of Poitiers, pp. 107, 108; William of Malmesbury, Book ii.; *Roman de Rou;* and *Chronique de Normandie, ut antè.*

[2] *Roman de Rou, ut antè.*

driven from England, or English enemies of Harold, or men outlawed by the Witán. These adventurers, a little later, formed part of William's army of invasion. It is strange that the duke did not stipulate for the restoration of these men to their homes and dignities. Their return would have been a pledge of Harold's sincerity, would have provided William with adherents, and would certainly not have been disagreeable to King Eadward. The omission of such an article implies that Harold's power was limited, as the stipulation that Dover should be surrendered proves that William anticipated having to enforce the treaty with his sword. It is probable, therefore, that the whole compact was a private one, witnessed only by the duke's chief councillors, and never divulged, until it suited William's diplomacy to excite European feeling by the charge of treachery against his rival.[1]

We have dwelt at some length upon this episode, because it may be said to have very materially influenced the course of events, and to have formed, in some wise, the prologue to the sad tragedy which was played out at Hastings. We now resume the thread of our narrative, and purpose to show how Harold's accession to Eadward's throne was regarded in England and Normandy.

The Witán met for the election of a successor to Eadward, even while the latter lay dead in his palace. There was no time for delay: the sceptre had fallen—it must be immediately

[1] Pearson, *Early and Middle Ages of England*, p. 238. A full examination of this curious passage in Harold's life—an exhaustive, but, as we venture to think, a too incredulous examination—will be found in Freeman's *History of the Norman Conquest*, ii. 216-254.

lifted up. Not long did the thegns and priests and citizens deliberate; not long, because all men's minds—or nearly all men's minds—had for some time been persuaded that Harold was their only possible ruler. A few voices were raised for Eadgar, still fewer for William, but the vast majority rang out in a mighty cheer for the English-born Harold. Mr. Freeman very forcibly remarks that we have no expression of those local jealousies which had divided England on more than one previous occasion. We hear nothing, he continues, of any rivalry between the house of Leofric and that of Godwine; nothing of any murmurs of the fierce Northern Danes against the establishment of a new West Saxon dynasty. If the sons of Earl Ælfgar dreamed, as is possible, of a divided kingdom —the northern half to themselves, the southern to Harold— their dreams were quickly dispelled. Such thoughts appear to have been agitating the minds of many; but at last, in this great Gemót of London, they found no utterance. It was not only London, ever foremost, says Mr. Freeman, in any patriotic cause;[1] it was not only Wessex, proud of her illustrious son; it was not only East Anglia, cherishing the recollections of his earliest rule; it was not only Hereford, rejoicing in her recovered king, safe alike against British foes and Norman governors;—it was the Witán, not of this or that shire or ancient kingdom, but of the whole realm of England, who chose Harold, the son of Godwine, to fill the vacant throne. His reign had long been looked for; and now the dying voice of Eadward had marked him out as the worthiest object of their choice. The wise ruler, the unconquered warrior, the

[1] When one remembers how noble and stirring a history London possesses, one is ashamed to think of the little pride which Londoners now-a-days feel in their mighty metropolis.

bountiful founder, the shield of the kingdom, the shelter of the oppressed, the judge of the fatherless and the widow, the Earl of the West Saxons, the conqueror of Gruffydd, the pacificator of Northumberland, the founder of Waltham,—stood forth before them as the foremost man of England. He, and he alone, stood forth above other men, sprung from no line of kings, but the son of a father greater than kings,—the man who, in long years of rule, had shown that there was none like him worthy to fill the throne of the heroes of old time,—worthy, as none of royal race were worthy, to wield the sword of Æthelstan, and sit upon the judgment-seat of Ælfred.[1]

The choice of the Witán was immediately communicated to Harold, who, though fully conscious, we may be sure, of the difficulties of his position, accepted the crown thus offered. He would have been no true Englishman had he shrunk from doing his duty because it was difficult! He could not but see that no other man was fitted to grapple with the arduous task which lay before the next occupant of the English throne; that no other man was fitted to reorganize the kingdom, to subdue internal dissensions, to defend it from external enemies. If he refused, who was to stand in the gap? The young Ætheling? He was no pilot to weather the storm that was then gathering about the cliffs of England. The hasty and impetuous Tostig? Or the treacherous Eadwine? Would Wessex and East Anglia submit to either? The Norman William? He was not less able as general or statesman than Harold himself: but think of the shame of the English realm, in once more submitting to the sway of a foreigner.

All these considerations must have been present to Harold's mind when he accepted the crown. But the path of duty

[1] Freeman, *History of the Norman Conquest*, ii. 21.

opened out straight before him,—a rough and thorny path; and, hero and patriot as he was, he resolved to tread it.

On Friday, January 6, 1066, Eadward was buried, and Harold was crowned. On the royal head of the latter the unction was poured by Ealdred, Archbishop of York; and all the people shouted with delight because Harold was king. And from the moment of his accession, as the old chronicler tells us,[1] he proceeded to abolish unjust laws, and to enact new and righteous ones; to become the zealous patron of churches and monasteries; to reverence and encourage the bishops, abbots, monks, and clergy; to show himself pious, humble, and courteous to all men; and to hold evil-doers in abhorrence. It was the inauguration of a new era; and who knows for what good it might have tended, had it not closed in blood and darkness on the field of Senlac?

We have now to see in what manner the accession of Harold was regarded by William the Norman.

The news was conveyed to him by a messenger from one of the Norman retainers who still hung about the English court.

> 'Un Serjant
> Ki d'Angleterre vint errant
> Al Duc vint droit.'

William is in his park near Rouen, trying some new arrows. Knights and squires and young nobles throng around him, waiting to join the chase.

> 'Mult aveit od li chevaliers,
> E damiseils et esquiers.'

He holds in his hand the mighty bow, which, like that of

[1] Roger de Hoveden, p. 133.

Ulysses, no arm but his own can bend. Suddenly the messenger approaches, takes him aside, and bowing low before him, says, 'King Eadward has ended his days, and Harold is raised to the kingdom.' A dark frown rises to his brow; he gives bow and arrows to a page; like a man in anger, he paces to and fro with hasty strides; he buckles and unbuckles his hunting cloak; he speaks not a word to knight or noble, and not a word does knight or noble speak to him. At last he moves down to the bank of the Seine, and taking boat, is ferried across to the other side. Then he enters his princely hall, and flinging himself down on a bench, rests his head against a pillar, and covers his face with his mantle. He will not let his attendants see how he is tortured by jealousy, and anger, and disappointed ambition. And thus he sits and muses in silence for a considerable period, while his counsellors ask one another with bated breath what ails their sovereign.

After a while there comes into the presence William's principal adviser and familiar friend, who is also his most powerful baron and his seneschal, the chief officer of his household, William Fitz-Osbern. He hums a tune as he walks,[1] for he is blithe of spirit; or perhaps he does it, that he may rouse the duke from his despondency. As he passes by the duke, the nobles pluck him by the sleeve, direct his attention to their master's unusual mood, and inquire of him, as his chief confidant, what ill news has so disturbed him.

'I know nothing certain,' answers the seneschal, 'but we shall soon learn.'

Then advancing to the duke, who, at his approach, uncovers his face, and looks up, he says:

[1] All these minute and interesting details are recorded in the *Roman de Rou*, and bring the scene before us in a singularly vivid manner.

'My lord, why dost thou seek to hide from *us* the tidings which are rumoured through every street in Rouen? It is said that the king of England is dead, and that Harold, violating his faith to you, has seized upon the crown.'

'The report is true,' replied the duke; 'and what can grieve me more than the death of Eadward, and the wrong done to me by Harold?'

'Sir,' answers Fitz-Osbern, 'chafe not at a thing that may be amended. For Eadward's death, indeed, there may be no remedy, but one may assuredly be found for the evil of which Harold has been guilty. The right is thine; thou hast brave and experienced knights; strike boldly; well begun is half done.'[1]

After due deliberation, William and his counsellor determined to despatch an embassy to Harold, and require him to resign the crown, which he had accepted in despite of his solemn oath and undertaking. On this point the chronicles are somewhat confused; and it is difficult to determine whether more than one embassy was sent, and whether the request conveyed by the second differed in scope from that conveyed by the first. Following the common version, we may believe that the first messenger, when he presented himself before King Harold, addressed him in words like these:[2]—

'William, Duke of the Normans, sends me to remind thee of the oath which thou didst take upon the holy relics, and to claim the immediate fulfilment of thy promises.'

Harold answered, we are told, in a half-serious, half-jesting manner:—'True it is that I took an oath to Duke William,

---

[1] *Chronique de Normandie*, p. 225.
Eadmeri, *Hist. Nor.* 5.

"What can grieve me more than the death of Eadward, and the wrong done to me by Harold?" LIVES OF OLD ENGLISH WORTHIES, *Page 202*

but I took it under grievous restraint. I promised what did not belong to me, and therefore my promise may not be fulfilled. My authority as king is given to me by my country, and against the will of my country I cannot put it off; nor against the will of my country can I wed a foreign wife. As for my sister, whom the duke would marry to one of his barons, alas, she died seven days agone. Does he wish me to send her corpse?'

A second messenger repeated the duke's reproaches, but in more moderate terms; only claiming, on behalf of his sovereign, the fulfilment of one condition, that Harold should marry the youthful Adeliza.

But Harold knew that the feeling of his subjects against foreign alliances was strong and bitter; and probably he also saw that no such connection would satisfy William's ambition. Open war was preferable to armed peace,—open war to hidden plotting; and therefore he refused the duke's demand, and boldly flung defiance in his face.

Unquestionably this result was the result which William had anticipated and hoped for. From the moment he heard of Harold's accession, he knew that his sole chance of gaining the coveted prize lay in the fortune of war. Yet the difficulties which lay in his path were numerous enough and formidable enough to have daunted a less resolute spirit. What he aimed at was no mere incursion or raid for the sake of plunder, but a permanent conquest; and though a permanent conquest had been effected by Cnut, it was under conditions which no longer existed. During the reign of Eadward, England had become more compact, more homogeneous, and her population had increased; her military strength was considerable, and was wielded by a commander not inferior in genius and skill to William himself. He had no English faction in his favour. He could not count upon the support of European opinion; he could hardly count upon the support of his own subjects. That he persevered in the face of all these obstacles, and eventually triumphed over them, is a signal proof of the force of his character, and of his ability as a soldier and a statesman.

His first care was to secure the assistance of his knights and barons.

For this purpose he assembled a council of his most intimate friends and advisers: his brothers, Odo of Bayeux, and Robert, Count of Mortain; his seneschal, William Fitz-Osbern, the trusted depository of his most secret thoughts; Iwan-al-Chapel, his sister's husband; Richard, Count of Evreux; Roger of Beaumont; Roger of Montgomery; Hugh of Grantmesnil; Walter Giffard; Hugh of Montfort; and William of Warrenne. To these he explained his designs, and appealed for their support in the great enterprise which he meditated. Such martial spirits, fired with the prospect of fame and booty, were unlikely to return any discouraging reply. They promised, so far as themselves were concerned, to serve him with body and goods, even to selling or pledging their inheritances. But they one and all perceived that something more was necessary than the assistance which even they, powerful barons as they were, could render,—that the undertaking was one which would need the employment of the entire resources of the duchy. 'Therefore,' said they, 'you must seek aid and support from all your barons; it *is* right that they should share in the council who are to share in the work.'

> 'Ceste parole lor mostrez,
> Bien deivent al cunseil venir,
> Ki il travail diebvent partir.'[1]

In obedience to this suggestion,—considering from whom it came, we might almost call it a command,—William convoked a great council of all classes of his subjects—warriors, and prelates, and merchants, the wealthiest and most illustrious in his realm. It was held at Lillebonne, and very numerously attended. With the fiery eloquence of which he was a consummate master, he laid his projects before this distinguished assemblage; he enlarged on his wrongs; he expatiated on the splendid prospects of a successful invasion of England; he praised their loyalty and their zeal; and concluded by assuming their consent as certain, and by demanding how many ships and men each of them would contribute.

The wary Normans made no immediate answer. They asked for time to consider all the weighty matters he had laid before them, and withdrew that they might consult among themselves, free from his personal influence. Then, as the chronicler tells us, they broke up into small parties of twenty, fifteen, forty, thirty, a hundred, sixty,—

> 'Par tropeaux si vunt cunseillant,
> Ci vint, ci quinze, ci quarante,
> Ci trente, ci cent, ci seisante,'[2]—

and vehemently discussed the great project of their lord. Opinions varied greatly: many were roused to ardour by its boldness, and professed themselves willing to assist it with men and munitions and ships; many recognised its temerity, and shrank from its dangers, foreseeing that its failure would involve all Normandy in ruin. England was rich and popu-

---

[1] *Roman de Rou*, lines 11171-3. [2] *Roman de Rou*, lines 11197-9.

lous; Harold had not only his own well-trained forces, but could hire as many foreign ships and soldiers as he willed. Moreover, he possessed a mighty fleet, with men thoroughly trained in nautical manœuvres, and accustomed to the perils and warfare of the sea.[1] How could they hope to prevail against so formidable an array?

In the midst of this confusion of angry voices—a confusion which boded no good to the duke's interests—William Fitz-Osbern sternly rose, and made an attempt to recall the disputants to what he conceived to be their legitimate duty. 'Why,' said he, 'why do ye thus dispute? William is your lord, and has need of your services. It would better become you to proffer them willingly, and not to tarry till he demands them. If you fail him now, and his need remains, and he still essays the adventure on which his mind is bent; then if he should fail, assuredly he will not forget that his failure was due to your want of loyalty. Prove, then, that you love him, by willing deeds.'

> 'N'atendez mie k'il vos priet,
> Ne ne demandez mil respiet,
> Alez avant, si li offrez
> Mult plus ke faire ne poez.
>
> Se la busuigne remaneit,
> Par adventure tost direit,
> A ço k'il est achoisonos,
> Ke tut areit perdu par nos;
> Fetes li tant ke il ne die
> Ke s'erre seit par vos faillie.'[2]

The barons, half in alarm and half in wrath at this bold

---

[1] William of Poitiers, 124; Ordericus Vitalis, 493.
[2] *Roman de Rou*, lines 11214–11225.

language, replied with a spirit worthy of the ancestors of the men who wrung Magna Charta from their reluctant king: 'Doubtlessly he is our lord; but is it not enough for us that we pay him his dues? Beyond the seas we do not owe him service; we have already suffered sufficiently from his many wars: if he fail in his new enterprise, our country is undone.'

> 'Sire, font il la mer doton,
> Ultre mer servir ne deron.'[1]

But, on further reflection, the council felt that it would be dangerous to place themselves in open opposition to their sovereign. Perhaps too, in spite of their prudence, they were somewhat dazzled by the glowing vision of a conquest of England. They therefore yielded so far as to request William Fitz-Osbern to speak for them in Duke William's presence; and as he knew the position of each knight and baron, to excuse the limited offers of service which they felt constrained to make. 'You know what we are willing to do,' they said, 'and we will do what you say.'

> 'Parlez por nos, ço vos preion,
> La parole sor vos meton:
> Vos direz ço ke vos voldrez,
> Nos feron ço ke vos direz.'[2]

Thereupon the Normans returned to the duke, and Fitz-Osbern stood forward as their lawful spokesman. But taking advantage of the commission with which they had entrusted him, he proceeded to lay their lives and liberties at William's feet. 'I do not believe,' he craftily exclaimed, 'that in the whole world there is a people more loyal or more devoted than are your subjects. Well do you know the liberal

---

[1] *Roman de Rou*, lines 11226, 11227.
[2] *Roman de Rou*, lines 11228-11331.

supplies they have at all times granted you, and the burdensome services they have taken upon themselves; but now, sire, they do more: they will cross the seas together, and they will double the aid each man has hitherto been accustomed to give. He who led to your banner twenty chevaliers, will now bring forty; the lord of a hundred will now bring two hundred. And as for myself,' he continued, 'out of my love and loyalty I will provide you with sixty ships, in full array for battle, and manned with fighting men.'

> 'Si bien l'ont fit, mielx le feront;
> Ensemble o vos mer passeront,
> Vostre servise dobleront.
> Ki solt mener vint chevaliers,
> Quarante en merra volontiers,
> E ki de trente servir deit,
> De sesante servir vos velt,
> E cil ki solt servir de cent,
> Dous cent en merra bonnement.
> E jo merrai en boen amor
> En la busoigne mon Seignor
> Sesante nés apareilleis
> De homes cumbatanz chargies.' [1]

At Fitz-Osbern's audacious misrepresentation of their wishes, the barons waxed justly indignant. 'We entrusted you,' they exclaimed, 'with no such answer; we did not say what you have said; and what you have said shall not and cannot be.' [2]

> 'Li Barunz heit se merveillerent,
> Mult fremirent è grondillerent
> Des paroles ke cil diseit,
> E des promesses ki' il faseit,
> Dune il ne aveit neil garant.'

---

[1] *Roman de Rou*, lines 11251–11263.
[2] *Roman de Rou*, lines 11264–11268.

'In matters,' they continued, 'within his own realm we will serve the duke, but we are not bound to assist him in conquering another man's country. And, moreover, if once we rendered him double service, and followed him across the sea, it would be held as a right and precedent for the future; and we should henceforth be fettered by it. It shall not be, it shall not be!'

And now a terrible tumult ensued, which not even the presence of William could overawe; voices grew louder, swords clanked ominously; and breaking up into groups of twenties and thirties, the angry Normans debated and gesticulated until the assembly was dissolved.

The duke had now to begin his work over again. Fitz-Osbern's stratagem had ended in utter failure; and to a less resolute and determined man it would have seemed that he had no resource but to abandon all idea of his enterprise. In this conjuncture, however, William may have remembered the old fable of the faggot of sticks, and how when the faggot could not be broken, each stick taken separately was broken with ease. He no longer thought of submitting his projects to the various wills of a popular assembly, but sent one by one for his leading barons; and in the privacy of confidential intercourse, he won over to his side those who had been loudest and angriest in their opposition. He solicited each man's aid, not as a service due to his prince, but as a special favour and a voluntary gift; he assured him that he had no intention of making it a precedent to bind him or his successors hereafter; he offered, it is said, to confirm his verbal assurance by letters sealed with the ducal seal; and with the fervid eloquence of which he seems to have been a skilful master, he so glowingly painted the certainty of a successful issue to his enterprise, and the prospects of wealth and honour to be easily won at the cost of the English, that the most reluctant were fired with a strange enthusiasm. And thus it came to pass that one man promised ships, and another armed soldiers, and another his own good sword; priests gave money, merchants their merchandise, and even the commonalty came forward with their voluntary offerings.

Meantime William had laboured, and not unsuccessfully, to obtain for his great enterprise the all-powerful sanction of the Church of Rome. And yet what reasons could he put forward to justify such a sanction? He had no rightful title to the English crown; he could neither claim it as his by inheritance, nor as his by election. It was true that he pretended that Eadward had bequeathed it to him on his deathbed, but the crown of England could not be disposed of by the voice of a dying monarch; and, besides, William adduced no trustworthy evidence that Eadward had made any disposition or recommendation in his favour. His real pleas were three in number, and flimsier pleas were never advanced: the murder of the youthful Ælfred and his Norman companions, the expulsion of Robert of Jumièges from the see of Canterbury, and the perjury of King Harold. To support these pleas, and advocate his cause, he despatched to the Papal court the monk Lanfranc,—his familiar counsellor and intimate friend, and a man of singular ability, whether as theologian, scholar, or diplomatist. Lanfranc arrived at Rome, and laid before the Pope the object of his mission. Harold was then summoned as a defendant to answer the charges made against him, but the English king denied that the Roman court had any jurisdiction in such a matter; he was too patriotic to place his crown at the disposal of a foreign power, and was too wise to believe in the impartiality of judges selected by an enemy.

The Roman tiara at this epoch was worn by Alexander II., but Alexander was but the puppet moved by the dexterous hand of Hildebrand, monk of Cluny,—the man who of all others has most largely contributed to the elevation of the Papal power. The one object of his life was to assert the supremacy of Rome over all the nations; and this object he laboured to carry out with indefatigable industry, with unfailing vigour, with masterly ability. England he had long regarded with jealous eye, for England, almost alone among European nations, had preserved her ecclesiastical independence. A land, says Mr. Freeman, where the Church and the nation were but different names for the same community; a land where the priest and the prelate, like the thegn and the yeoman, were subject to the civil law; a land where the king and his Witán deposed and elected bishops,—where, only recently, Robert of Jumièges had been driven from the see of Canterbury, and his place filled by the obnoxious Stigand,—was a land more hateful to Hildebrand and the Roman court than a land of pagans. And now the opportunity had come for punishing both the people and their rulers, and for bringing rebellious England within the fold of the infallible Church. It was an opportunity which Hildebrand was not likely to neglect. The claims of William were brought before the curia of the cardinals, and strongly advocated by Hildebrand, who inveighed bitterly against Harold's violation of his oath, without seeing, apparently, that his personal wrong, this individual sin, could not attach to his subjects, nor in any wise justify a foreign invasion of a peaceful country. To the honour of the curia be it said, that several of the cardinals had the honesty to dissent from Hildebrand's opinion, and to deny the existence of sufficient grounds to justify the Church in sanctioning an armed aggression against a Christian people. When Hildebrand repeated and enforced his arguments, a loud murmur arose, and many scrupled not to tell him that it was infamous to authorize and encourage homicide.[1] But he cared little for such pious scruples, and eventually his influence prevailed. A crusade was ordered against England, of which William was declared the leader, and he was directed to bring back the rebellious kingdom into obedience to the holy see, and to re-establish there the tax of 'St. Peter's pence.' Lanfranc was made the bearer of a bill of excommunication against Harold and all his partisans and followers; and he also carried to William, as special marks of the Pontiff's favour, a banner of the Roman Church, and a ring containing one of the hairs of St. Peter, set beneath a diamond of great price.

> 'Un gonfanon e un anel
> Mult precios è riche è bil ;
> Si corre il dit, de soz la gueire
> Aveit un des cheveuls Saint Pierre.'[2]

The sacred banner, which was to herald the invasion of England by William the Norman, was the same that, a few years before, the Norman knights, Raoul and William de Montreuil, had planted, in the name of the Church, on the castles of Campania.[3]

---

[1] Thierry, *Conquest of Normandy*, i. 158, 159. See authorities quoted by him.

[2] *Roman de Rou*, lines 11452-11455.

[3] Orderius Vitalis, Hist. Eccles., in *Script. Rerum Normann.* p. 473.

CHAPTER V.

Harold organizes his Kingdom—Shadows of Coming Events—The Hairy Star—England invaded by Harold Hardrada of Norway—Scandinavian Visions—March of the English.

FROM the plots and devices of William and his counsellors, we return to trace the manly proceedings of King Harold.

Fully aware of the dangers which threatened his realm, he hastened to complete its organization. He left his brothers-in-law, Eadwine and Morkere, in their respective earldoms of Northumbria and Mercia, and entrusted them with the defence of northern England. The eastern coast was in charge of his own brothers, the devoted Gyrth and Leofwine. The West Saxon earldom he retained in his own hands; partly because he knew of no lieutenant fitted for so important a charge, partly because the shores of Kent and Sussex were the most vulnerable parts of the kingdom, and needed to be watched by the most jealous eye. While thus providing for its military supervision, he did not neglect its internal affairs; but, as Roger of Hoveden tells us, he abolished unrighteous and established righteous laws, founded and benefited churches and monasteries, displayed due reverence towards bishops and abbots, and all ecclesiastics, and showed himself pious and lowly, and the enemy of all evil deeds and evil-doers. He formulated strict orders to his earls and thegns to arrest and punish all robbers and violators of the public peace. He issued a new coinage, with the legend *Pax* on the reverse, and his own portrait, crowned, on the obverse. He was ever ready to hear in person the complaints of his subjects. From morn to night he laboured actively for the public weal.

Yet the minds of the people, though fully trusting in the valour and sagacity of their king, were haunted by vague apprehensions of coming evil,—apprehensions which seemed to receive a powerful confirmation from the appearance of a comet blazing in the heavens, as a portent of evil, for seven days and nights. Æthilmer, a monk of Malmesbury, who addressed to the celestial visitant a sort of poetical rhapsody, probably did but express the national feeling when he exclaimed, 'Thou, then, hast returned at last; thou wilt be the cause of weeping to many mothers! Often before have I seen thee shine; but thou seemest to me more terrible, now that thou announcest the ruin of my country.'[1]

From some indications in the chronicles, we gather that Northumbria was not wholly satisfied with the election of Harold, though its primate had consecrated him king, and its earl had vowed to him allegiance. To remove the disaffection of his fierce northern subjects, Harold made a progress through Northumberland, accompanied by Wulfstan, Bishop of Worcester; and such was the influence of his charm of manner, his kingly presence, and unstudied eloquence, that he completely won them over to acknowledge his authority. Then, indeed, he was king over *all* England, and king by the best of titles, the affection of those over whom he ruled.

For the moment peace prevailed from the Channel to the Tyne, and the safety of his crown seemed ensured.

It may therefore have been with a not unnatural feeling of exultation that Harold returned to Westminster, where he celebrated his Easter festival. But in the lives of kings at that epoch of storm and convulsion, shadow quickly succeeded to sunshine; and it is not impossible that it was at this very festival Harold received Duke William's challenge of his crown,—a challenge which, as we have seen, he repudiated with fitting scorn,—and it was immediately on its close that his treacherous brother Tostig sailed with an armed force to ravage the English coast. With Duke William's sanction he had raised a body of Norman and Flemish mercenaries, whom with a double treachery he proceeded to employ against his own brother and his own countrymen (May 1066).

The events which followed are thus summarily related by the Saxon chronicler :—

'There was over all England such a token seen in the heavens as no man ever saw before. Some men said that it was *Cometa*, the star, which some men call " the hairy star." And it appeared first on the eve Litania Major, the 8th before the Kalends of May, and it shone all the seven nights. And shortly afterwards came in Tostig, the earl from beyond sea (*i.e.* the Cotentin), with as great a fleet as he could procure ; and the inhabitants were compelled to give him both money and food. And King Harold, his brother, gathered so great a ship force and so great a land force as no king in England had ever done before, because he had received information that William the Bastard would come to conquer his realm : all as it afterward happened. And meanwhile Tostig the earl sailed into the Humber with sixty ships ; and Eadwine the earl came with a land force, and drove him out. And the boatmen forsook him; and he went to Scotland with twelve vessels. And there he was met by Harold, king of Norway, with three hundred ships; and Tostig submitted to him and became his man.'[1]

Such is the brief but pregnant story told by the oldest and best of our early English chroniclers. The narrative in Roger de Hoveden's *Annals* is almost as bare of details:[2]—

'Shortly after this [the apparition of the comet], Earl Tostig, returning from Flanders, landed in the Isle of Wight; and having compelled the inhabitants to supply him with provisions and pay him tribute, he took his departure and collected plunder all along the [Kentish and Sussex] shore, until he came to the port of Sandwich. News of his invasion being brought to King Harold, who was then staying at London, he ordered a considerable fleet to be equipped, and an army of horse to be levied, and himself made preparations to set out for Sandwich. When this was reported to King Harold, he took with him some of the mariners who were well inclined, and some [probably prisoners] who were ill-wishers to him, and he directed his course to Lindesey, where he burned a great number of towns, and slew many men.

'Thereupon Eadwine, Earl of Mercia, and Morkere, Earl of Northumbria, flew to their rescue with an army, and drove him out of the country. On his departure thence he repaired to Malcolm, king of the Scots, and remained with him all the summer. . . .

[1] *Saxon Chronicle*, A.D. 1066.
[2] Roger de Hoveden, *Annals*, pp. 133, 134.

'After this Harold Hardrada, king of Norway, and brother of St. Olaf, came with a very strong fleet, amounting to upwards of five hundred large ships, and anchored unexpectedly at Tynemouth,—on which Earl Tostig met him, as they had previously arranged, with his fleet; and making all speed, they entered the estuary of the Humber.'

From these accounts, and from other sources, we gather that Earl Tostig was repulsed in his attempts on the northern coast by the vigour of Earls Eadwine and Morkere. Harold would seem to have left to them at this crisis the defence of their own provinces, while he was keeping watch in the south for the expected arrival of his most formidable opponent. His fleet cruised in the Channel, and his army was stationed at all the most vulnerable points of the shores of Kent and Sussex; and thus, for a period of four months, he waited for the foe that did not come. Early in September he was forced to disband his army[1] from want of supplies; and, probably thinking the danger was over for that year, he rode back to London, whither he also ordered his fleet to sail. He had scarcely reached his capital, before he was again summoned into the field by the arrival of a new competitor for his crown, Harold Hardrada, king of Norway.

Harold Hardrada has been invested with such an air of poetry and romance by the writers of the old Norse Sagas, that it is a difficult task to distinguish the historical from the legendary hero, and to decide what is truth and what is fiction in the extant narratives of his wonderful career.[2] But,

---

[1] With the exception of his house-carls, or household troops, Harold's army was entirely composed of the *landfyrd*, or militia, who were not accustomed to serve for a longer period than thirty or forty days.

[2] See Snorro Sturleson's poem in Laing's edition, vol. iii.

looking back through the mists of the past, we can at least see that he was a reckless and dauntless warrior—of a generous temperament—fierce in battle, but mild in council—ever ready for the most desperate adventures—nursed in the lap of battle, and scornful of the arts of peace. He was the last of the true Norse rovers, of those long-haired 'children of Odin' who broke up the Roman polity in the west, and infused their wild love of enterprise into the slower spirit of the Saxon. In a life of more than ordinary change he had been soldier and seaman, alternately a sea-pirate and a land-rover, *viking* and *varing*. He had served in that remarkable imperial guard, composed of the boldest spirits of all nations, who kept the gates of the palace of the Byzantine emperors. Acquiring wealth, he wished to return to his own land of snow and ice; and when it was designed to detain him by force, he escaped by sea, carrying with him a high-born beauty. For a while, if the Saga may be credited which narrates his exploits, he harassed the rich coasts of Sicily, amusing his leisure intervals, few and far between as they were, with the composition of wild pæans and dithyrambics in praise of war and wine and love, in boundless exultation over his deeds of prowess, and equally boundless scorn of his defeated enemies. Returning at length to Norway, he dispossessed its sovereign, and caused himself to be crowned king. But he soon grew weary of peace, and his ambition led him to meditate the conquest of England. Whether he evolved this design out of the 'depths of his own inner consciousness,'—whether it was suggested to him by Earl Tostig, or the earl's messengers,—or whether having conceived it, he was encouraged to put it into execution by Tostig's promises of help, we are unable to decide. It is enough to say that he resolved on the conquest of England, and levied for this purpose an immense naval and military force.[1]

Harold's fleet is estimated by some authorities at three hundred, by others at five hundred, and by others at even one thousand ships. It was manned by skilled seamen, and carried a host of Scandinavian warriors. Yet it did not set forth under the brightest auspices. The magnitude of the enterprise seems to have weighed on the minds of the many, and the consequent depression produced, as is usual under such circumstances, an abundant harvest of sinister omens and prophetic superstitions. A soldier dreamed that he saw his comrades landed on the English coast, in presence of the English army, and that in front of this army rode a demon-woman of gigantic stature, mounted on a wolf: the wolf held in his jaws a human body dripping with blood, which no sooner had he devoured than his rider fed him with another victim. A similar vision vexed the sleep of Harold himself, to whom his martyred brother St. Olaf appeared, and warned him that he in his turn would feed the jaws of the ravenous wolf. And a second soldier, Gyrd, an intimate friend of the king's, dreamed that the fleet had sailed, and that a flock of crows and vultures, and other obscene birds, perched on the masts and rigging of the vessels; on a rock which they approached was seated a 'witch-wife' of forbidding countenance, holding a fork in one hand and a trough in the other, and counting the ships: 'Go,' she exclaimed, 'go, ye birds, without fear, for food shall not be wanting to ye, and ye shall have an abundant choice, for I go with them.'[2]

[1] Lord Lytton, *Harold*, Bk. ix. c. xi.
[2] Snorro Sturleson, in Laing's edition of the *Heimskringla*, iii. 151, 152.

> ' Thoro' wind, over water,
>   Comes scent of the slaughter,
>   And ravens sit greeting
>   Their share of the bones.
>
> ' Thoro' wind, thoro' weather,
>   We're sailing together;
>   I sail with the ravens,
>   I watch with the ravens,
>   I snatch from the ravens
>   My share of the bones.'

But, scorning dream and witch-wife, Hardrada set sail with his fleet for England. At the Orkney Islands, which were peopled by men with Norse blood in their veins, he was joined by two chiefs and 'a bishop.' Then he skirted the east coast of Scotland, and received the reinforcement of Tostig's vessels. Landing at Cleveland, on the Yorkshire coast, the king and his ally secured much plunder; and then, with spirits revived, sailed onward to Scarborough. Here the inhabitants were brave, and the walls were strong. The Norsemen therefore ascended the high hill behind the town, and lighting a huge pile of wood, they rolled the burning brands and logs down on the roofs of the town; and as house after house caught fire, and confusion and tumult spread through the streets, they rushed into the *mêlée* sword in hand, and committed terrible havoc. The town surrendered, but not the less was it pillaged.[1]

The fleet next doubled Ravenspur, after a similar scene of rapine had been enacted at Holderness, and sailed up the Humber. Thence it passed into the Ouse, and anchored at Richall, in the neighbourhood of the great city of York. Here, at Tostig's instigation, the army landed, bearing before them

[1] Snorro Sturleson, ed. by Laing, iii. 152.

Hardrada's famous standard of the 'Land-Ravager' (*Land-Ode*); and presently found themselves face to face with the forces mustered by Morkere and Eadwine, the two earls,—forces who numbered in their ranks a large body of priests and monks. The Norwegians advanced to meet them along the high ground between York and Selby; and at Fulford, about two miles from the northern capital, the battle took place. Harold Hardrada drew up his array on the acclivity which at this spot rises from the Ouse, his right wing defended by a broad and deep marsh. Here the Anglo-Danish attack was made with great fury, under the direct conduct of Earl Morkere; and at first it proved successful. But King Harold immediately brought up his left wing to the support of his retiring troops, and restored the fortune of the battle. He himself with his two-handed sword clove a passage into the very midst of the Northumbrians, who were seized with a panic, and fled in wild disorder. Hot and fierce was the pursuit of the Land-Ravager; nor did it terminate until the gates of York were reached. The city surrendered on the following Sunday, and agreed to receive Hardrada as king of England. Tostig assumed the title of Earl of Northumberland, and issued a proclamation from the Norwegian camp: 'a few weak-minded men,' as Thierry says, 'acknowledged him, and a small number of adventurers answered his appeal.'

On receiving the unexpected news of this enemy in the north of his kingdom, Harold resolved to march immediately against him. It was true that by doing so he left the south unguarded; but as winter was approaching, he might reasonably suppose that Duke William had delayed his adventure until the following spring. At all events, the one enemy was within the realm, and had even seized a portion of it;

the other had not yet set foot in England; and there was the hope that by rapid and well-conceived movements he might reach the scene of battle, encounter and defeat the Norwegians, and return in time to oppose, if need be, the Normans. Harold reasoning thus, summoned his troops, and gave orders for the march northward.

According to a legend, which is probably based on some slight foundation of truth, the king was at this time suffering from bodily disease. The heart of a hero, however, at such a crisis, invariably rises superior to physical suffering, and Harold in the sight of men bore himself with his customary cheerfulness. The day he spent in collecting troops, and providing for their due equipment; the night in prayers and sighs before the Holy Rood of Waltham. His patriotic endurance, according to the old chroniclers,[1] was rewarded by help and consolation from above. The deceased Eadward came from his world of bliss to take pity on his successor, and on the kingdom over which he ruled. In the watches of the night he appeared to Æthelsiga, the Abbot of Ramsey, and gave him a message for King Harold. Bid him, he said, be strong, and of good courage, and go forth to battle with the enemies of England. He himself by his prayers would guide and defend his people, and direct their efforts to certain victory. The abbot hastened to convey these comforting words to the king; and Harold, cheered by the supernatural message, recovered from his sickness, and addressed himself to his task with hopeful confidence.

At the head of his thousands, he set forth upon that great northern march, which must rank among the grandest exploits

---

[1] Æthelred of Rievaux; and the *Vita Haroldi*, quoted by Freeman, vol. iii. pp. 358, 359.

of the kind recorded in history. As he moved forward, his ranks were constantly swelled by fresh levies; so that his progress resembled the course of a great river, which as it flows towards its goal, receives the augmentation of many waters.

The camp of the Norsemen was pitched at Stamford Bridge, where a structure of timber carried the main road across the Ouse. The fleet lay in the river; the army, not fearing the approach of any foe, occupied both banks, in somewhat straggling array. It was a hot autumnal day; and because of the heat, the soldiers had laid aside their heavy coats of mail, and wore only their helmets and their bucklers. The following morning they were to take formal possession of York, and they were making merry over their easy conquest, when suddenly they saw in the distance a great cloud of dust rolling between them and the great northern city, and in the midst of this cloud spear and shield shone as ice glistens in the sun.[1]

'Who are these men advancing towards us?' inquired Harold Hardrada of Earl Tostig.

'It can only be men from the city,' replied the earl, 'to demand pardon, and implore our protection.'

Nearer and nearer came the cloud; and soon it resolved itself into an army, marching in seven divisions.

'The enemy! the enemy!' shouted the Norwegians; and they flew to arms, while three of their swiftest horsemen were despatched to bring up in all haste the soldiers who remained behind in the camp or on board the ships. Harold Hardrada advanced the 'Land-Ravager,' drawing up his soldiers around it in a long narrow line, curving at either extremity; those who

[1] Snorro Sturleson, ed. Laing, iii. p. 158.

occupied the first rank setting their spear-shafts on the ground, with the points turned towards the enemy, and level with the breast of a horseman; those in the second with spears still lower, and level with the breast of a horse: thus forming a double defence against any charge of cavalry. Round the standard was ranged a rampart of shields. Tostig and his Northumbrians took up a position in front; while Hardrada, if we may believe the Saga, rode to and fro among his warriors, mounted on a jet-black steed, and chanting aloud extemporaneous verses: 'Let us fight, let us advance, though without our cuirasses, to the edge of the blue steel! Our helmets glitter in the sun; and what more can brave men need?'[1]

Harold had rested neither day nor night on his northward march; and on Sunday evening (September 24), the evening of the day that had witnessed the capitulation of York, he arrived at Tadcaster, on the river Wharfe, where the Northumbrian fleet had retired on the Norwegian invasion. Thence he pushed on, by the Roman road or 'High Street,' to York, which he entered on Monday morning. He was received by the citizens as a deliverer; but he tarried not for loyal welcome, or to refresh his soldiers. He had his work to do, and scant time to do it in; and so onward through the shouting streets he passed to Stamford Bridge, and before sunset, came in sight, as already stated, of the Norwegian army.

[1] Snorro Sturleson, ed. Laing, iii. pp. 159, 160.

CHAPTER VI.

The Battle of Stamford Bridge—Harold and his Brother—The Struggle—Death of Hardrada—Victory of the English—King Harold at York—The Messenger from the South.

THE two armies have met face to face on the low acclivity which, at Stamford Bridge, slopes down to the sluggish waters of the Derwent. Each is eager to 'fall to;' but before spears are crossed, a score of cavaliers suddenly emerge from the English ranks, and spur forward to the spot where floats the Northumbrian banner of Earl Tostig. One of them, evidently their foremost man, suddenly checking his steed, exclaims:[1]

'Where is Tostig, the son of Godwine and Gytha?'

At this summons, the earl lifts his helmed cap, and replies:

'I am he: what dost thou want of me?'

The Englishman answers in a deep but tender voice:

'Thy brother Harold greets thee, and bids me say, that if thou wilt return to thy allegiance, thou shalt receive again thine earldom of Northumberland, and the king will bestow his late earldom of Wessex upon Morkere; nay, thou shalt have a third of the kingdom to rule together with the king.'

'And what,' rejoined Tostig,—who, false to his brother, could

---

[1] The following incident is related by Snorro Sturleson. Mr. Freeman rejects it as mythical, but, we venture to think, on insufficient grounds.

yet be faithful to his ally,—' what shall be given to King Harold of Norway?'

The stern, contemptuous answer has become historical:

'Seven feet of ground for a grave; or, seeing that he is taller than other men, as much more as his corse may require!'

'Go back, then,' said Tostig, 'and tell King Harold, my brother, to make ready for the battle. Never shall men say in Norway, that Earl Tostig brought Harold, the son of Sigurd, to England, and then betrayed him to his foes.'

As the horsemen turn away, and ride slowly towards their own ranks, Harold Hardrada comes forward and asks of Tostig,

'Who is the man that spoke so well?'

Tostig answers, 'King Harold of England.'

'How then!' exclaims Hardrada; 'thou shouldst have told me, and never should he have returned to tell hereafter of this day's doom!'

Tostig's heart is not altogether dead to brotherly impulses, and he boldly replies:

'He came in peace, and to offer me dominion. If one of us must die, let him slay me rather than that I should slay him!'

Hardrada makes no rejoinder, but turning to his warriors, observes:

'The king of the English is shorter than some of us, but he rides firmly in his stirrups.'[1]

Another incident, recorded in the Saga of Snorro Sturleson as occurring before the beginning of the battle, seems to a great extent mythical, and yet may have a basis of truth.[2]

[1] Snorro-Sturleson, ed. Laing, iii. 87.   [2] *Ibid.* iii. 88.

The Norwegian king is riding round his ranks; his black horse stumbles and falls. It is an evil omen, shout his men; but with opportune wit he answers, 'No; a fall is lucky for a traveller.' The mishap, however, is noticed by Harold of England, and he inquires of his chiefs, 'Who is the tall man that fell from his horse—the man with the blue cloak and shining helm?' He is told it is King Harold of Norway. 'A tall man and a goodly,' says his rival; 'but his good fortune hath surely left him.'

The English army was drawn up in the form of a wedge or phalanx, with the apex or point turned towards the Norwegians. At the orders of its king, it moved upon the enemy with swift but resolute step, preceded by a small body of cavalry, who harassed the hostile array by their persistent charges, but could not break through that living wall of flesh. The unprepared detachments on the right bank of the river were speedily swept away, and the Englishmen reached the bridge across the Derwent.[1] Here their progress was arrested by the valour of one man, who 'kept the bridge' unaided, as did Horatius Cocles in 'the brave days of old.' It is said that forty men fell beneath his axe; arrows and javelins flew over him in vain; he seemed to bear a charmed life: nor did he succumb, until an Englishman, floating in a small skiff underneath the bridge, thrust his spear up through the open planks, and pierced his enemy's corselet. The English army, led by Harold, then poured, with defiant shouts, across the shivering timbers, and attacked the main body of the Northmen. Loudly rang axe

[1] We must suppose the preceding colloquy to have taken place while the English and Norwegians occupied the different banks of the river, which is a narrow and unimportant stream.

and spear on shield and helm; the swift arrows whistled through the air; the stern, deep cheer of the English mingled with the wild battle-songs of 'Northman, Scot, and Fleming.' Conspicuous among the *mêlée* loomed the mighty form of Harold Hardrada, and beneath his huge two-handed sword man after man went down. But an arrow from an unknown hand smote him in the throat; and the Norse viking, the last of the ancient sea-rovers, 'the warrior of Africa, the pilgrim of Jerusalem,' passed away, as he doubtlessly desired, in the very throe and tumult of battle.

After the king's death, the command seems to have been taken by Tostig; and from the narratives of the different chroniclers, we can gather that the fight was fiercely fought out to the very last; that Englishman and Northman displayed an equal courage, worthy of warriors sprung from the same lineage. The English king made a second effort to save his brother; but his messenger was sent back with the proud defiance, that he and his warriors would rather die than owe life to the English. The battle, however, was going against them: the steady, resolute courage of Harold's soldiers gradually prevailing over the wild valour of the Norwegians. Inch by inch the ground was won. Tostig fell, and with him the 'Land-Ravager' ceased to wave its once triumphant folds. Inch by inch the English drove back their enemies, dealing around a terrible slaughter, until the whole slope was covered with dead bodies, and the waters of the Derwent ran red with blood. And thus was fought and won the great battle of Stamford Bridge,—the last in which Northman and Englishman met upon English soil.

After the fight was over, Harold caused the corpse of his brother to be searched for. It was recognised by a peculiar body mark,[1] removed to York, and buried, doubtlessly, with the usual solemnities. Whether Hardrada found his seven or eight feet of ground for a grave, we know not; but it is certain that to few of his followers were any funeral rites accorded; and as late as the days of Ordericus Vitalis, a mass of whitened bones—'magna congeries ossium mortuorum'—bore witness to the desperate heroism with which the Norse invaders had contended for the prize of victory.

At York, for a few days, King Harold held his court, reorganizing the administration of the Northumbrian earldom, and securing the fruits of his triumph. The Norwegian fleet still lay in the Ouse. Anxious to avoid further slaughter, he sent messengers to its chiefs, and to Olaf, the son of Hardrada, offering peace. They gladly accepted the proffered olive branch; and repairing to the royal presence, gave hostages, according to the custom of the time, and vowed that from thenceforth they would ever keep peace and amity towards the English and their king. Then, in four-and-twenty galleys, the survivors of Hardrada's splendid army sailed away from the English shores. And since the great day of Stamford Bridge the kindred nations of Scandinavia, linked to us by so many ties—akin to us in character, genius, and language—have never set foot on English ground 'in any guise but that of friends and deliverers.'[2]

The last invader had quitted the shores of England; and Harold remained at York to celebrate his victory with a royal banquet. We may imagine with a modern novelist,[3] that the

---

[1] Indicio verucca inter duos scapulas (a mole between the two shoulders)—William of Malmesbury, iii. 152.

[2] Freeman, *Norman Conquest of England*, iii. 375.

[3] Lord Lytton, *Harold*, Bk. xi. c. xii.

wassail was gay and boisterous; and that 'lively song, long neglected in England, woke, as it wakes ever, at the breath of Joy and Fame.' But the shadow of the coming fate drew nearer and yet nearer to the side of the English king. While all went merry as a marriage bell, a messenger broke in upon the revel;[1]—a messenger who with swiftest pace had traversed England from the chalky cliffs of the Sussex coast to the old royal city on the Ouse; and who startled the banqueters with the ominous intelligence, that William of Normandy had landed on English ground with a mighty host; that his fleet covered the waters of the Channel; and that Harold would have to contend, if he would preserve his crown, with an abler and more powerful competitor than he who lay dead on the field of Stamford Bridge.

And so the course of our narrative bids us change the scene from the regal halls of York, to

> ' Those heights,
> Where the Norman encamped him of old,
> With his bowmen and knights,
> And his banner all burnished with gold.' [2]

---

[1] Henry of Huntingdon, p. 762.
[2] Thomas Campbell, *Lines on the Camp Hill, near Hastings*.

CHAPTER VII.

Duke William's Preparations—Seeks for Allies—Mysterious Fate of Conan of Brittany—The Norman Army and Fleet—Waiting for a Fair Wind—The Invasion of England.

HAVING obtained the support of his barons and the sanction of the Roman Church, Duke William proceeded, with characteristic vigour and high administrative ability, to collect the naval and military forces necessary to a successful achievement of his great enterprise.

His first and most important task was the creation of a fleet,—a fleet to carry over his soldiers and their supplies, and yet capable of contending with Harold's war-ships. From the pictorial narrative of the Bayeux tapestry, and from the Homeric couplets of the *Roman de Rou*, we may gather a vivid idea of the energy with which he set to work to execute this part of his mighty project.

> 'Fevres è charpentiers manda;
> Dunc véissiez à granz esforz
> Par Normendie a toz li porz,
> Mairrieu atraire è fust porter,
> Cheviles fere et boiz doler,
> Nés et esquiz apureillier,
> Veiles estendre, must drecier
> A grant entente et à grant cost.'[1]

---

[1] *Roman de Rou*, lines 11473-11480.

The stoutest trees were felled in every wood; not a port in Normandy but rang with the clash of axe and hammer. The wealthy nobles and prelates of the duchy came forward liberally to the assistance of their sovereign. William Fitz-Osbern undertook the building and equipment of sixty ships, and a similar quota was contributed by Roger of Beaumont, by Roger of Montgomery, and by Hugh of Avranches. Hugh of Montfort furnished fifty; Fulk the Lame and Gerald the Seneschal, forty each. Walter Giffard supplied thirty ships and a hundred knights; the Bishop of Le Mans the same number of ships, with their crews. But, as Mr. Freeman points out,[1] magnificent as were these donations, those made by the duke's own kinsfolk far exceeded them. The Count of Mortain contributed no fewer than one hundred and twenty ships; his brother Odo, the warlike Bishop of Bayeux, one hundred; William of Evreux, eighty; Robert of Eu, sixty. 'The monk Nicolas, the son of Duke Richard the Third, now Abbot of the great house of Saint Ouen, gave twenty ships, with a hundred knights. Others of less degree gave one ship or more, according to their means. And among those was another monk, of less lofty birth, but of higher personal renown, than the princely Abbot of Saint Ouen's. A single ship with twenty knights was the offering of Remigius, then almoner of the house of Fécamp, but who was in after times to be the last prelate of the ancient see of Dorchester, the first who placed his throne on the lordly steep of more famous Lincoln. But one gift, though the gift of a single ship only, had a value beyond all others in the eyes of the duke. The ship which was destined for his own use, the ship which was to bear William and his fortune,

---

[1] Freeman, *Norman Conquest*, iii. 379, 380.

was the offering of the conjugal love of the Duchess Matilda. This chosen vessel bore the name of the *Mora*, a name not very easy to explain. Either at its prow or at its stern it bore the likeness of a boy wrought in gold, blowing an ivory horn pointing towards England.'[1]

The total number of the armada which William collected is very differently estimated by different authorities, ranging from six hundred and ninety-six to upwards of three thousand. Probably we shall do well to strike a mean between the highest and lowest of these sums, and to allow that William had about four hundred ships with large sails, and one thousand open boats with one mast, or towed by the ships, used solely for purposes of transport.

Meantime—as we have written elsewhere [2]—William began to assemble an army corresponding in magnitude to this formidable fleet. High pay and boundless booty were promised to every good and true man content to serve him with lance or sword or bow. Religious enthusiasm was employed to stir up the feelings of the masses; and so successful was the agency of this powerful but dangerous lever, that many a widowed mother sent her sons to enrol their names,

---

[1] The foregoing statement is founded on several chronicles, which we have thought it needless to quote, as Mr. Freeman has condensed their details into so lively a narrative. In reference to the 'boy wrought in gold,' the *Roman de Rou* says :

> 'Sor li chief de la nef devant . . .
> (Out de coivre fet un enfant),
> Saete et arc tendu portant,
> Verz Engleterre out son viaire,
> Ea la faseit semblant de traire.'
> *Roman de Rou*, lines 11574-11599.

[2] *Scenes from the Drama of European History*, p. 70.

in the hope of salvation for their souls. Priests gave their money, merchants contributed their merchandise, peasants gladly parted with their scanty stores. The brave brought their prowess, the man of genius his skill, the wealthy their wealth and credit. Hither sped the tawny-haired sons of the Goth, reeking with the purple of the Rhenish vineyards; and the quick-eyed children of the south, from their homes in the shadow of the snow-crested Alps. The stalwart descendants of Scandinavian heroes came with their heavy battle-axes swinging in their brawny hands. For once the tardy Fleming quickened his step, charmed by a vision of English ale and English beauty. Ready and alert, then as in all times, the Frank hastened as blithely to the *mêlée* as to the feast. From Anjou and from Maine, from Brittany and from Poitou, from Aquitaine and from Burgundy,—from the frowning highlands of Norway and the pine-clad slopes of the Apennines, —from the iron-bound coast of the Baltic and the shining shores of the Mediterranean,—knights and men-at-arms, pikemen and bowmen, on horse and on foot, richly equipped, or travel-worn and weather-beaten,—they came, they came!

But with respect to the total number of this motley host, as with respect to the total number of William's fleet, a great discrepancy exists between the different authorities,—arising from the circumstance, perhaps, that one counts only the knights or men-at-arms, the other includes every man who carried a weapon. If we accept the latter mode of calculation, it does not seem improbable that the army gathered for the invasion of England numbered sixty thousand men in all.

William was too able a statesman not to seek the help of allies in the prosecution of his enterprise. He repaired to the court of Philip, the French king, at St. Germains, and respectfully saluting him as his feudal superior, solicited his assistance. 'You are my overlord,' he said; 'and should you be pleased to aid me, and should I, by the grace of God, obtain my right over England, I promise to do you homage for it, as though I held it direct from you.'

> ' Ke se tant aidia li voleit,
> Ke par s' aïe éust son dreit,
> Engleterre de li prendreit,
> E volentiers l'en servireit.' [1]

Philip assembled his council of nobles, and laid before them the duke's request; but they seem to have been unanimously of opinion that it should not be complied with.

'You know,' said they to their sovereign, 'how ill the Norman obeys you now, and worse would it be if he were master of England. Moreover, it would cost us heavily to assist the duke; and should he fail in his adventure, the English would be our enemies for ever.'

> ' Quant Engleterre ara cunquise,
> Poiz jà n' areiz de li servise;
> Petit sert, maiz meins servira,
> Quant plus ara, meins vos fera.' [2]

Baffled in his expectations, William left the presence of the French king, greatly discontented.

In his application to the Count of Flanders, his brother-in-law, he was almost as unsuccessful, though numerous Flemings swelled his ranks, either with or without the tacit consent of their sovereign. Count Eustace of Boulogne, however, came

---

[1] *Roman de Rou*, lines 11330-11333.
[2] *Ibid.*, lines 11362-11365.

forward openly, and not only contributed men and arms, but repaired in person to William's camp. A more powerful prince, and a man of daring and ambitious character, Conan, Count of the Bretons, regarded the proposed enterprise with great disfavour. He looked upon William as a usurper; he accused him of having had a share in the murder of his father; and he now took advantage of his difficulties to declare war against him. He sent to him by his chamberlain the following message:[1]—

'I hear that you meditate crossing the sea to conquer the realm of England. Now Duke Robert, whose son thou pretendest to be, on setting out for Jerusalem, remitted all his heritage to his cousin, and my father, Count Alan. But you and your accomplices poisoned my father; you have appropriated to yourself his lordship; and to this day have detained it, contrary to all justice, seeing that thou art a bastard. Restore to me, then, the Duchy of Normandy, which is rightfully mine, or I will pursue thee to the last extremity with all the forces at my disposal.'

In William's circumstances, a threat of this nature was well calculated to alarm him: Conan was a powerful enemy, and a war with him would probably overthrow William's carefully laid scheme of conquest. He contrived, however, to free himself from the danger. Conan's chamberlain anointed the hunting-horn, the gloves, and the reins of his master with poison. Count Eudes, his successor, took warning by his fate; and, far from threatening William with a disputed claim to his ducal crown, he formed with him a close and cordial alliance,

---

[1] Some doubt has been thrown upon the authenticity of this narrative, which, however, is recorded by a trustworthy Norman chronicler, William of Poitiers.

and sent his two sons, Brian and Alan, to fight under his banner. Others of the Bretons, such as Robert de Vitry, Bertrand de Dinan, and Raoul de Gaël, also volunteered their services.

The host gathered together with such indefatigable energy was encamped on the high ground above the mouth of the Dive, and the fleet intended to transport it, and to guard its transportation, lay anchored in the harbour formed by the estuary of that river. Leaving his wife Matilda, assisted by a council of wise men—at whose head was placed the venerable and experienced Roger de Beaumont — to administer the affairs of the duchy, William, in the month of August, hastened to take the command of the expedition; and only waited for a south wind to set sail on the enterprise which would make or ruin him. But for one whole month the south wind would not blow, and William's motley host was condemned to endure all the lingering tortures of delay. It is a striking proof of the duke's abilities as a commander, and of his influence over men, that the discipline of his army was preserved unbroken through this dangerous interval; and it is a no less signal proof of his powers of organization, that the soldiers received their pay and provisions with unerring regularity, and were entirely prevented from plundering the surrounding country.

Not unmindful of the storm that was gathering on the shores of Normandy, King Harold sent over his spies to ascertain the strength and disposition of William's army. One of them was detected, and brought before the duke; who, however, instead of putting him to death, suffered him to return to England, and charged him with a message for his sovereign. 'Tell him,' he said,[1] 'that I shall appear before him much sooner than he thinks of, or wishes for, and will teach him the real power of Normandy.'

A month had elapsed; the supplies which the surrounding country afforded had been exhausted: a change of position became imperative; and taking advantage of a westerly wind, William moved his fleet and army to a port much nearer than the Dive to the English coast. This was the roadstead of St. Walaire or St. Valery, at the mouth of the Somme,—a capacious and sheltered estuary, capable of accommodating William's immense flotilla. Here another long and tedious delay occurred:

> 'Tuque, velis nolis, tandem tua litora linquens,
>   Navigium vertis litus ad alterius.
> Portus ab antiquis Vimaco fatur haberi,
>   Quâ vallat portum, Somana nomen aquâ.
> Desuper est castrum quoddam Sancti Walarici,
>   Hic tibi longa, fuit difficilisque mora.'[2]

The bad weather returned, and it became necessary to anchor the fleet and encamp the troops, who suffered severely from the heavy and incessant torrents of rain.

During the delay which ensued, some of the ships, tossed and shattered by the tempest, sank with their crews,—a calamity which greatly disheartened the Norman army, already weary of spirit through their enforced inaction. In this dull leisure time, the soldiers spent hour after hour in dismal reflections upon the perils of the voyage and the difficulties of the enterprise. No battle had yet taken place, said they, and yet already many a goodly man was missing: they counted, and exaggerated, the number of dead bodies which the sea cast

---

[1] William of Poitiers, 123.
[2] Widon, *Carmen de Hastingensi Prælio* (*Chron. Angl. Norm.* iii. 3).

upon the strand. Lest this disaffection should extend and increase, the duke caused the drowned to be secretly interred, and doubled the rations of provisions, and served out to each soldier a liberal supply of spiced wines; but all these precautions did not hush the murmur of discontent. 'The man is mad,' they exclaimed, 'in endeavouring to seize the land of another. God is wroth at so nefarious a design, and proves it by refusing to us an auspicious wind.'

Even the iron heart of William himself was somewhat shaken by the wearisome period of inaction to which he was compelled. If it lasted much longer, and the winter came on, he knew that he must abandon his enterprise for that year; and in such a case, his army would melt away like snow before the sun, with but little prospect of his ever gathering it together again. He would frequently repair to the church of St. Valery, the patron of the town, and remain for hours lost in devotion and meditation before his shrine; each time that he quitted it, turning a wistful glance towards the weathercock on the belfry tower, and if it seemed veering in a southerly direction, kindling with evident joy,—if it showed a northerly or westerly wind, growing more and more depressed. At length, in a strange access of superstition,—or, as some would say, in a genuine enthusiasm of devotion,—or, it may have been, with the politic view of reviving the hopes and spirits of his warriors, he caused the abbot and monks of St. Valery to bring from their church the coffer containing the relics of the saint, and carry it in solemn procession through the camp. As it came in view, baron and man-at-arms and bowman knelt in prayer. The chiefs proved their devotion by liberal offerings, and their example was followed by the commonest soldier, so that the shrine of the saint was covered with pieces of money.

> 'Als cors saint vinrent tuit orer
> Cil ki debveient mer passer;
> Tant i ont tuit deniers offert,
> Tot li cors saint en ont covert.'[1]

And lo, on the following night, as if Heaven had been won by this magnificent act of fanatic zeal, the wind changed, and the weather grew calm and serene. On the following morning, the 27th of September, a soft southern breeze blew across the rippling channel, and the sun, so long obscured in mist and cloud, broke forth in all its splendour. Every man seemed filled with a new life—an unwonted vigour; and with shouts and songs of praise, testified their joy that the dull protracted pause of 'sick expectancy' was over. The duke, more ardent than his youngest follower, urged and commanded them to lose not a minute of the favourable season, but to hasten on board their vessels. They needed neither commands nor exhortations. They rushed to the shore in hot disorder, some carrying their weapons and coats of armour, others seeking a missing companion in the press; each endeavouring to be foremost—each in trouble, lest by some mishap he should be left behind; many voluntarily dragging down the waggons loaded with munitions and supplies to the place of embarkation; some, already on board, yarely shipping the masts and hoisting the sails, while their labours were cheered by the sound of music, of drum, and trumpet, and cymbals, uniting in a spirit-stirring swell of martial harmony![2]

At last, all was completed; and after a final act of devotion before St. Valery's altar, William went on board his ship, whose sails were emblazoned with the three lions of Normandy, and

---

[1] *Roman de Rou*, lines 11582-11585. [2] Guy of Amiens, 78-94.

from whose mast-head streamed the banner consecrated by the Pope. The fleet set sail, each vessel carrying a light, while his own bore a huge lantern, designed as a cynosure for every eye. But being a swift sailer, she speedily left all her consorts vastly in the rear. When morning dawned, the duke sent a sailor to the mast-head to look out for the laggards, but he declared that nothing was in sight save sea and sky.[1] The duke then cast anchor; breakfast was served up; with wine the hearts of the crew became merry; and William encouraged them with brave and cheerful words. They were the servants of God, he said, who would not fail to provide for their safety. The sailor again ascended, and now four ships were visible on the horizon. A third time, and he joyously declared, ' I see in the distance a dense forest, as it were, of leafy trees!' How, at this intelligence, Duke William, from his inmost heart, glorified the divine goodness, we leave, as the old chronicler says, the reader to conjecture!

On the morning of Thursday the 28th of September the Norman fleet arrived in the Bay of Pevensey, and the future conqueror landed upon the English shore.[2]

'He landed,' as Mr. Freeman reminds us,[3] 'at a spot so memorable in the earliest English history, that, to one who muses there, the landing, even of William himself, seems but of secondary interest. William came, as it might seem, to pour a new Latin and Celtic infusion into Teutonic England. He brought his Romanized Northmen, and the Welsh of the Lesser Britain, to bear rule over Saxons, Angles, and Danes, who had never fallen away from their Teutonic heritage. He

---

[1] William of Poitiers, 126.   [2] Guy of Amiens, 123.
[3] Freeman, *Norman Conquest*, iii. 400, 401.

came to begin his work on a spot where the Saxon of old had dealt one of the heaviest of all his blows against the Roman and the Briton. He came to subdue England on one of the spots which had seen most done to turn Britain into England.

'At Beechy Head to the west, and near Hastings to the east, the high ground comes down to the sea. Between these points lies a long flat shore, where the waves now break on a vast mass of shingle, which at some points stretches a long way inland, forming a wilderness of pebbles, slightly relieved by small patches of gorse and thin herbage. Between the coast and the hills—the hills which form a part of the great *Andredes-weald* [or "uninhabited forest"]—there lies a wide level; but here and there, slight and low projections, feeble offshoots from the high ground, struggle down towards the coast. One such post, commanding alike the sea and the inland country, had been chosen as the site of a Roman city; and Anderida, the *Andredes-ceaster* of our forefathers, became, in the later days of Roman occupation, one of the chief of the fortresses which guarded the Saxon shore.'

Anderida, so called from the great *Andredes-weald* which overspread all this part of Sussex, was one of the most considerable fortresses built by the Romans on the southern coast, and placed under the command of their *Comes Saxonici Littoris*, or 'Count of the Saxon Shore.' Towards the close of the fifth century it was attacked by the Saxons under Ælle, who 'slew all that dwelt therein,' says the *Saxon Chronicle;* 'nor was there one Briton left.' So complete was the destruction, that for centuries the true site of the luckless city was unknown; and it is only of late years that antiquarian researches have identified it with that of Pevensey.

The outer wall of the castle is of Roman workmanship, and

consists of a casing of neatly squared stones, filled in with well cemented flints, which at intervals are bound together by courses of broad, thoroughly baked, red tiles. It is strengthened by nine circular towers, two of which anciently flanked the Decuman or western gate. The city itself enclosed an irregular parallelogram of three sides, the fourth side having been washed by the sea, which now flows several miles off.

These remains, interesting as they are now, must have been far more interesting, because far more extensive, when William of Normandy landed in the Bay of Pevensey. Their admirable strategetical position appears to have caught his eye; for one of the first castles erected after the conquest was the castle of Pevensey, and the land here and in the vicinity was bestowed upon his trusty follower and lay brother, Robert de Moreton.

There are some writers who profess not to see the workings of Providence in the course of human events, who regard history as a mere philosophical sequence of cause and effect. To such we would commend for consideration the circumstances under which William disembarked his army at Pevensey. As Mr. Freeman reminds us, and as others have previously pointed out, had he been a little earlier or a little later, he would probably have met with a successful resistance. That westerly wind which so long vexed his spirit, proved his chief security. The English fleet, weary of their apparently fruitless watch, and short of provisions, had withdrawn from the Channel, and left the route to England open. Had he sailed a few days earlier, he must have encountered it; and we can easily believe that it would have dealt swift destruction among his overloaded ships. A few days later, and Harold would have been at Pevensey, at the head of a gallant army, flushed with the victory of Stamford Bridge. But in the great designs of Providence William had a mighty work to do, and all things so wrought together as to favour its being done.

Without the slightest show of opposition, William's army was disembarked; but with the wariness of an able commander, he provided for every possibility, and was careful that they should land in military order. After the ships had been run in shore, the horses were released from their captivity; and then began the process of landing the motley thousands of the Norman host. The first to set foot on English soil was their leader. As he touched the sand he slipped, and fell forward on his face. A murmur of apprehension and alarm arose, and many voices exclaimed, 'Heaven preserve us! This is an evil omen.' But William rising immediately, replied with his usual presence of mind, '*Par le resplendor Dé*, by the splendour of God, I have taken seizure of this kingdom with my hands, and all that it contains shall be mine and yours.'[1]

> 'Seignors, par la resplendor Dé,
> La terre ai as dous mainz seizie;
> Sans chalenge n'iert maiz guerpil;
> Tote est nostre quant qu'il ì a;
> Or verrai ki hardi serra.'[2]

A soldier, not less ready-witted than his leader, snatched a handful of thatch from a neighbouring hut, and offered it to William as seizure of the land, and of its wealth. 'I accept it,' said the duke, 'and may God be upon our side.'

---

[1] This story, be it said, is suspiciously like the one narrated of Julius Cæsar by Suetonius (*Julius*, 59).

[2] *Roman de Rou*, lines 11716–11720.

> 'Sire, dist il, avant venez,
> Ceste saisine recevez ;
> De ceste terre vos saisis,
> Vostre est sainz dote li pais.
> E li Dus respont : Je l'otrei,
> E Dex i seit ensemle od mei.'

The first to land of the Norman army were the archers, who carried their quivers at their sides, and their bows bent, as if in the presence of an enemy; and threw out skirmishers in every direction, but without discovering a single armed man. Then came the knights, in full armour; and mounting their horses, they formed in array of battle, with their men-at-arms gathering under their respective banners. After a brief pause, they proceeded to occupy Pevensey, where a garrison was stationed, and some rude works were constructed, chiefly for the defence of the ships, which had all been drawn on shore. On the following day, Friday the 29th, the great host moved eastward to Hastings, which thenceforth became what we should now call 'the headquarters' of the invader. It was a position of conspicuous importance, for it commanded both the eastern and the western roads; and, moreover, was the terminus, so to speak, of the great highway from London to the west.

Here a wooden castle was erected,[1] and surrounded by a deep trench,—probably on the site afterwards chosen for the Norman fortress whose ruins still crown the central hill. Thierry speaks of '*two* wooden towers;' but he would seem to have confused the separate erections of Pevensey and Hastings. A nucleus of defence and a *point d'appui* for future operations being thus secured, William sent out foraging parties in every direction; partly with the view of obtaining

[1] William of Poitiers, 127.

supplies, and partly with the view of attracting Harold to the coast by the extent of his ravages. On this point Mr. Freeman's remarks deserve to be studied :[1]—

'There can be little doubt that William's ravages were not only done systematically, but were done with a fixed and politic purpose. It was William's object to fight a battle as soon as might be; but it was not his object to advance for this purpose far into the country, to seek for Harold wherever he might be found. So to do would have been to cut himself off from his own powerful base of operations, and from his only hope of retreat in case of defeat. It was William's object to bring Harold down to the sea-coast, to tempt him to an attack on the Norman camp, or to a battle on the level ground. In either of these cases the Norman tactics would have a distinct advantage over the English. It is impossible to doubt that the systematic harrying of the whole country round Hastings was done with the deliberate purpose of provoking the English king, and of bringing him in all haste to defend his subjects. The work was done with a completeness which shows that it was something more than the mere passing damage wrought by an army in need of food. The tracts of the ravages done at this time are recorded in the great Survey [the Domesday Book] twenty years later. The Bayeux Tapestry not only vividly sets before us the way in which provisions of all sorts were brought in for the use of the camp; it also represents an incident which at once goes to the heart. A house is being set on fire : the inmates, a woman and a child, are coming forth from their burning dwelling. This is doubtless one instance among thousands of the cruel destruction which was fast spread over the

[1] Freeman, *Norman Conquest*, iii. 411, 412.

country, as far as William's plunderers could reach. Men fled everywhere with such of their goods and cattle as they could save, and sought for shelter in the churches and churchyards. It would doubtless be the policy of the pious duke to keep his followers back, as far as might be, from all damage towards those who thus put themselves under the direct protection of religion. Elsewhere all was havoc. It was to save his people from the horrors of war in their most barbarous form that King Harold jeoparded his life and kingdom.'

Meantime news was brought to his great rival of the victory of Stamford Bridge, and the news was supplemented by the advice—given apparently by an 'English landowner of Norman birth,' who would fain have mediated between his sovereign by natural ties and his sovereign by allegiance—that he should abandon his perilous enterprise, and return in peace to Normandy. If he remained in England, there could be no escape for him or for his soldiers. The English king was at the head of an army of one hundred thousand men, and inspired with boundless confidence in themselves and their leader by the great victory they had obtained over the warriors of the north. The Normans were wholly unfit to cope with them; nay, they were but as despicable dogs compared with the valiant English. William was a prudent chief,—hitherto had been conspicuous for prudence both at home and abroad: let him, then, return to Normandy, or if he would not, let him keep safely within his camp, and refrain from the hazard of a battle.[1]

William chafed at the sage words of his self-constituted counsellor. He haughtily replied that he would neither return to Normandy nor keep within his entrenchments, but

[1] William of Poitiers, 128.

would fight King Harold at the earliest possible moment; and that he would have done so, even if he had had but ten thousand instead of sixty thousand gallant soldiers. In truth, return was for William impossible: he had ventured life and fortune for the English crown; and if he failed, his sole resource was a soldier's death.

We have told the reader how the feast of triumph at York was interrupted by the messenger who carried to his king the sad tidings of the Norman invasion of England. It was mournful intelligence to break in upon the hour of triumph,— mournful intelligence for a monarch who had already fought one great battle to save his crown. Yet it was received by Harold in a spirit not unworthy of an English king. 'Had I been on the spot,' he exclaimed, proudly confident in his own military genius and the courage of his soldiers,—'had I been on the spot, the foreigners should never have landed, or had they landed, they should have been cut down where they stood. But it has otherwise pleased the King of Heaven, and it is impossible for me to be everywhere.'

> 'Tant en féisse en mer plungier,
> E tant en féisse néier,
> Jà à la terre ne venissent,
> Jà neient del nostre ne préissent;
> Jà de morir garant n'éussent,
> Se la mer tote ne béussent;
> Maiz issi plout el Rei celeste,
> Je ne poiz mie par tut estre.'[1]

After holding council with his nobles and chiefs, who unanimously took oath[2] that they would rather die than

---

[1] *Roman de Rou*, lines 11841-11846.

[2] With the exception, apparently, of the Earls Eadwine and Morkere.

submit to the yoke of any other king, Harold immediately commenced his march southwards, and in due time [1] reached London. Here he hastily collected what levies he could from the midland and southern counties, not forgetting the 'men of Kent, whose right it was to deal the first blow in the battle, and the men of the great city itself, whose high privilege it was to guard the king and his standard;' and having made the needful military preparations, repaired on a brief pilgrimage to his minster at Waltham, to implore, kneeling at the feet of the holy Lord, the blessing of Heaven on his supreme effort to defend the liberties of England.

'Before the great object of his life's reverence,' says Mr. Freeman, ' King Harold bowed himself low, and lay for a while flat on his face on the consecrated pavement. Then, as men said at Waltham in after days, the holy image, whose head had hitherto stood erect, bowed itself towards the king, who lay prostrate beneath it. One eye alone, that of the saint Thurkill, was privileged to behold the actual working of the divine wonder. But many there were who had seen the image in former days, and who bare witness how its head had been from that day bowed towards the ground, as if to say, "It is finished,"—as if to say that all was over with the hopes and the career of him who had so devoutly honoured it.' [2]

It was perhaps directly after this memorable circumstance that the Duke of Normandy proposed terms of accommoda-

---

[1] In about ten days. He probably reached London on the 5th or 6th of October.

[2] Freeman, *Norman Conquest*, iii. 429, 430. The primary authority is the tractate *De Inventione Crucis*, written by a monk of Waltham.

tion to the King of the English, and despatched for this purpose a monk of Fécamp, one Dom Hugues Margot, to the court at Westminster. The monk, when admitted into the royal presence, duly set forth his master's pretended claims, enlarged on Harold's perjury, referred to the blessing which the Pope had bestowed on the Norman expedition, and concluded by suggesting that the dispute should be referred to the Roman Pontiff, or should be determined by the issue of a single combat.

Harold haughtily replied, 'I will not surrender my crown; I will not refer the matter to the Pope; nor will I meet Duke William in single combat.'

A second message was sent by the Norman: 'Go and say to Harold, that if he will fulfil the compact he made with me over the holy bones of the saints, I will leave him all the land lying beyond the Humber, and will give his brother Gyrth all the land that Godwine held. If he refuse my offer, then shalt thou say to him, before all his people, that he is a perjurer and a liar; that he, and all who aid him, are excommunicated by the Pope; and that the bull of excommunication is in my hands.'

According to the old chronicle, many of the English nobles were at first dismayed by the awful threat of excommunication. But true patriotism rose superior to artificial terrors, and from out the crowd which gathered round Harold's royal seat, stepped forth a bold and loyal thegn, who cried:

'Whatever the dangers which beset us, we must fight! It is no question now of acknowledging a new lord, as if our king were dead, but the peril and need is this: the Duke of Normandy has apportioned our land among his barons, his knights, and his people, most of whom have already rendered him homage, and will claim their gifts immediately the duke becomes king. And he, on his part, will be pledged to yield up to them our estates, and our wives, and our daughters; for hath he not already promised them? They come, then, to ruin not only ourselves, but our descendants, and to deprive us of the heritage of our forefathers. And what are we to do? Whither shall we go when we no longer possess a country of our own?'

These arguments convinced the doubtful; this example inspired the timid; and every English chief immediately swore that he would make neither truce nor treaty with the invaders, but would drive them into the sea, or perish.

Harold was now eager for the battle; he longed to measure himself against the Duke of the Normans, who had so long been the shadow on his path; he longed, moreover, to hasten to the rescue of his suffering subjects. But his levies came in slowly, and his wisest counsellors saw that his best chances of victory lay in delay. His brother Gyrth came forward at this juncture with counsel as prudent as it was patriotic. 'It would be wiser,' he said,[1] 'that thou shouldst tarry in London, and gather together thy reinforcements, while I go forth with thy army and do battle with the Normans. If thou hazardest thy life, thou hazardest the safety of England. Thou canst not deny, O Harold, that, whether through constraint or of thine own will, thou didst swear to Duke William an oath upon the relics of saints: why enter the strife with this burden on thy conscience? For me, who am not forsworn, the war is just, for it is waged in defence of my country. Leave me, then, to meet the Norman: if I am defeated, thou wilt succour

[1] See *Roman de Rou*, 12040-12070; and William of Jumièges, vii. 35.

me; if I die, thou wilt avenge me. But if *thou* art defeated, or if *thou* diest, there is no one to take thy place.' And then he added: 'While thou stayest in London and collectest thy troops, see thou that the whole country between Hastings and London be swept bare; burn the houses, lay waste the cornfields; and then if William advance, there shall be neither food nor shelter for his host, and he will be constrained to make peace, and return to his own dominions.'

> 'Alez par cest paiz, ardant
> Maizons è viles destruisant;
> Pernez la robe è la vitaille,
> Pors et veilles et aumaille,
> Ke Normanz vitaille ne truissent
> Ne nule rien donc vivre puissent.
> Fetes la vitaille esluingnier,
> Ke il ne truissent ke mengier,
> Si les porrez mult esmaier
> E faire ariere repairer;
> Li Dus meisme s'en ira,
> Quant la vitaille li faldra.'[1]

Sounder military advice could not have been given than Gyrth gave to his brother; and Harold's principal nobles and chiefs acknowledged its wisdom, and strongly recommended its adoption. But Harold was something more than a statesman or a king,—he was an Englishman; he loved the fierce tumult of the battle; and his heart bled within him at the thought of the sufferings that had already been inflicted on his subjects. 'I can never,' he answered, 'burn English house or English village; I can never injure the lands or goods of my people. How can I do harm to the people whom I govern? How can I harass or destroy those who look to me for protection?'

[1] *Roman de Rou*, lines 12065-12076.

And so, on Thursday the 12th of October, King Harold and his army set out from London.

He marched straight along the great road which struck through Kent and Sussex right to the sea-coast; and there, on the hill of Senlac, commanding the communications with the metropolis, and overawing both the eastern and western roads, he pitched his tent, and prepared to give battle to the invaders. His movements were evidently planned with the object of forcing William to engage him at a disadvantage. The country on his right and left was covered with a dense and almost impracticable forest, through which no army could effect a passage. The duke must either advance along the main road to London, in which case he would first have to fight the English army; or he must adopt the circuitous route along the coast to Dover, and thence by way of Canterbury, in which case he would be at a loss for supplies, and the English army would hang upon his flank and rear, until fresh levies swelled their numbers, and enabled them to crush him easily. Nothing could be better conceived than Harold's rapid march, and his position on the heights of Senlac: if William had drawn him to the coast, he in his turn had taken up ground where William could only fight him at a disadvantage.

English Worthies.

BOOK IV.—HAROLD II.
Continued.

THE BATTLE OF SENLAC (OR HASTINGS).—A.D. 1066.

'Long was the day, and terrible. The cries
Of "God to aid!" "The Cross!" "The Holy Cross!"
With songs of Roland and of Roncesvalles,
Were heard, then lost in dumbness and dismay.
A mighty roar ensued, pierced through and through
By shrillest shrieks incessant, or of man
Or maddened horse that screamed with fear and pain—
Death agonies. The battle, like a ship
Then when the whirlwind hath it, torn and tost,
Staggered from side to side. The day was long:
By dreadful charge of onset or feigned flight,
And rout and rally, direfully drawn out,
Disastrous, dismal. Night was near, and still
The victory undetermined, when a shaft
Pierced Harold to the throat. He fell, and died.
Then panic seized the Saxon host, pursued
With hideous rage till utter darkness hid
From human sight the horrors of the field.'

      Henry Taylor, *The Eve of the Conquest.*

AUTHORITIES.

[The young student will thank us, perhaps, for indicating the principal authorities to be consulted in reference to the Battle of Hastings :—Wace, *Roman de Rou*, edit. Taylor; Chronicle of William of Poitiers (Guglielmus Pictaviensis); Chronicle of Henry of Huntingdon; Chronicle of William of Malmesbury; Chronicle of Robert of Gloucester; the Bayeux Tapestry; Florence of Worcester; Guy of Amiens, *Carmen de Bello Hastingensi;* Chronique de Geoffroi Gaimar (*Chroniques Anglo-Normandes*); 'L'estoire è la généalogie des dux qui unt esté par ordre en Normandie,' by Benoit Sainte Maure (*Chroniques Anglo-Normandes*).

The best modern authorities are :—Freeman, *History of the Norman Conquest of England* (ed. 1868),—a work of the greatest research, to which I have been largely indebted; J. A. St. John, *The Four Conquests of England;* Thierry, *Histoire de la Conquête de l'Angleterre;* Sir F. Palgrave, *History of England and Normandy;* Sharon Turner, *History of England;* M. A. Lower, *Contributions to Literature*.

The reader may also consult Roger of Hoveden, Matthew of Westminster, Chronicle of the Abbey of Battle, and Chronicle of William of Jumièges.]

CHAPTER I.

The Battle of Senlac, or Hastings—The Morning of Battle—Speeches of William and Harold—The Norman Charge—Repulse by the English—Deeds of Valour—William's Stratagem—Harold's Death—Disorder of the English—The Battle Lost and Won.

THE English army halted on the hill of Senlac,[1]—a spur or offshoot of the Sussex downs, about 260 feet above the sea-level. Like a peninsula, it stretches out to the south-west, with low ground—now field and dale, once wood and marsh—surrounding it on three sides. Across a kind of valley the ground rises again to the south, and attains an elevation of 280 to 360 feet, forming a bold undulating ridge of the Hastings sand, along which the great London and Hastings road is carried, and which, at one point, is known by the name of Telham. The surrounding country is of a very broken surface; and in the days of which we are speaking, its aspect must have been that of a dreary wilderness.

On the summit of the Senlac hill Harold posted his troops, surrounding it on the east, west, and south by a triple palisade and a triple entrance, and further defending it on the south by an artificial ditch. On the south-eastern slope was planted the royal standard.

---

[1] So called by Ordericus Vitalis, who is followed by Mr. Freeman. Hastings was seven miles distant.

These preparations seem to have occupied the whole of Friday the 13th of October. We read of further messages sent by William to Harold; but their details are very doubtful. Mr. St. John seems to think that they were dictated by a conscience shrinking from the great act of imposture and injustice in which he was engaged.[1] More probably they sprang from policy, and were intended to reassure his own soldiers as to the justice of his cause, and to damp the ardour of the English by holding out hopes of accommodation. According to some authorities, he offered to submit his claims to the ordeal of a single combat; but this, as Mr. St. John remarks, is so little in keeping with his character for prudence, sagacity, and caution, that we may safely dismiss it as a fiction.

The night before the battle was spent in a very different manner by the hostile armies. The English awaited the coming struggle like men confident in their leader, themselves, and their cause. They had, but a few days before, met the Land-Ravager and his rovers in the valley of Derwent, and won a glorious victory. Why, then, should they tremble before the spears of the Normans? These audacious invaders, on the morrow, should feel the weight of English battle-axes, and so much of English ground should be granted to them as was needed for their graves. Free from apprehension, they caroused and made merry, they danced and sang: 'Bublie,' they cried, and 'waeshael, and laticome, and drinchael, and drinc-to-me.' At least, so says the Norman chronicler:

'Quant la bataille dut joster,
La nuit avant, ço oï conter,

---

[1] J. A. St. John, *Four Conquests of England*, ii. 265.

> Furent Engleiz forment haitiez,
> Mult riant e mult enveisiez;
> Tote nuit mangièrent e burent,
> Unkes la nuit el lit ne jurent.
> Mult les veissiez démener,
> Treper e saillir e chanter;
> *Bublie,* crient, *e weissel,*
> E *laticome,* e *drincheheil,*
> *Drinc Hindrewart* e *Drintome,*
> *Drinc Kelf,* e *drinctome.*'[1]

Far differently, if we may believe the Norman narratives, the night was spent in the Norman camp, where William and the priests did their utmost to stimulate among the soldiery a frenzy of devotion. A broad fosse ran in front of his camp; and behind, in regular rows or avenues, were planted the bough-twined huts of the 'rank and file.' In their rear stood the tents of the men-at-arms, and the pavilions of the knights and nobles. The centre was occupied by the splendid pavilion of the duke, before which drooped the heavy folds of the *gonfalon,* or banner, blessed by the Pope himself. The steady tramp of the sentinels, the clang of the armourers' hammers, the neighing of the war-horses,—all told of busy preparation for the morrow. Suddenly these sounds were hushed; a silver bell tinkled upon the night; from every hut and tent and pavilion came forth their inmates; and afar through the kneeling ranks wound a solemn procession of priests and monks, with censer and with crucifix, headed by Odo of Bayeux and Geoffrey of Coutances, in their magnificent pontificals. Then arose the low murmur of confession, and hands were uplifted in absolution and benediction. Solemn litanies pealed upon the night breezes, and voices round the distant watch-

[1] *Roman de Rou,* lines 12465-12476.

fires echoed each holy chant. And the excited soldiery vowed that, if God granted victory to their swords in the coming strife, they would never eat flesh upon a Saturday, long as life endured.

> 'E li Normanz e li Franceiz
> Tote nuit firent oreisons,
> E furent en aflicions.
> De lor péchiez confez se firent,
> As proveires les regehirent,
> Et qui n'en ont proveires prez,
> A son veizin se fist confez.
> Por ço ke Samedi esteit,
> Ke la bataille estre debveit,
> Unt Normanz pramis e voé,
> Si com li cler l'orent loé,
> Ke à cet jor mez s'il veskeient,
> Char ne sanne ne maingereient.'[1]

At length the morning came; the morning of the 14th of October,—of the birthday both of Duke William and King Harold. After hearing mass, and receiving the sacrament of the Lord's Supper, the Norman leader drew forth his troops, and addressed them in spirit-stirring words. His speech is recorded with slight variations by three of the old chroniclers.[2] We give it as it stands in Wace's Homeric narrative :—

> ' "Mult vos deis," dist-il, "toz amer,
> E mult me pois en vois fier,
> Mult vos dei e voil mercier
> Ke por mei avez passé mer,
> Estes venu en cele terre,
> Ne vos en puiz, ço peiz mei,
> Tel graces rendre comme jo dei,

---

[1] *Roman de Rou*, lines 12478-12491.
[2] Wace, Henry of Huntingdon, and William of Poitiers.

Maiz quant jo porrai, les rendrai,
E ço aureiz ke jo aurai :
Se jo cunquier, vos cunquerrez,
Se jo prens terre, vos l'aurez.
Maiz jo di bien veraiement :
Jo ne vins mie solement
Por prendre ço ke je demant,
Maiz por vengier li félunies,
Li traïsans, li feiz menties,
Ke li homes de cest païs
Unt fet à notre gent toz dis.
Mult ant fet mal à mes parenz ;
Mult en ant fet à altres gens ;
Par traïsan font kank' il font,
Jà altrement mal ne feront.
La nuit de feste Saint Briçan [1]
Firent orrible traïsan,
Des Daneiz firent grant dolor
Toz les veistent en un jor.
Ne kind mie ke péchié seit
D'ocire gent ki miex ne creit :
Ensemle od els mangié aveient,
E en dormant les occeient ;
D'Alwered avez bien oï
Come Guigne mult le traï :
Salua li, poiz cil beisa,
Ensemle od li but è menga,
Poiz le traï, prist e lia,
E à felun rei le livra,
Ki en l'isle d'Eli le mist,
Les vils li creva, puiz l'ocist.
A Gedefort fizt toz mener
Cels de Normendie e diesmer :
Et quant la diesme fu partie,
Oez com fait felonie,
Por ço ke trop grant le sembla,
La diesme de rechief diesma,

---

[1] The massacre of the Danes took place on St. Brice's day.

Teles félunies e plusors
K'il unt fete à nos ancessors
Et à nos amis ensement,
Ki se contindrent noblement,
Se Dex plaist nos les vengeron,
Et kant nos veincu les aron,
Ke nos feron légièrement,
Lor or aron e lor argent,
E lor aveir donc plenté ont,
E li maneirs ki riches sont.
En tot li mond n'a altretant
De si fort gent ne si vaillant
Come vos estes asemblez ;
Vos estes toz vassals provez."
E cil commencent à crier :
"Jà n'en verrez un warder,
Nus n'en a de morir poor,
Se mestier est por vostre amor."
Il lor répont : "Les vos merciz,
Por Dex, ne seiez esbatriz,
Forez les bien al comencier ;
N'entendez mie à goaingner ;
Li guain nos cirt tot comun ;
A plenti en ara chascun ;
Vos ne porreiz mie garir
Por estre en paiz ne por fuir,
Jà Engleiz Normanz n'ameront
Ne jà Normanz n'esparneront,
Félons furent e felons sont,
Faus furent e faus seront.
Ne fetes mie malvaistié,
Kar jà n'aront le vos pitié.
Ne li coart por bien fuir,
Ne li hardi por bien férir,
N'en iert des Engleiz plus preisiez.
Ne n'en sera plus esparniez.
Fuir poez jusk' à la mer.
Vos ne poes avant aler ;
N'i troverez ne nef ne pont,
Et esturnians vos faldront ;

> Et Engleiz là vos ateindront,
> Ki à honte vos ociront.
> Plus vos morreiz en fuiant
> Ke ne fereiz en combatant ;
> Quant vos par fuir ne ganeiz,
> Cumbatez vos e si veincrez.
> Jo ne dot pas de la victoire,
> Venuz somes por aveir gloire ;
> La victoire est en notre main,
> Tuit en poez estre certain." [1]

That these are the words actually employed by William, the chronicler does not pretend, and the reader will not believe ; but in all probability they embody with tolerable accuracy the sentiments he made use of, and the arguments with which he endeavoured to inflame the courage of his soldiers. We can fancy we hear his voice, 'loud as a trumpet with a silver sound,' pealing over the serried ranks, as he thus addressed them :—

'Knights and soldiers! remember ye to fight your best, and put every one to death; and if we conquer, rich shall be each man among us! What I have, you shall have; if I conquer, you too will conquer; if I win this land, it shall also be yours! But, in all truth, I say that I come not here for my own right alone, but to avenge the felonies, perjuries, and treacheries which this people have inflicted upon our nation. They slaughtered our kinsmen the Danes, on the night of St. Brice ; they blinded and afterwards murdered Alfred, the brother of their last sovereign, and decimated his companions. Behold, then, your enemies! Felons they were, and felons they are; false they were, and false they will be! Never, even in a just cause, were they famous for warrior blood or martial glory. On, on! and with God's help we will

[1] Wace, *Roman de Rou.*

chastise them for their evil deeds! The victory lies in your own hands!'[1]

William Fitz-Osbern, at the conclusion of this harangue, addressed his sovereign, and begged of him to tarry no longer. Then, as the sunrise reddened the eastern heaven, the Norman host quitted its intrenchments, and commenced its stately march along the greensand ridge which strikes inland from the cliffs of Hastings. Keeping to the north of the modern village of Hollington, it rolled onward over field and dale, until, ascending the height of Hetheland or Telham, it faced

[1] We subjoin an abridged version of William's speech, given by Benoit de St. Maure:—

'Cum sage, proz e diserez,
Les ont li dux amonestez ;
Remembre lor lor grant honor,
Que puisqu'il l'orent à seignor,
Ne furent en nul leu veneuz,
Or est li termes avenuz
Que lor valors estuet dobler,
Creistre e pareistre e afiner.
Ci n'a mestier hobeleiz,
Mais od les branz d'acer forbiz
Deffendre les cors et les vies,
Kar od tant seront acomplies
Les granz paines e les travailles,
Ici finiront les batailles,
Ci recevront les granz loiers
Qu' aveir deivent bons chevaliers
Les terres, les filus, les honors,
Plus c' unc n'orent lor anceisors.
Par lor valor, par lor procces,
Auront dès or les granz richesses,
Les granz tenures e les fieus ;
Mais trop estperillos li gieus.
Si la victoire n'en est lor
Et se il ne sunt venqueor,

the 'ramparted ground' of the English on the opposite height of Senlac. The array then halted; and the knights, clothed in coats-of-mail reaching even to the knee, put on their conical helmets, fixed their 'prick-spurs' to their heels, seized their kite-shaped bucklers, emblazoned with many a quaint device, and grasping their heavy swords or long ponderous lances, vaulted nimbly upon their richly caparisoned war-horses.

Odo, Bishop of Bayeux, and William's half-brother, a truculent member of the Church militant, next donned a hauberk under his pontifical rochet, and swaying to and fro his formidable mace, mounted a large white courser.

Then Duke William himself prepared to arm, and called for

> Mort sunt, en ce n'a recovrer;
> Kar fuie n'i aureit mestier,
> Recet ne chastel ne boschage;
> Mais qui or sera proz e sage
> S'il monstre e face apareissant,
> E il sera par tot aidant
> Chadel et eseuz et deffense;
> E si chascun d'eus se propense,
> Si trovera c'une Engleterre,
> Ne vont gaires nus hom conquerre,
> Qu' Engleis la peussent deffendre;
> Et si deivent à ce entendre,
> Que mult poent estre seur
> Dunt Heraut est vers lui parjur.
> Faus, enchoaiz, vient al estor
> Od tote sa grant déshonor;
> Morz est, vencuz e trespassez,
> E il vivront mais honorez
> Del grand conquest qu'iloc feront,
> Qu' ensemble od lui départiront.
> Or n'i a plus mais del férir
> E de vassaument contenir
> Que la bataille aient veneue
> Ainz que la nuit seit avenue.'

his coat-of-mail, which, by some misadventure, his squire handed to him with the wrong side foremost. Observing the cloudy countenances of the onlookers at an accident which they regarded as an omen of the most disastrous character, William Fitz-Osbern blithely cried,[1] that it should rather be looked upon as an augury of good fortune, for it showed that circumstances previously unchangeable would thenceforth acknowledge the duke's power. William himself having made the sign of the cross, donned his hauberk with his usual composure, saying, 'Truly, my friends, I know that I ought not, if I put any trust in omens, to enter the battle-field to-day. But I never had, nor will have, any faith in such superstitions, confiding in God, who shapes the future according to His will. I love not wizards, and I believe not in diviners. Let us imagine that the hauberk turned awry signifies that my duchy will be changed into a kingdom, and king shall he be who but a duke has been.'

' " Maint home," dist-il, "ai veu :
Si issi li just avenu,
Jà hui maiz armes ne portast
Ne en hui maiz en champ n'entrast,
Mais ankes en sort ne crei
Ne ne creirai; en Dex me fi,
Kar it fet d'el tot son pleisir,
E ço k'il velt fet avenir.
Unkes n'amai sortiseors,
Ne ni crei devineors;
A Dam le Duc tut me comant,
Ch' à mon haubert n'alez dotant;
Li haubert ki fre tresturné,
Et puiz me r'est à dreit doné

---

[1] According to some of the authorities, this makes a portion of Duke William's speech.

> Senelie la tresturnée,
> De la chose ki ert muée.
> Li nom ki ert de duché
> Verreiz de duc en rei torné;
> Reis serai ki duc ai esté,
> N'en aiez mie altre pensé."[1]

Next, having girded on his iron mace and laced his casque, which his valet handed to him, he called for his good steed. Nor better could there anywhere be found than the Spanish barb which Walter Giffard, the Lord of Longueville, had brought him on his return from a pilgrimage to the shrine of St. Iago of Compostella. Taking the bridle in his hand he sprang into the saddle, and seated himself with so royal a bearing that the Norman chivalry broke into loud murmurs of approbation. 'Never have I seen,' said the Vicomte de Thouars, 'a man more admirably armed, nor one who rode so gallantly, nor one who bore his hauberk better. Never knight brandished lance more bravely, nor managed his horse with greater skill. There lives not under the heaven a knight to equal him: so noble a count shall soon become a noble king!'

> 'Home mez si bel armé ne vit,
> Ke si gentement chevalchast,
> Ne ki si bel arme portast,
> N'a ki haubert si avenist,
> Ne ki lance si bien brandist,
> Ni en cheval si bien seist,
> Ki si tornast ne si tenist.
> Soz ciel tel chevalier n'en a
> Beau quens è beau rei sera.'[2]

At this moment, one Vital, a follower of Bishop Odo, who had been reconnoitering the English army, came upon the

---

[1] *Roman de Rou*, lines 12649-12668. [2] *Ibid.* lines 12688-12696.

scene; and when William asked him to point out his rival Harold, he replied that the English king stood, as he thought, in the thick of the array on the summit of Senlac, where the royal standard was flying. The duke then piously vowed that, if God granted him the victory, he would build a noble minster in His honour, on the very spot where that standard stood. The vow was heard by a monk of Marmoutiers, William Faber, or the Smith; and stepping forward, he besought the duke that the minster should be dedicated to the famous St. Martin. This the duke promised; and such was the origin of the Abbey of Battle, whose magnificent ruins still excite the admiration of the pilgrim.

The Normans were divided into three massive columns. In the first, or the right wing, led by Roger of Montgomery and William Fitz-Osbern, rode the horsemen of Boulogne and Picardy, the Rhenish mercenaries, and the men-at-arms of France and Flanders, Burgundy and Aquitaine. The centre, commanded by William in person, was composed of the flower of the Norman chivalry, flanked by the men of Coutances and Bayeux, and the archers of Evreux. And the third division, or left wing, under Alan of Brittany and Aimery of Thouars, consisted of the men of Maine, the Bretons, and the Poitevins.

William was supported by his two brothers, Odo of Bayeux and Robert of Mortain; and all three were armed with the heavy iron mace of the Normans.

The equipment of the army, as might be expected from its heterogeneous constituents, was very various. The archers, who went on foot, were clad in jerkins, with caps on their heads, or they wore a close-fitting body armour, and a conical helmet, with no defence for the face but a nose-piece. The men-at-arms carried the straight and heavy Norman sword, and were encased in helmets and coats-of-mail, and further protected by the kite-shaped shield.

Duke William now called to his side Raoul of Conches, whose hereditary privilege it was to carry the ducal standard in the day of battle, and offered him the guardianship of the Papal gonfalon, or consecrated banner. 'I shall need my right arm,' was the reply, 'for my sword, my left for my horse and shield.'

> '"Portez," dist-il, "mon gonfanon,
> Ne vos voil fere se dreit non ;
> Par dreit è par anceissorie
> Deivent estre de Normendie
> Vostre parent gonfaunonier,
> Mult furent tuit boen chevalier.
> Grant merci, dist Raoul, aiez,
> Ke nostre dreit reconoissiez ;
> Maiz li gonfanon, par ma fei,
> Ne sera hui porté par mei.
> Hui vos claim quite cest servise ;
> Si vos servirai d'altre guise,
> D'altre chose vos servirai :
> En la bataille od vos irai,
> Et as Engleiz me combatrai
> Tant ke jo vis estre porrai."'[1]

Next he summoned Walter Giffard, a white-haired warrior, who had borne the burthen of arms for many years. But no: the stalwart knight was still eager for the thick of the fray. He was feeble; but with such strength as was left to him, he would wield his sword against the enemy.

> 'Tant i kind ferit od m'espée,
> Ke tot en iert ensanglantée.'[2]

---

[1] *Roman de Rou*, lines 12719-12734. [2] *Ibid.* 12752, 12753.

So the sacred standard was finally entrusted to young Torestain the White, son of Rou, who showed himself on that day not unworthy of the important charge. And every preparation being thus completed, the Norman army descended the slope of Hetheland like the billows of a heavy sea, and prepared to attack the English position. In advance of the serried ranks rode a strange warrior of gigantic stature, the great Norman minstrel, Taillefer, or the Cleaver of Iron; and as he rode,

> He sang aloud a lusty strain
> Of Roland and of Charlemain,
> And Oliver and the heroes all
> Who fell at bloody Roncesvalles.

> Devant li duc alout cantant
> De Karlemaine è de Rollant,
> E d' Oliver è des vassals
> Ki morurent en Renchevals.[1]

'Sir,' he exclaimed, turning to the duke, 'in my time I have served you loyally, and now in recompense I do but ask that you will permit me to strike the first blow in to-day's battle.' And the duke granted him the favour, and the daring troubadour galloped forward :—

> Before the array he blithely rode,
> And many a feat the Saxons showed ;
> His ponderous lance his right hand took,
> And like a tender sapling shook,
> Then swang it in the air amain,
> And caught it dexterously again ;
> Three times aloft 'twas lightly whirled,
> Next at the enemy was hurled,
> And lo, heart-struck, a Saxon fell ;
> His sword he also handled well,

---

[1] *Roman de Rou*, lines 13151–13154.

And thrice it leaps, and thrice it falls,
Till soldier unto soldier calls,
'This, truly, is a sorcerer's deed!'
Headlong now sped his gallant steed,
With jaws so wide the Saxon coward
Trembled lest he should be devoured;
And pressing 'mid his Saxon foes,
Two fell beneath those fatal blows.[1]

We may add that this valiant jongleur slew an English standard-bearer and an English soldier before he was himself overpowered.

[1] Imitated from the Chronique de Geoffroi Gaimar:—

    'Devant toz li altres se mist,
    Devant Engleiz merveilles fist;
    Sa lance prist par le tuet
    Si com ces fast un bastonet,
    Encontre mont halt l'engetta
    Et par le par receue l'a.
    Treiz fois issi getta sa lance,
    La quarte foiz puis s'avance:
    Entre les Englois la launca,
    Parmi le cors un en navera,
    Puist trest s'espée, arère vint
    Et getta l'espée, qu'il tint,
    Encontre mont haut le receit,
    L'un dit à l'altre, qi ço veit,
    Que ço estoit enchantement.
    C'il se fiert devant lagent
    Quant treiz foiz ont getté l'espée.
    Le cheval ad la goule baée,
    Vers les Englois vint eslessé,
    Auquanz quident estre mangé
    Pur la cheval q'issi baout.
    Li jûgléour enprès venout,
    De l'espée fiert un Engleis,
    Le poign li fet voler maneis;
    Un autre férit tant cum il pout,
    Mau guerdon le jour en out.'

But we must now direct the reader's attention to the movements of Harold and his gallant army. Its numbers it is utterly impossible to compute, as we possess no other data than those furnished by the Norman chroniclers, whose object would necessarily be to exaggerate the strength of the conquered. We may doubt, however, whether they equalled the numbers of the Normans; and, for various reasons, we are inclined to believe they fell considerably below them.

Behind the defences which he had hastily constructed, Harold drew up his forces in two compact and solid bodies of infantry: the first consisting of the men of Kent, who formed the van, and of the levies from Essex and Hertfordshire, Sussex and Surrey, Lincolnshire, Somersetshire, Norfolk, and Gloucestershire; the whole drawn up in the shape of a wedge or triangle. The front ranks were clothed in coat-of-mail, armed with battle-axes, and protected by long kite-shaped shields, which they linked into one another, so as to form an almost impenetrable barrier. The rear ranks were occupied by the bowmen.

The second division was a solid mass of veteran soldiers,— Harold's famous house-carls, the stout soldiers of London and Middlesex, the trained and faithful men of East Anglia. Most of these wore mail, and carried shield, like the Normans, and swung the 'massy battle-axe,' the favourite Norse weapon. But others were lightly armed, bearing clubs and javelins, swords and spears, and being attired in tunics of hide, or quilted linen.

Harold's standard, embroidered with gold, set with precious stones, and blazoned with a figure called 'The Fighting Man,' was pitched on the summit of the hill. The king's post was near at hand, and under a 'lone apple tree,' which long afterwards marked the spot where the battle-fray was fiercest.

While the Norman leader was marshalling his array, an English spy, it is said, brought to Harold the latest intelligence of the Norman dispositions, of their numbers, and their approach.

The Norman chronicler records for our benefit the speech of Harold to his army, as he records that of William. The purport, if not the words, of the latter, he might easily have become acquainted with; but it is difficult to understand how he should know aught of the English king's harangue. Probably the speeches in the *Roman de Rou*, like those in Thucydides, are the result of ingenious conjecture and lively imagination. Still the subjects on which Harold is made to discourse are undoubtedly those which at such a time would naturally have stimulated his eloquence.[1]

> 'Li dus, ço dist, le deit requerre,
> Ki conquerre velt Engleterre,
> Et il, ço dist, le deit attendre,
> Ki la terre li deit défendre.
> A sa gent dist e comanda,
> Et à ses baronz cunseilla
> Ke tuit ensemble se tenissent,
> Et ensemble se défendissent.
> Quer se dilve se disparteient,
> A grant peine se rescovreient.
> Normanz, dist-il, sunt boen vassal,
> Vaillant à pié et à cheval;
> A cheval sunt boen chevalier
> Et de cumbatre costumier;
> Se dedenz noz poent entrer
> Nient iert pinz del recovrer.

---

[1] *Roman de Rou*, lines 12879-12905.

> Lungues lances unt et espées,
> Ke de lor terres unt aportées,
> E vos avez lances aigües,
> Et granz gisarmes esmolues.
> Cuntre vos armes ki bien taillent
> Ne kind les lor gaires ne vaillent;
> Trenchiez quant ke trenchier porriez
> Et jà mar rien espaveriez.'

'Stand firmly in your ranks,' said Harold to his soldiers, 'keep close together, and the victory will be yours. The Normans are good knights, and ride gallantly on horseback: if they once break through your line, it will be difficult for you to recover your former ground. They have long lances and swords; but you too have your sharp spears, and more, your heavy battle-axes. Against such weapons theirs will avail them nothing if you stand stedfast, overwhelming them with javelins as they advance, or if they draw near, cleaving them with your axes to the very earth.'[1]

---

[1] Harold's speech is thus conceived by Lord Lytton, expanding the brief outline given in the Norman chronicles:—'This day, O friends and Englishmen, sons of our common land, this day ye fight for liberty. The Count of the Normans hath, I know, a mighty army; I disguise not its strength. That army he hath collected together, by promising to each man a share in the spoils of England. Already in his court and in his camp he hath parcelled out the lands of this kingdom; and fierce are the robbers who fight for the hope of plunder! But he cannot offer to his greatest chief boons nobler than those I offer to my meanest freeman,— liberty and right and law in the soil of his fathers! I have heard of the miseries endured in the old time under the Dane, but they were slight indeed to those which ye may expect from the Norman. The Dane was kindred to us in language and in law; and who now can tell Saxon from Dane? But yon men would rule ye in a language ye know not, by a law that claims the crown as the right of the sword, and divides the land among the hirelings of an army. We baptized the Dane, and the Church tamed his fierce soul into peace; but yon men make the

And now, before the battle begins, let us glance at the scene presented on the crest of the hill of Senlac, this memorable 14th day of October, in the year of grace 1066.

On the very crown and topmost point, where the ground

Church itself their ally, and march to carnage under the banner profaned to the foulest of human wrongs! Outscourings of all nations, they come against you! Ye fight as brothers under the eyes of your fathers and chosen chiefs; ye fight for the women ye would save from the ravisher; ye fight for the children ye would guard from eternal bondage; ye fight for the altars which yon banner now darkens! Foreign priest is a tyrant as ruthless and stern as ye shall find foreign baron and king! Let no man dream of retreat; every inch of ground that ye yield is the soil of your native land. For me, on this field I peril all. Think that mine eye is upon you, wherever ye are. If a line waver or shrink, ye shall hear in the midst the voice of your king. Hold fast to your ranks; remember, such amongst you as fought with me against Hardrada, remember that it was not till the Norsemen lost, by rash sallies, their serried array, that our arms prevailed against them. Be warned by their fatal error,—break not the form of the battle; and I tell you, on the faith of a soldier who never yet hath left field without victory, that ye cannot be beaten. While I speak, the winds swell the sails of the Norse ships bearing home the corpse of Hardrada. Accomplish this day the last triumph of England; add to these hills a new mount of the conquered dead! And when, in far times and strange lands, scold and scop shall praise the brave man for some valiant deed wrought in some holy cause, they shall say, "He was brave as those who fought by the side of Harold, and swept from the sward of England the hosts of the haughty Norman."'—LORD LYTTON, *Harold*, Book xii. c. 6.

It is unnecessary to say that this glowing oration is for the most part imaginary; yet we may well believe that some such arguments as are set forth therein were actually employed by Harold to encourage his gallant soldiers. Lord Lytton, it will be observed, makes use of the word 'Saxon' with an erroneous signification. There were no Saxons in Harold's time: the whole population of the land was purely English. Saxon and Teuton had been successively absorbed in the great wars of the English nation, who spoke, not what is strangely called the Anglo-Saxon language, but genuine English.

begins to slope towards the south-east, were planted the two great 'ensigns of England,—the Dragon of Wessex, which had led Englishmen to victory at Ethandune and at Brunanbush, at Penselwood and at Brentford, and which had sunk without dishonour in the last fight beneath the heights of Assandun.'[1] But a few days before, it had waved victorious on the field of Stamford Bridge, in the last encounter between Norsemen and Englishmen on English land, and now it was doomed to see the last king of English blood overcome by the Norman invader.

Close at hand was also pitched the Standard, the personal ensign of King Harold, 'a glorious gonfanon, blazing with gems, and displaying, wrought in the purest gold, the figure of an armed warrior advancing to the battle.'

And round about this post of honour was gathered the flower of the English chivalry, the retainers of Harold and his house, the thegns and house-carls of Wessex, the men who had stormed the mountain-fastnesses of the Welsh, and driven back the impetuous onset of the warriors of the north. 'And there,' says Mr. Freeman, 'between the Dragon and the Standard, stood the rising hopes of England's newly chosen dynasty. There, as the inner circle of the host, were ranged the fated warriors of the house of Godwine. Three generations of that great line were gathered beneath the stdanrad of its chief. There stood the aged Ælfwig, with his monk's cowl beneath his helmet; there stood young Hakon, the son of Swegen, atoning for his father's crimes; and closer still than all the innermost centre of that glorious ring, stood the kingly three, brothers in life and death. There, in their stainless truth, stood Gyrth the counsellor, and Leofwine the

---

[1] Freeman, *Norman Conquest*, iii. 475, 476.

fellow-exile;[1] and there, with his foot firm on his native earth, sharing the toils and dangers of his meanest soldier, with the kingly helm upon his brow, and the two-handed axe upon his shoulder,[2] stood Harold, King of the English.'

[1] So in the *Roman de Rou*, lines 12971, 12972:

> 'Lewine è Guert furent od lui,
> Frere Heraut furent audui.'

[2] Or hanging from his neck. So Wace says, line 13111:

> 'Granz haches tindrent en lor cols.'

We venture to think that here the chronicler should be strictly followed. How would it have been possible for the English to use their spears, if at the same time they were supporting their heavy battle-axes on their shoulders? It is more probable that they were suspended from the neck by a loose thong or strap.

CHAPTER II.

The Battle of Hastings—*continued*.

IT was at nine o'clock in the morning that the Battle of Hastings, as it is popularly though erroneously called, began. The Norman divisions crossed the low land lying between the hills of Hetheland and Senlac, and attacked the English with great fury. The onset was preluded by a heavy discharge of arrows, and the heavily armed troops then endeavoured to break down the palisade, while they were met with incessant discharges of stones and javelins, and with vigorous blows from axe, sword, and massive club. The English, standing firm as a tower, and apparently rooted to their native soil, shouted again and again, 'Holy Cross! God Almighty! Out! Out!' To which the Normans, though ignorant of the meaning of their opponents' cries, responded with '*Dex aie!* God help us!'

> '*Olicrosse* sovent crivent
> E *Godemite* reclamvent;
> *Olicrosse* ess en Engleiz
> Ke *Sainte Croix* est en Franceiz;
> E *Godemite* altretant
> Com en Franceiz Dex tot poissant. . . .
> Normanz escrient, "*Dex aie;*"
> La gent Englische, "*Ut* s'escrie."'[1]

---

[1] *Roman de Rou*, lines 13119 to 13124, and 13193, 13194.

It seems impossible, as Mr. St. John remarks,[1] through the defective nature of the accounts transmitted to us, to represent distinctly the manœuvres and evolutions of the contending armies. Swayed by the ideas of chivalry, and ignorant of military science, the chroniclers neglect the strategic movements of the day, to dwell on examples of personal hardihood, relating how Harold at once displayed the abilities of the general and the courage of the common soldier, now directing the movements of the army, and now plunging, battle-axe in hand, into the densest masses of the foe; how Gyrth and William fought hand to hand,—how the youthful earl speared the duke's horse, while the rider escaped unhurt; how, later in the day, William had two other chargers killed under him; how the lines of assailants and assailed, agitated by various impulses, swayed to and fro like the surges of a troubled sea; and how, as long as Harold's soul and body kept together, the fierce small army of the English continued invincible.

Weary with fruitless efforts, the Norman infantry at length recoiled, and the mounted knights pressed forward in their turn to break down the English defences, and penetrate the living barrier of armed men. They fought with brilliant valour, but were repulsed by the steadiness of the English, before whose swinging battle-axes knight after knight went down. Not an English soldier quailed; not an inch of ground was yielded: the mass was as solid and as stedfast as those squares of infantry which stood rock-like before the billowy charges of the French cavalry at Waterloo.

At this time a body of Bretons on the left of the Norman army could no longer endure the incessant blows of the

[1] J. A. St. John, *Four Conquests of England*, ii. 269, 270.

English, and fairly broke and fled. The spectacle of a flying enemy proved too much for the equanimity of the English right, whose light-armed soldiery quitted the line of their defences, and pursued their beaten assailants down the slope. In the *mêlée* which ensued, the slaughter of the Normans seems to have been terrible. The fugitives falling back on the centre of their army, threw it into confusion, and a general panic seizing the Norman ranks, the English drove them pell-mell into a ravine which ran across the intermediate plain. Both men and horses were hurled into its depths, and the finest warriors of Normandy and Brittany, of Maine and Anjou, were to be seen rolling over one another with their faces to the earth, and fruitlessly struggling to regain their feet. Some of them flung their arms about their foes, and in a terrible embrace dragged them down to a common death; until the ravine was choked up, and, it is said, made level with the plain, by the number of the unfortunate who found in it a fearful grave. For long years afterwards survived the memory of this great slaughter, and the place where it occurred retained the significant name of *Malfosse*, or the Accursed Ditch.

To increase the panic, a rumour spread abroad that William himself had perished in the affray; and the retreat becoming a rout, the day seemed utterly lost. Then the duke spurred forward into the *mêlée*; he threw back his vizor, that all might see his face; he waved his iron mace in his sinewy hand, and flinging himself in front of the fugitives, he dealt heavy blows on every side, and reproaches not less heavy. 'Behold me,' he cried, 'I live, and, with God's blessing, will conquer. What madness induces ye to fly? Turn, turn and strike, for I tell ye the day shall be ours!'

> 'Qu' avez oï, genz senz valor?
> Ne veiz-vos vostre seignor
> Déhore e bien aidanz e sains
> E de victorie tot certains?
> Tornez arière au féréiz,
> Kar jà les verreiz desanfiz.'[1]

Nor in this critical moment was Odo of Bayeux wanting in promptitude of courage. The Norman chronicler gives us a striking picture of the truculent prelate, with his hauberk under his white vestment, mounted on a snow-white charger, and carrying a heavy mace of iron in his hand. 'Stand fast, stand fast,' he exclaimed, 'be calm and fear not! With the grace of God we yet shall conquer!'

> 'Quand Odes li boen corenez,
> Ki de Baienes ert sacrez,
> Porrist, si lor dist, "Estez, estez,
> Seïez en paiz, ne vos morez;
> N'aiez poer de nule rien,
> Kar se Dex plaist nos viencron bien."
> Issi furent asséuré,
> Ne se sunt mie remué,
> Odes revint puignant arière
> U la bataille esteit plus fière.
> Forment i a li joi valu,
> Un haubergeon aveit vestu,
> Desor une chemise blanche;
> Le fut li cors, juste la manche;
> Sor un cheval tot blanc sceit,
> Tote la gent le congnoisseit
> Un baston teneit en son poing.'[2]

Through the exertions of the two great leaders, the Normans were rallied, and their ranks restored to something like

---

[1] Benoit de St. Maure, in the *Chroniques Anglo-Normandes.* See also William of Poitiers, p. 134.

[2] *Roman de Rou,* lines 13243-13250.

order; and once more they advanced to the attack of the English position. William and his choicest knights pressed towards the standard of the 'Fighting Man.' Observing their approach, Gyrth, the Earl of the East Angles, threw himself across the Norman leader's path, and hurled at him his javelin, which missing the rider, wounded to the death his horse. William quickly freed himself from the stirrups, and springing to his feet, dealt his assailant a blow with his heavy mace, which crushed in his skull.[1] Almost at the same time fell his brother Leofwine, either by the hand of Odo of Bayeux or Robert of Mortain.

But the fortune of the day—and here we borrow an episode from Mr. Freeman's historical epic—was still far from being determined. The two earls had fallen, but the fight at the barricades went on as fiercely as before. The men of the earldoms of the two fallen chiefs relaxed not because of the loss of their captains. The warriors of Kent and Essex fought manfully to avenge their leader.

> 'Là à la presse ert plus espesse,
> Là cil de kent è cil d'Essesse
> A merveille se cumbateient,
> E li Normanz urser faiseient,
> En sus les faiseient retraire,
> Ne lor poeient grant mal faire.'[2]

As for the duke, he called to a knight of Maine to give him up his horse. Whether from disloyalty or cowardice, or both, the knight refused. A blow from the duke's hand soon brought him to the ground; and William, once more mounted,

---

[1] Both Wace and Guy of Amiens agree that Gyrth was slain by William, but Wace makes Gyrth's death one of the latest incidents of the battle.

[2] *Roman de Rou*, lines 13874-13879.

"William, springing to his feet, dealt his assailant a blow with his heavy mace which crushed in his skull."—LIVES OF OLD ENGLISH WORTHIES, *Page 202.*

was soon in the hottest part of the fray, encouraging his soldiers by voice and example. But the deed and the fate of Gyrth were soon repeated. Another English spear felled William's second horse; and another Englishman, like the East Anglian Gyrth, paid the penalty of his exploit by death at the duke's own hand.[1] Count Eustace of Boulogne then offered his charger to his chief, and a knight of his own following did him the same good service. The two led their men-at-arms against the English lines, and vigorously pressed on the attack. To some extent it was successful: the English had lost the two brothers of their king; they had lost many meaner, though not less gallant men; the palisades were partly broken down: but in the tumult that ensued, the English firmly held their ground, and as one of the foremost fell, another from the rear rank stepped forward to take his place. The living ring was unbroken; within the charmed circle of these hero-patriots no invader had set his foot.

The chronicler records numerous instances of individual valour as occurring in the course of this great battle.

Thus: an English thegn rushed impetuously forward at the head of a company of one hundred men, each provided with a different weapon. He himself wielded an axe whose steel was fully a foot in length; and wherever the press was greatest he leaped more swiftly than a stag, marking his path by dead and wounded Normans. Rushing against a knight who bestrode his war-horse with chivalrous bearing, he delivered a blow at his head with his heavy axe, but it slipped aside, and the keen steel shore right through the horse's neck and shoulder, bringing both horse and rider to the earth. The Normans who beheld the deed were so astonished, that they

[1] William of Amiens, 503-518.

fell back from the assault; whereupon Roger of Montgomery rode hastily to the spot, and little heeding the Englishman's long-handled axe, dealt him so lusty a blow that he fell dead. Then cried Montgomery, 'Strike, Normans! the day is ours!' and again the warriors mingled in the fray, with push of lance and stroke of sword.

> 'Bien le faseient li Normant,
> Quant un Engleiz vint acorant;
> En sa cumpaigne out chent armez,
> De plusors armes atornez,
> Hache Noresche out mult bele,
> Plus de plain pié ont l'alemele,
> Bien ju armé à sa manière,
> Grant ert e fier, o bele chiere.
> En la bataille el primer front,
> La à Normanz plus espez sont,
> En vint saillant plus tost ke cers;
> Maint Normant mit li jor envers
> Od sa cumpaigne k'il aveit,
> A un Normant s'en vint tot dreit,
> Ki armè fu sor un destrier;
> Od la hache ki fa d'acier
> El helme férir le kuida,
> Maiz li colp ultre escolorja;
> Par devant l'arcon glaceia
> La hache ki mult bien trencha
> Li col del cheval en travers
> Colpa k'a ture vint li fers,
> E li cheval chaï avant
> Od tot son mestre à terre jus.
> Ni sai se cil le féri plus,
> Maiz li Normanz ki li colp virent,
> A grant merveille s'esbahirent.
> L'assalt aveient tot guerpi,
> Quant Rogier de Montgomeri
> Vint poignant, la lance beissié;
> Onc ne leissa por la coignié

> K'il aveit sus el col levée,
> Ki mult esteit lonc enhanstée,
> Ke il Engleiz si ne férist,
> K'a la terre platir le fist ;
> Dunc s'écria, "Ferez, Franceiz ;
> Nostre est li champ sor les Engleiz."'[1]

There was an Englishman who notably distinguished himself by the slaughter he made among the enemy. His wooden helmet was so laced around his neck that not a single blow could reach the head ; and while with his massive battle-axe he delivered the most terrible blows on every side, it seemed as if he himself bore a charmed life.

His prowess was observed by one of the Norman knights, who rode, according to the chronicler, a steed that neither fire nor water could arrest in his course when once his rider spurred him on. Charging straight against the Englishman, he smote him upon the helmet in such wise that it fell over his face. Then, as he lifted up his right hand to remove it from his eyes, the knight struck off his hand, which immediately dropped on the ground. A Norman soldier, leaping forward, and stooping, seized the axe. He held it but a moment, and for that moment paid very dearly: even as he stooped, an Englishman smote him on the shoulders with such force that his bones were broken, and the lungs forced through the yawning wound. In the meantime, the knight and his war-horse had regained his ranks unwounded ; and meeting, face to face, another foe, he rode him down and trampled him under his horse's hoofs.

The foregoing incident is thus described by Wace :—

> 'De l'altre part out un Engleiz
> Ki leidesseit mult li Franceiz ;

---

[1] *Roman de Rou*, lines 13386-13422.

Od une hache mult trenchant,
Les alout mult envaïssant.
Un helme aveit tot fait de fust,
Ke kolp el chief ne receust ;
A ses draz l'aveit atachié,
Et envirun son col lacié,
Un chevalier de Normendie
Vit li forfeit à l'estoltie
K'il alout des Normanz faisant ;
Sor un cheval sist mult vaillant ;
Eau ne feu nel retenist,
Se li sire bien le poinsist ;
Li chevalier l'esperuna
E li cheval tost le porta.
Sor li belure l'Engleiz feri,
De suz les oils li abati,
Sor li viaire li pendi
E li Engleiz sa main tendi
Li helme voleit suz liver,
E son viaire délivrer ;
E cil li a un colp doné,
Li puing destre li a colpé,
E sa hache à terre chaï.
Et un Normand avant sailli ;
Od ses dous mains l'a relevée,
Ke il aveit mult golosée ;
Maiz mult li out corte dure,
K'il l'out sempres cumperée.
Al beissier ke il faseit
A la hache ke il perneit,
Un Engleiz od une coignié,
Ke il aveit lungue emmanchié,
L'a si féru parmi li dos
Ke toz li fet croissir les os :
Tote poet l'en veir l'entraille,
E li pomon e la coraille.
Li chevalier al boen cheval
S'en retorna ke il n'ont mal ;
Maiz un Engleiz ad encuntre,
Od li cheval l'as si hurté,

> Ke mult tost l'a acraventé,
> Et od li piez tot défolé.'[1]

We read also of two Englishmen, sworn brothers-in-arms, who fought side by side, and wielded their axes with a prowess which seemed to render them invulnerable. A French knight encountered them: his heart for a moment failed him, and he thought upon saving himself by flight. But he regained courage, and lifting his shield as a safeguard for his head, he pierced one Englishman through with his lance, which, as the Englishman fell, broke in his body; then he seized the mace suspended to his saddle-bow, and crushing in head-piece and head, slew the other Englishman with a single stroke.

We subjoin the story in its original Norman-French:—

> 'Dous Engleiz vit mult orguillos,
> Ki s'esteient acumpaignié
> Por çe ke bien erent preisié.
> Ensemble deveient aler,
> Li uns debveit l'altre garder,
> En lor cols aveient levées
> Dui gisarmes lunges e lées;
> As Normanz feseient granz mals,
> Homes tuoent e chevals.
> Li soldeier les esgarda,
> Vi li gisarmes, si dota;
> Son boen cheval perdre creincit,
> Kar ço ert li mielx k'il aveit;
> Volentiers altre part tornast,
> Se cuerdise ne semblast.
> Maiz tost fu en altre pensé,
> Sun cheval a esperuné;
> Poinst li cheval, li frein lascha
> E li cheval tost le porta.
> Por la crieme des dous gisarmes
> L'escuz leva par les enarmes:

---

[1] *Roman de Rou*, lines 13503-13545.

> Un des Engleiz féri tot dreit,
> Od la lance ki il teneit,
> Sos li menton en la petrine;
> Li fer passa parmi l'eschine.
> Endementrez ke il versa,
> Se lance chaï e froissa,
> Et il a le gibet seisi
> Ki a sun destre bras perdi;
> L'altre Engleiz a féru amont
> Ke tot li chief li casse e font.'[1]

With one other episode of individual valour, we close our extracts from the Norman chronicler's spirited ballad-poem :—

Robert Fitz-Erneis, a daring young cavalier, endeavoured to cut his way towards the standard of the 'Fighting Man,' in the hope that he might carry it off as a splendid trophy of his valour. He struggled onward through the press with dauntless resolution. His sword struck down several Englishmen, but he was soon surrounded, and he fell beneath the battle-axes of their comrades. On the morrow his body was found outstretched beneath the drooping folds of the standard.[2]

> ' Robert ki fu Filz-Erneis,
> La lance aluigne, l'escu pris,
> A l'estandart en vint puignant;
> De son glaive ki fu tranchant,
> Fiert un Engleiz ki ert devant,
> Mort l'abati de maintenant,
> Puiz trait l'espée demaneiz,
> Moint colp féri sor les Engleiz.
> A l'estandart en alout dreit,
> Per ço k'abatre le voleit,
> Maiz li Engleiz l'avironèrent,
> Od lor gisarmes le tuèrent:

---

[1] *Roman de Rou*, lines 13431-13461.   [2] *Ibid.* lines 13751-13764.

> Lor fu herí quant il fu quis,
> Lez l'estandart mort et occis.'[1]

These individual deeds of daring were unable, however, to exercise any great influence on the fortune of the fight. For the greater part of the day it had gone in favour of the English; and Duke William plainly saw that unless he could break their solid array, he could not hope for success. But he remembered that when his left wing fled, a large body of the victors had been beguiled from their ranks by the fierce excitement of the pursuit; and his quick eye saw that if he could again induce such a movement, he might be able to pour in his troops at the gap so created in the unyielding barrier. He resolved, therefore, on attempting the stratagem, and gave orders that his left wing should again retire, but this time only in simulated flight, and without confusion. His hopes were more than realized. The English right, wearied probably with the long day's battle, saw before them, as they thought, a flying enemy; and exulting in the belief that victory would at last reward their exertions, they broke from their lines, and rushed in pursuit. As soon as they had been enticed to a sufficient distance, the Norman left turned suddenly upon them and drove them back, though not without a desperate struggle, to their position, which they entered simultaneously with them. Meanwhile the main body of the Normans, profiting by this fatal error, had ascended the hill, turned the flank of the English centre, and poured in

---

[1] There is so much spirit and so much vigorous simplicity in the *Roman de Rou*, that it is a wonder no enterprising publisher has reprinted it, with a new metrical translation. Not a few passages have all the fire and terseness of Scott; and we think it a matter to be regretted, that this valuable contemporary narrative of the Conquest should be neglected in our schools, and so little known to the general reader.

irresistible numbers against the defenders of the Standard. Now came the crisis of the battle. The ring of shields which encircled the ensigns of England still stood immoveable, and on both sides prodigies of valour were displayed, worthy to be sung of by an English Homer. Harold was the soul and brain of the defence. His valour was so brilliant, his resolution so indomitable, that even the Norman chroniclers have felt compelled to do him justice. They extol not only his heroism as a knight, but his skill as a commander. It is strange that he and his great rival never met. True it is, the historians assert, that William eagerly sought him;[1] yet the duke was as prudent as he was brave, and perhaps he may have shrunk from a personal encounter which might not have ended to his advantage.

After a heroic resistance, the English, overpowered by numbers, began to slacken in the struggle. They had lost so many of their bravest knights,—they were so weary of killing! Not a man had fled; they had died where they stood; and the ground was covered with the slain. But Harold fought on, with an arm that no exertion enfeebled, for his country and his crown; and so long as Harold lived, the issue of the battle remained doubtful. Evening was drawing in; and if darkness came, the English might well draw off from the battle-field in gallant order, and retire upon London to gather reinforcements. William saw that the issue was still uncertain. He resolved upon a new device, and ordered his archers to shoot up in the air, so that their arrows might, as it were, fall straight from heaven. His orders were obeyed, with a result that was terrible for the English. The heavy rain of steel-pointed shafts passed through the helmets and visors, and struck

[1] William of Poitiers, 136.

their wearers in the eyes. They lifted their shields to ward them off, but this action laid them open to the Norman spears. A mighty shower of arrows was specially directed against Harold and his co-defenders of the Standard; and one of these, 'more charged with destiny than its fellows,' pierced the king's right eye. In his agony he plucked out the accursed weapon, and breaking it with his hands, flung the pieces aside. His axe fell to the ground, and for a moment he leaned helplessly upon his shield. This accident decided the fortune of the day in favour of William the Norman; and the English were long accustomed to say to their conquerors, that the arrow so sent up against their king was well shot, and that the bowman won signal glory for his country who thus put out King Harold's eye.

Seeing the condition of the English sovereign, four Norman knights rushed in upon him,[1]—Eustace of Boulogne, the son of Guy of Pontheiu, Giffard, and Montfort. One stabbed him in the breast, another struck off his head with a sword, a third wreaked his rage on the dead body, and a fourth smote off the king's leg. It is to the honour of William of Normandy that he expelled from his army the perpetrator of the last most inglorious and dastardly exploit.

The closing scenes of the battle, which we have thus briefly described, are told by Wace in spirit-stirring verse:—

> 'Normanz archiers ki ars tenient,
> As Engliez mult espez traient
> Maiz de lor esarz se covreient,
> Ke en char férir ne s' poeient;

---

[1] A previous attempt had been made by twenty knights to carry off the royal standard. Most of the twenty fell, but the banner was beaten to the ground, and the golden Dragon borne off in triumph.

> Ne por viser, ne por bien traire,
> Ne lor poeient nul mal faire.
> Cunseil pristrent ke halt traireient ;
> Quat li sactes descendreient,
> De sor lor testes dreit charreient,
> Et as viaires les fureient.
> Cel cunseil ont li archier fait,
> Sor li Engleiz unt en halt trait ;
> Quant li sactes revencient,
> De sor les testes lor chaient,
> Chiés e viaires lor porçoent,
> Et à plusors les oilz crevoent ;
> Ne n'osvent les oilz ovrir,
> Ne lor viaires descovrir.
> Sactes plus espessement
> Volvent ke pluie par vent
> Mult espès volvent sactes
> Ke Engleiz clamoent wibetes.
> Issi avint k'une sacte,
> Ki deverz li ciel ert chacte
> Féri Heraut desus l'oil dreit,
> Ke l'un des oilz li a toleit ;
> Et Heraut l'a par aïr traite,
> Getée a les mains, si l'a fraite.
> Por li chief ki li a dolu
> S'ast apuié sor son escu.
> Por ço soleient dire Engleiz,
> E dient encore as Franceiz
> Ke la sacte fu bien traite
> Ki à Heraut fu en batte traite,
> E mult les mist en grant orgoil,
> Ki al rei Heraut neva l'oil."[1]

And now, their standards beaten down or carried off, their king dead, their best and bravest slaughtered, the English no longer offered any resistance; and those who had survived the long day's carnage—chiefly men of low degree—endeavoured

[1] *Roman de Rou*, lines 13275-13310.

to save themselves by flight. In hot haste the victors pursued them. No quarter was given,—none was asked : amid the foldings of the hills, on the plain, in the forest, the Normans wreaked their vengeance on the fugitives as long as the moonlight enabled them to distinguish foe from friend. But the dark, tangled, and intricate recesses of the wood soon rendered the continuance of the carnage unsafe. Though far from satiated with blood, the pursuers therefore were reluctantly compelled to interrupt their gratification and return to the battle-field, where they found their leader's tent pitched in the midst of the dead and dying, close to that symbol of fraud and cruelty which the Popes denominated 'the standard of St. Peter.'[1]

And thus, on the 14th of October 1066, was the Battle of Senlac, or Hastings, fought and won; and thus in blood and darkness set the star of our English Harold. The victory was with the Normans; but seldom has victory been more dearly purchased: fifteen thousand of their host fell on the perilous field.

[1] J. A. St. John, *Four Conquests of England,* ii. 273.

CHAPTER III.

Night on the Field — Harold's Character considered — Search for his Body — Its Interment at Hastings — Removal to Waltham Abbey — Harold and Edward the First.

THE victors, as we have said, passed the night on the field they had so dearly won, William's tent being pitched among the bodies of the slain, and his supper made ready within it. His knights and nobles stood around him, praising his prowess and his generalship, and rejoicing in the prospect of the spoil of conquered England. 'And he sate among them,'—a man of lofty stature and noble mien; and, with the devout hypocrisy of the age, gave thanks to the Lord of hosts, through whose interposition he had gained the fight. Mourning and lamenting for the lost, he thanked his knights for their dauntless courage; and 'he ate and drank among the dead, and slept that night upon the field.'

The character of Harold, the last of the English kings, the last of the race of native-born princes, has been variously painted by historians, according to their prepossessions, their prejudices, or the influence of traditions. The Norman chroniclers naturally depict him in the blackest colours, though constrained to bear witness to his heroic courage, and his skill as a leader of armies. Some of our later writers have allowed themselves to be swayed by the evidence of these hostile witnesses, and have shown themselves more disposed to extol the successful qualities of the conqueror, than to consider impartially the noble virtues of the unsuccessful patriot. Happily, Mr. St. John and Mr. Freeman have, in our own time, risen superior to the force of prejudice. The latter, it may be, errs on the side of eulogy, for he almost disallows, in his turn, the possession of a single error to cast a shadow on the brilliant picture. Mr. St. John's estimate seems to us more temperately and more justly considered. The greatest of the sons of Godwine, Harold, as he remarks, inherited his father's courage, but not his prudence. Anticipating the virtues and faults of chivalry, he was 'the very embodiment of honour, bravery, magnanimity, and all knightly qualities.' If ambition be a sin, he was guilty of this sin ; for, from an early age, he seems to have aimed at the throne, to which, at last, he was honourably called by the spontaneous suffrage of his countrymen. Incapable of fear, he was, for that very reason, too apt to underrate the suggestions of policy. Confident in his own resources, he sometimes undervalued the difficulties which lay in his path. And though of eminent ability as a military commander, he suffered his natural impetuosity to lead him into the battle at Senlac, when a fortnight's delay would probably have saved his crown and country.

Harold, we say, was the greatest of the sons of Godwine ; but we think him as much inferior to his father in art and subtle statesmanship, in self-control and the knowledge of men, as he was unquestionably his superior in those chivalric qualities which dazzle the multitude, and win the popular favour. He did not possess his father's power of waiting : his genius was of a more brilliant, but less stedfast character; his temperament was more sanguine and passionate.

At the time of his fall, Harold stood, says Mr. St. John,[1] on the very keystone of the arch of manhood, when the mind and body are in perfection, and his athletic frame, tall and majestic, and invested, in a proportion which rarely falls to the lot of man, with beauty, it was but too natural that he should think lightly of danger. Moreover, he united in his own person the blood of the two brave races which had contended during nearly three hundred years for mastery in England: by his father he was a West Saxon, by his mother a Dane. Hot and impetuous, therefore, was his blood; and he did not live long enough for it to be tempered by the cooler current of mature manhood. He died at the age of forty-three.

Our narrative now brings us to the day after the great battle. The summit of Senlac—whose name was afterwards corrupted into the expressive perversion of *Sangue-lac*, or the lake of blood—was literally heaped with dead bodies,—not fewer, it may be, than twenty to twenty-five thousand;[2] and down the hill-side trickled a rill of gore. The peasant, we may add, long believed that the ruddy chalybeate waters of the brook, which still flows across the battle-field, derived their peculiarity of colour from the blood of the slaughtered. Drayton, in his 'Poly-Olbion,' preserves the tradition:

> 'Asten once distained with native English blood;
> Whose soil yet, when but wet with any little rain,
> Doth blush, as put in mind of those there sadly slain.'

---

[1] J. A. St. John, *Four Conquests of England*, ii. 277.

[2] The loss of the Normans, from the nature of the battle, must have largely exceeded that of the English, though the latter were defeated.

The first duty was the burial of the dead. With politic compassion, William permitted the English women to remove the bodies of their husbands, sons, and brothers for interment in the neighbouring churches and minsters.[1] Among the first to be recognised, were thirteen with a monk's habit under their armour, —Ælfwig, Abbot of Hide, and his twelve brethren, who had fought and bled in defence of their country's freedom. Those whom no loving eye distinguished, and no loving hand tended —and so mutilated were the bodies, that recognition was frequently impossible—were left to rot where they lay, or to be devoured by 'worms, and wolves, and birds, and dogs.' Two monks of Waltham, Osgod and Æthelric the 'childe-maister,' who from a distance had watched the varying fortunes of the preceding day, undertook to search for the corpse of their noble founder. Their labours proved fruitless, until they called to their assistance one who had loved him, 'not wisely, but too well,'—Eadgyth Swanneshals, or Edith the swan-necked. Her eye detected it by certain secret marks, and the body was then wrapped in purple linen, and buried, by the conqueror's command, on the cliffs of Sussex. Fain would Harold's mother, the noble Gytha, have ransomed the dead :—' I have lost three of my sons,' said she—' I have lost three of my sons in this dread battle; return to me the bones of but one, and I will pay you for them, weight by weight, in pure gold.' William coldly replied, that he through whose ambition so many had perished, and now lay unburied, was unworthy of Christian sepulture.[2] So he was buried on the wind-swept rocks, where the complaining seas, to the ear of fancy, murmur an everlasting dirge; and a stone placed over his remains long bore the

[1] William of Poitiers, 139 ; *Roman de Rou*, lines 14083-14092.
[2] Ordericus Vitalis, 532.

Norman's taunt, which the patriotic sympathy of the modern Englishman converts into an appropriate epitaph for the last of the English kings :[1]

> 'By the Duke's will, thou restest here, to be,
> O Harold! guardian of the shore and sea.'[2]

> 'Corpus enim Regis citò sustulit et sepelivit,
> Imponens lapidem, scripsit et in titulo :
> "Rex mandata Ducis, ex lui Heraldi, quiescis,
> Ut custos maneas littoris et pelagi." '

'Guardian of the shore and sea' he would in truth have shown himself, had fortune dealt with him more gently; and guardian of the shore and sea the hero yet may prove, if in the hour of danger he shall inspire the hearts of Englishmen with his own unquailing courage!

If anything be certain in history, it is that Harold died at Senlac, and was at first interred on the cliff at Hastings. '*Heu, ipsemet cecidit crepusculi tempore!*' But tradition loves to be busy with the memory of heroes, and a superstitious patriotism shrinks from believing in the loss of those who are recognised as the only possible saviours of their country. And thus it is that the closing scene of Harold's career has been embroidered with the wildest legendary details. Just as the Portuguese long

---

[1] Mr. Freeman justly observes, that William's conduct in this matter was not dictated by any personal spite, but by motives of policy, which led him to brand the perjurer, the usurper, the excommunicate of the Church, the despiser of the holy relics, with the solemn judgment of a minister of righteous vengeance. — Freeman, *History of the Norman Conquest*, iii. 512.

[2] Guy of Amiens, *Carmen de Bello Hastingensi*, 589-592. See also William of Poitiers, p. 228.

looked for the reappearance of the dead Sebastian, so did the English for the coming of the king, who should deliver them from the bonds of Norman oppression. It was said—and the story was repeated from mouth to mouth—that Harold had been found on the field of Senlac, dangerously wounded, but still living, by some of the women engaged in searching the dead. By two franklins, or yeomen, he was carefully removed to Winchester, where he resided for a couple of years, and was tended by a Saracen woman of wonderful skill in potions and medicaments.[1] On his complete recovery he repaired to Germany and Denmark, to obtain assistance in recovering his crown. Unsuccessful in his solicitations, he abandoned the cares and projects of the world, returned to England in disguise, and withdrew to an anchorite's cell attached to St. John's minster at Chester. Here he died at a ripe old age, revealing himself to the attendants by his deathbed, as Harold, once King of the English.

Another and more credible story relates to his burial-place. In the old monastic chronicle it is claimed for Waltham Abbey, that it had the honour of affording a Christian grave to its founder and benefactor; and while there is a weight of evidence in support of the claim, there seems none to invalidate it. Whether the body was removed from the lonely cairn on the sea-cliff with the conqueror's consent, or whether its translation was secretly effected, it is impossible to say; but that such a translation *did* take place, we have but little doubt.[2] So that Harold finally lay at rest in his own minster

---

[1] See the curious romance called the *Vita Haroldi*, in the *Chroniques Anglo-Normandes*, 2d vol.

[2] The author of the *De Inventione Crucis* (temp. Henry I.) both saw and handled the bones of the dead king.

at Waltham, in the place of honour—that is, by the high altar—with the significant inscription on the stone,

'HAROLD INFELIX.'

Mr. Freeman closes his account of the interment of our hero with an eloquent and suggestive passage, which we take leave to borrow, as a fitting termination to our own briefer and less elaborate record :[1]—

Once only, he says, since Harold's burial, has Waltham seen a royal corpse ; but then it was one worthy to rest even by the side of Harold. Two hundred and forty years after the fight of Senlac, the body of the great Edward was borne with all royal honours to a temporary resting-place in the church of Waltham. Harold was translated to Waltham from a nameless tomb by the sea-shore ; Edward was translated from Waltham to a still more glorious resting-place, beneath the soaring vault of the apse of Westminster. But for a while the two heroes lay side by side—the last and the first of English kings, between whom none deserved the English name, or could claim honour or gratitude from the English nation. The one was the last king who reigned purely by the will of the people, without any claim either of conquest or of hereditary right. The other was the first king who reigned purely as the son of his father, the first who succeeded without competitor or interregnum. But each alike, as none between them did, deserved the love and trust of the people over whom they reigned. With Harold our native kingship ends ; the Dragon of Wessex gives place to the Leopards of Normandy ; the crown, the laws, the liberties, the very tongue of Englishmen, seem all fallen, never to rise again. In Edward the line of English

[1] Freeman, *Norman Conquest of England*, iii. 521, 522.

kings begins once more. After two hundred years of foreign rule, we have again a king bearing an English name and an English heart,—the first to give us back our ancient laws under new shapes; the first, and for so long the last, to see the empire of his mighty namesake [Eadward the son of Ælfred] was a worthier prize than shadowy dreams of dominion beyond the sea.

Such, concludes Mr. Freeman,[1] such were the men who met in death within the now vanished choir of Waltham. And in the whole course of English history we hardly come across a scene which speaks more deeply to the heart, than when the first founder of our later greatness was laid by the side of the last kingly champion of our earliest freedom—when the body of the great Eadward was laid, if only for a short space, by the side of

HAROLD THE SON OF GODWINE.

[1] Freeman, *Norman Conquest of England*, iii. 522.—We must here again repeat our obligations to this masterly work, the most complete and philosophical of all histories of the stirring period of which it treats. It is due to ourself to state, however, that we have carefully verified all our references to the contemporary authorities; though in a field already reaped by Mr. Freeman, nothing is left for any later gleaner.

English Worthies.

BOOK V.

STIGAND, ARCHBISHOP OF CANTERBURY.

'STIGAND was neither a hero nor a saint. He did not possess the moral force or the intellectual power which enables a great mind to make adverse circumstances a stepping-stone to usefulness and honour; and he did not possess the meaner ambition of those who, failing in the arena of manly contest, are satisfied with the effeminate applause which is elicited by sentimentalism and romance. But Stigand was a sturdy patriot, in whose breast beat an honest English heart. He hated the French, and their hatred was more powerful than his; for the Norman had not only the power of the sword,—he was master also of the literature of the age.'

DEAN HOOK.

> 'Hark! 'tis the tolling curfew! the stars shine;
> But of the lights that cherish household cares
> And festive gladness, burns not one that dares
> To twinkle after that dull stroke of thine,
> Emblem and instrument, from Thames to Tyne,
> Of force that daunts, and cunning that ensnares!
> Yet as the terrors of the lordly bell,
> That quench, from hut to palace, lamps and fires,
> Touch not the tapers of the sacred quires;
> Even so a thraldom, studious to expel
> Old laws, and ancient customs to derange,
> To Creed or Ritual brings no fatal change.'

WORDSWORTH.

AUTHORITIES.

[THE authorities for the life of Archbishop Stigand are necessarily identical, in the main, with those for the history of the 'troublous times' in which he lived. For accounts of the principal incidents in which he figured, or which occurred in his day, the reader will refer to the old monkish historians and chroniclers already enumerated:—William of Poitiers, Ordericus Vitalis, Ailred, *Life of Edward the Confessor;* the *Saxon Chronicle;*—and, of later date, William of Malmesbury, Matthew of Paris, Roger of Wendover, Henry of Huntingdon, Higden's *Polychronicon*, and the like.

Many interesting details will be found in the *Chronica Magistri Rogeri de Hovedene* (Roger of Hoveden), edited by Stubbs, the older portion of which (A.D. 732-1148) is supposed to be copied from a Northumberland compilation of the date of 1164.

See also Mr. Luard's edition of *Lives of Edward the Confessor* :—(1.) *La Estorie de Seint Edward le Roi* (in Norman French; a poem of 4686 lines), *circa* 1245; (2.) *Vita Beati Edwardi Regis* (a Latin poem of 636 lines); and (3.) *Vita Ædwardi Regis* (supposed to have been written for Queen Edith), *circa* 1070-1074.

For later authorities consult Osbern's *Anglia Sacra*, a treasury of English ecclesiastical history; Wilkin's *Concilia* ; Maskell's *Monumenta Ritualia Ecclesiâ Anglicanâ* (vol. iii.). See, too, Dean Hook's *Lives of the Archbishops of Canterbury*, vol. i. pp. 504-530, which contains a lucid sketch of Stigand's life.]

For *Chronological Landmarks* and *Contemporary Sovereigns*, see pp. 341-3.

BOOK V.—ARCHBISHOP STIGAND.

A.D. 1013 (?)–1070.

Stigand's early Career—King Eadward's Court—Stigand promoted to the See of Winchester—Is elevated to the Primacy—Consecration of Westminster Abbey—Death of Eadward—Coronation of Harold—Coronation of William—Stigand's Policy—Visits Normandy in the Conqueror's Train—Retires into Scotland—The Camp of Refuge—Stigand made prisoner and deposed—His Death—His Character.

OF the last Archbishop of Canterbury before the Conquest,[1] of the last Englishman who held the primacy from the death of Harold until the reign of Henry II., it seems desirable to offer the reader a brief biographical sketch; the more so, inasmuch as the last pre-

---

[1] The Archbishops of Canterbury before the Conquest were:—Augustine, 597-604; Laurentius, 604-619; Mellitus, 619-624; Justus, 624-627; Honorius, 627-655; Deusdedit, 655-667; Theodore, 668-690; Brihtwald, 693-731; Tatwine, 731-734; Northelm, 735-740; Cuthbert, 741-758; Bregwin, 759-765; Jaenbert, 766-790; Æthelbard, 793-805; Wulfred, 805-832; Feologild, 832-833; Ceolnoth, 833-870; Æthelred, 870-889; Plegmund, 890-914; Athelm, 914-923; Wulfhelm, 923-942; Odo, 942-958; Dunstan, 960-988; Æthelgar, 988-989; Siric, 990-994; Ælfric, 995-1006; Ælfege, 1006-1012; Living, 1013-1020; Æthelnoth, 1020-1038; Eadsige, 1038-1050; Robert of Jumièges, 1051-1052; Stigand, 1052-1070. The first date is that of the prelate's accession; the second, that of his death

Conquest or Anglo-Saxon archbishop was in many respects a remarkable character.

Of Stigand's parentage or birth, we know nothing. No record is extant of the place where he was born, or where he was educated. It is impossible to say who were his early patrons, or what events first brought him into notice. But as we first find him brought before us on the historical canvas as the chaplain and counsellor of Queen Emma, the wife of King Cnut, we may reasonably conjecture that he was of Danish descent, and had gained in some way or other the favour and confidence of the great Earl Godwine.

In 673 the kingdom of the East Angles had been divided into two dioceses, Elmham and Dunwich. These were re-united a century later. To the united see of the East Angles Stigand was appointed towards the close of Hardiknut's reign; and we first meet with him in history on the occasion of his consecration, in 1043, at the same time that Eadward was consecrated king. Thus says the *Saxon Chronicle:*

'A.D. 1043.—This year was Eadward consecrated king at Winchester, on the first day of Easter, with exceeding pomp. Archbishop Eadsige consecrated him, and before all the people well-instructed him; and for his own advantage and the people's, admonished him. And Stigand the priest was blessed Bishop of the East Angles (or Elmham).'

But as Stigand's prosperity was dependent upon that of his royal patron, Queen Emma, he fell into adversity when her star declined. The *Saxon Chronicle* continues:

'And soon after, the king caused all the lands which his mother possessed to be seized into his hands, and took from her all that she possessed in gold and in silver, and in things unspeakable, because she had before held it too closely with him. And soon after Stigand was deposed from his bishopric, and all that he possessed was seized into the king's hands, because *he was nearest to his mother's counsel*, and, as people thought, she acted even as he advised her.'[1]

From this passage it is safe to conjecture that Stigand's influence over the widow of the great Cnut was all-powerful, and that he took a foremost part in the court intrigues and political transactions of the time. Either by the exercise of his diplomatic skill, which seems to have been considerable, or through the interposition of Earl Godwine, he regained his mitre in the following year, and rose so quickly in Eadward's esteem that he was attached to his court, and made one of the royal chaplains. It is a signal illustration of his honourable character, that he did not, in his renewed prosperity, forget his patroness. He obtained the payment of Queen Emma's dower, and the grant of a residence at Winchester for her behoof. Thither she retired; and, on Stigand's counsel, refrained from further meddling in court plots, devoting her old age to charitable and devout works. She was also, by Stigand's exertions, reconciled to Earl Godwine, with whom for a brief period she had been at variance: and thus the bishop came to be recognised as one of the principal leaders of Godwine's, or, as it might more correctly be designated, the English or patriotic party. In this capacity something like a constant opposition must necessarily have arisen between him and Robert of Jumièges, the Norman Bishop of London. The latter was craftily scheming to surround the king with Norman monks and courtiers, and to enthral him with Norman customs; Stigand laboured as zealously to

[1] *Anglo-Saxon Chronicle*, A.D. 1043.

support the influence of Godwine and Harold, whom he recognised as the natural chiefs and protectors of the English people. We can fancy, too, that, apart from all political causes, there was that in the character and disposition of the two prelates which must have brought them into constant collision. Stigand was gifted with a strong, clear, independent mind, which was by no means prone to superstitious observances or bigoted fears; Robert, either really or from subtlety, affected to believe in the superstitions so dear to the narrow soul of Eadward, surnamed the Confessor. We can well believe that he would regard such an incident as the following with the contempt of an honest, blunt understanding :[1]—

'Once upon a time, when the king, being at Westminster on Easter-day, had been holding a court in royal fashion, and was sitting at table, suddenly he lifted up his voice and laughed aloud, so that the eyes of all the guests were turned upon him; and when they wondered at his laughing thus, without any apparent cause, they said to the king, after dinner, he having retired into his private chamber, " O lord king, we saw an unusual circumstance to-day, at which we all marvelled, because never before did we see you laugh so openly, nor could we discover the reason for your laughter."

'The king replied : "A strange thing I saw, and therefore it was not without reason that I laughed."

'Then the nobles who were sitting round, not at all supposing that one so illustrious had laughed without cause, humbly besought him to condescend and explain the cause of his excessive mirth.

[1] Matthew of Westminster.

'And when he had been persuaded by their frequent entreaties, he said: " More than two hundred years have passed by since the Seven Sleepers in the cave of Mount Cœlries, near Ephesus, have been resting on their right sides; but now, since we first sat down at table, they have turned on their left sides, and so will lie for seventy years more."

'And when those who were present heard this saying, they asked of the king what the turning of the sleepers forebode.

'And he said: " Of a truth, their turning is an omen of dreadful import to mankind. For wars and oppressions of nations will intolerably vex the human race, and there will be changes of many kingdoms, and through the virtue of Christ the pagans will be crushed by the Christians."'[1]

It is difficult to see in the royal 'vision' any matter for laughter; and, so far as the omen was concerned, after events certainly bore no relation to it, unless King Eadward looked upon the Normans as Christians, and his own subjects as pagans.

Unfortunately, we possess no information which will enable us to write a connected biography of Stigand, though there was so much of what we are accustomed to call English pluck and good sense in his character, that we would willingly have known the *man* more intimately. All we can do, however, is to take note of the principal scenes in which he figured. During Godwine and Harold's exile, we may well believe that his influence at court declined, and that he confined himself in the main to the administration of his diocese;[2] but, on the great earl's return, he again came prominently forward,

---

[1] For this dream of the Seven Sleepers, see the note at the end of this chapter.

[2] He was removed to the see of Winchester in 1047.

and he presided over the Witán who reinstated Godwine and Harold in their respective governments. At this time he was privately consulted by King Eadward; and it was in obedience to his advice that the foreigners were dismissed, and the sentence against the English leaders reversed.

The Witán which reinstated Godwine and Harold, also deposed, with the king's consent, Robert, the Norman Archbishop of Canterbury, and, as a reward for his services, Stigand was promoted to the vacant see. The ex-archbishop immediately proceeded to Rome, and solicited the Papal interposition on his behalf. The Pope (Leo IX.) decided that his deposition was irregular, and ordered him to be replaced on the archiepiscopal throne. But, as Dr. Hook remarks,[1] once only in the history of the Church of England, during the 'Anglo-Saxon period,' had an English prelate presumed to appeal to Rome from the decisions of an English tribunal; and then, though the judgment was in his favour, his disloyalty availed him nothing, for by both Church and State the Papal rescript had been treated with contempt. And now, though the old English dynasty was going down into shadow and oblivion, the same independent spirit in matters ecclesiastical was manifested. In defiance of the Pope and his cardinals, Robert of Jumièges was deposed, and Stigand installed as Archbishop of Canterbury.

It was not without difficulty, however, that he obtained the *pallium*, or archiepiscopal robe, which was the outward and visible sign of his dignity, and was invariably transmitted by the Pope on the accession of a new primate. Until his own arrived, he officiated, we are told, in the *pallium* which Robert had incautiously left behind him.

[1] Dr. Hook, *Lives of the Archbishops of Canterbury*, i. 504.

The Papacy at this time was in the hands of a man whom the great Roman families had selected in defiance of the will of the German emperor, who, in virtue of his title of 'Cæsar,' transmitted to him from his ancestors, claimed the right to nominate, or confirm the nomination of, the sovereign pontiff. This 'Anti-pope,' as he is called in the history of the Church, was Benedict X., and was disposed to be indulgent, because he knew the insecurity of his position, and needed support. On Stigand's application, in 1058, he granted him the coveted *pallium;* but in the January following, on the advance of an Imperial army, Benedict was expelled,[1] and Nicolas II. reigned in his stead.

Archbishop Stigand now found himself in an unfortunate plight. In the eye of Rome he had been guilty of two great crimes: first, that of usurpation; and second, that of having accepted investment at the hands of an excommunicated anti-pope. He was summoned before the Papal court to justify himself; but the journey from Canterbury to Rome was, in the year 1059, an enterprise of no small difficulty and peril: nor was Stigand specially desirous of placing himself in the power

[1] 'Hildebrand, the archdeacon, seized him by force, and placed him before Nicolas and a council in the Lateran Church. They stripped him before the altar of his pontifical robes, set him thus despoiled before the synod, put a writing in his hand, containing a long confession of every kind of wickedness. He resisted a long time, knowing himself perfectly innocent of such crimes; he was compelled to read it, with very many tears and groans. His mother stood by, her hair dishevelled and her bosom bare, with many sobs and lamentations. His kindred stood weeping around. Hildebrand then cried aloud to the people, "These are the deeds of the Pope whom ye have chosen!" They rearrayed him in the pontifical robes, and formally deposed him. He was allowed to retire to the monastery of St. Agnes, where he lived (and died) in the utmost wretchedness.'—DEAN MILMAN, *History of Latin Christianity,* iii. 424.

of the successful rival of Benedict x.[1] He continued to perform the duties of the primacy, therefore, without any formal recognition on the part of Pope Nicolas; and this was, undoubtedly, one of the circumstances which afterwards induced the court of Rome to look so favourably upon Duke William's invasion of England.

The archbishop next appears conspicuously in the annals of his time, on the occasion of the consecration of Westminster Abbey, towards the close of the year 1065. The king's illness, as the old Norman chronicler tells us,[2] rendered it desirable to hurry forward the solemn dedication of the sacred edifice which he had reared with so much energy and devout persistence.

> 'On Christmas night seizes him
> A fever, which much inflames him.
> The king lies down, cannot eat,
> For long time seeks to repose himself;
> Feebleness in the morning troubles him,
> Nevertheless, the king gets up
> For the great feast: during the day
> He dissembles and hides his pain:
> The feebleness quite prostrates him;
> Nevertheless, on this day, crown
> And regalia he carries with difficulty;
> And for the three days of the week,
> At table, though it troubles him,
> In the palace at dinner he sits.
> On the fourth day, which was that of the Innocents,
> The prelates come, the chiefs come,
> To punish whatever appertains
> To so great a dedication.

---

[1] Osbern, *Anglia Sacra*, i. 791.
[2] Luard, *Lives of Eadward the Confessor*, pp. 281, 282.

The king forces himself to come there,
Since for it he had a great longing;
But so weak and ill is he,
So much doubt has his head, and feebleness has his heart,
He cannot be, according to his wish,
Present, which much afflicts him;
But much he commands and admonishes
That the feast should be full.'[1]

---

[1] The same old chronicler furnishes us with an animated description of the abbey:—

'Now he (the king) laid the foundations of the church
With large square blocks of grey stone;
Its foundations are deep,
The front towards the east he makes round,
The stones are very strong and hard.
In the centre rises a tower,
And two at the western front,
And fine and large bells he hangs there.
The pillars and entablature
Are rich without and within,
At the bases and capitals
The work rises grand and royal;
Sculptured are the stones,
And storied are the windows;
All are made with the skill
Of a good and loyal workmanship.
And when he finished the work,
With lead the church completely he covers.
He makes there a cloister,—a chapter-house in front,
Towards the east, vaulted and round,
Where his ordained ministers
May hold their secret chapter;
Refectory and dormitory,
And the offices in the tower.
Splendid manors, lands, and woods
He gives, confirms [the gift] at once;
And, according to his grant, he intends
For his monastery royal freedom.

The foundation of the abbey is an event which must not be passed over with a cursory notice. The abbey was the chief work of the Confessor's life, the last relic of the royal house of Cerdic; and therefore, as Dean Stanley observes, it was a portent of the mighty future. It inaugurated the greatest change which, with one exception (that of the Reformation), the English nation has witnessed from that time to this. 'When Harold stood by the side of his brother Gyrth and his sister Eadyth on the day of the dedication, and wrote his name with theirs as witness to the charter of the abbey, he might have seen that he was signing his own doom, and preparing for his own destruction. The solid pillars, the ponderous arches, the huge edifice, with triple tower, and sculptured stones, and storied windows, that arose in the place, and in the midst of the humble wooden churches and wattled tenements of the Saxon period, might have warned the nobles who were present that the days of their rule were numbered, and that the avenging, civilising, stimulating hand of another and a mightier race was at work, which would change the whole face of their language, their manners, their church, and their commonwealth.'[1]

No such thoughts animated the minds of those who assisted at the consecration of King Eadward's abbey. Undoubtedly, to none of them occurred any suspicion that the crown of

> Monks he causes there to assemble,
> Who have a good heart there to serve God,
> And puts the order in good condition,
> Under a holy and ordained prelate;
> And receives the number of the convent,
> According to the order of St. Benedict.'
> —LUARD, *Lives of Eadward the Confessor*, p. 244 (lines 2298-2323).

[1] Dean Stanley, *Memorials of Westminster Abbey*, pp. 34, 35.

England would shortly rest on a foreign brow. Nor, we suspect, did Stigand imagine that the archiepiscopal tiara would in a few short months be the precious spoil of a Norman ecclesiastic. They were looking forward—priests and nobles —to a brighter day, under the rule of an English-born king of proved valour and sagacity. They were not ignorant of the dangers which menaced the kingdom's peace from the ambition of William of Normandy, but they entertained no fear that his designs would not be readily baffled. They had confidence in their country; they had faith in its future. And well has that faith been justified. The wave of conquest broke over the land, but as soon as it had passed, men saw that the ancient landmarks still survived. And to this day the abbey stands as a memorial of the inherent vitality of the English character,—as a conspicuous monument of the continuity by which the old England has ever been linked with the new,—so that the changes inaugurated by successive generations seem but the natural developments of the principles laid down by our forefathers. Thus, to the thinker, a special sacredness, a peculiar interest, must always attach to the ancient foundation of Eadward the Confessor, consecrated as it is by the associations of ten centuries:

> 'A million wrinkles carve its skin;
> A thousand winters snowed upon its breast
> From cheek, and throat, and chin.'

'At midwinter King Eadward came to Westminster, and had the minster there consecrated, which he had himself built, to the honour of God, and St. Peter, and all God's saints.'[1]

Surrounded by his nobles and attendants, he appeared on

---

[1] *Saxon Chronicle*, A.D. 1065.

Christmas-day, wearing his royal crown; but on the Christmas-night his feeble energies, which had been preternaturally stimulated, suddenly gave way. The shadow of death fell upon him. Yet for the next three days he resisted, as best he could, the progress of his mortal malady, and even presided at the splendid banquets which were customary at this season of rejoicing. But on St. John's day his weakness became so apparent that he could struggle no longer, and he gave orders that the abbey should be consecrated on the morrow.[1] The morrow was Childermas, the Feast of the Holy Innocents, and in the morning he summoned up strength sufficient to sign the foundation charter. Among the witnesses we read the names of Eadgyth the Queen, of Harold and his brother Gyrth, of Stigand, Archbishop of Canterbury, and Ailred, Archbishop of York.

In the Middle Ages, and down even to the last century, it was considered of ill omen to commence any undertaking on the Feast of the Innocents.[2] 'If this belief,' says Dean Stanley, 'existed in the time of the Confessor, the selection of the day is a proof of the haste with which the dedication was pushed forward. It is, at any rate, an instance of a most auspicious work begun (if so be) on the most inauspicious day of the year.'

[1] Ailred, *Vita Eadwardi*, c. 399.
[2] From Hearn's *Letters* (i. 234) we learn that Eadward IV.'s coronation was deferred until Monday, because the preceding Sunday was Childermas. Bourne says (c. xviii.) that, 'according to the monks, it was very unlucky to begin any work upon Childermas-day.' And Philip de Comines tells us, 'that on this day Louis XI. would not debate any matter, but accounted it a sign of great misfortune towards him if any man communed with him of his affairs, and would be very angry with those about him if they troubled him with any matter whatsoever.'—See *Brand*, i. 535, 536.

On the evening of Innocents' day[1] Eadward sank into a profound lethargy, and was removed to the room in Westminster Palace, afterwards known in many a later scene and legend of England's troubled history as 'The Confessor's,' or 'The Painted Chamber.' At its further end, on raised platform, and underneath the regal canopy, was placed the bed of death, surrounded by Harold and Queen Eadgyth, by all the greatest thegns, and by Stigand, with the holy rood in his hand.

On the third day the king suddenly awoke from his stupor; his voice seemed to recover its clearness, his countenance its brightness. But it was the effect of a delirious ecstasy. His eyes glowing with a strange fire, he recounted to his astonished hearers how he had seen two holy monks whom he remembered in Normandy, and how they had foretold to him the perils looming near at hand, which should only be ended when

> 'The green tree which springs from the trunk,
> When thence it shall be severed,
> And removed to a distance of three acres,
> By no engine or hand (of man),
> Shall return to its original trunk,
> And shall join itself to its root,
> Whence first it had origin;
> The head shall receive again its verdure,
> It shall bear fruit after its flower;
> Then shall you be able for certainty
> To hope for amendment.'[2]

---

[1] We are compelled to repeat here, for the sake of continuity, some of the details already given on pp. 187, 188.

[2] *La Estorie, etc.*, in Luard's *Lives of Eadward the Confessor*, p. 285.— Evidently this was a prophecy framed 'after the event.' The 'three acres' are the illegitimate kings, Harold II., William I. and II. The parent-stem is represented by Maud, wife of Henry I.

While he was indulging in wild vaticinations, his queen Eadgyth sat on the ground, nursing his cold feet in her lap. Beside her rested her brother Harold, and around were gathered the great officers of State, all terror-stricken. At this moment Stigand's cool common-sense stood his country in good stead. Whispering in Harold's ears to take no heed of a dotard's dreams, he pressed forward to the royal bed, and besought the dying king to name his successor. For a moment Eadward reflected; and then anticipating, or recollecting, the wishes of his chief counsellors,—aware, indeed, that no other man of English birth could possibly be chosen,—he fixed upon Harold the son of Godwine.

A calm ensued; and on the fifth day, with various incoherent speeches,[1] and the hope 'that he was passing from the land of the dead to the land of the living,' he peacefully expired; and 'St. Peter, his friend, opened the gate of Paradise, and St. John, his own dear one, led him before the Divine Majesty.'

On the following day—Friday, January 6th, 1066—the king was buried; and on the same day took place the coronation of Harold his successor.

The exact share taken by Stigand in the coronation ceremony is matter of dispute. The Norman historians, anxious to throw discredit on the rites which made Harold king, assert that the consecrated oil was poured on his head by Stigand,—that is, by a prelate whom the Roman pontiff had not confirmed; but though Stigand undoubtedly was present,[2] there seems little doubt that the anointing was performed by Ealdred, or Alred, the Archbishop of York. It seems

---

[1] See Note, 'Death of King Eadward,' at the end of this chapter.
[2] This is evident from the record borne by the Bayeux tapestry.

certain, too, that Harold placed the crown on his own head, as Charles the Great had done before him, and as Napoleon did after him.

The year passed away, and within a few days of its close another coronation took place within the walls of Westminster. Ealdred of York was again present, holding in his hand 'the golden crown of Byzantine workmanship,' which in due form he placed on the head of William the Conqueror (December 25, 1066). Stigand, loyal to his country in its deepest need, was absent: he had fled into Scotland.

As William advanced before London, after the victory at Senlac, he was met at Swanscombe by a large body of armed Kentishmen, commanded by Stigand the archbishop, and Ægelsige, abbot of the monastery of St. Augustine at Canterbury.[1] What passed on this occasion is not precisely known,—whether a contest took place, followed by a treaty between the two armies, or whether the capitulation was concluded before they crossed swords; but a belief long prevailed, that the Kentishmen agreed to offer no further resistance, if William confirmed them in the enjoyment of their ancient privileges.

> 'Then said the dreadful Conqueror,
>   "You shall have what you will,
> Your ancient customs and your laws,
>   So that you will be still;
>
> 'And each thing else that you will crave,
>   With reason at my hand,
> So that you will acknowledge me
>   Chief King of fair England."'

---

[1] The circumstances here narrated are involved in very great doubt.
[2] Evans, *Old Ballads*, i. 36.

Archbishop Stigand would seem to have taken no part in this capitulation (if indeed the whole story be not a myth), but retired to London, where a Witán was hastily assembled to determine on the choice of a successor to the unfortunate Harold. The claimants most powerful in renown and fortune were Eadwine and Morkere, the great Earls of Northumbria and Mercia, and their pretensions were supported by all the men of northern England; but the men of the south and the citizens of London put forward, in opposition, King Eadward's nephew, a scion of the old royal house, Eadgar the Ætheling. His claim was strongly advocated by Archbishop Stigand, whose influence finally prevailed, and Eadgar was elected king.

But the Normans were rapidly drawing their toils around the metropolis; and as the English had no leader fitted to cope with a situation so perilous, they began to perceive that further resistance was impossible, or at least hopeless. The prelates, thegns, and magistrates resolved, therefore, to carry the keys of the city to Duke William, and make the best terms they could. In this submission, the government, if government it could be called, not unwillingly joined; and Archbishop Stigand led the Ætheling to the conqueror's camp at Berkhampstead, and did homage, and swore the oath of fidelity.[1]

In acting thus, Stigand, as it seems to us, did the best he could for his country. The Ætheling, as he must have found, was unfitted to cope with a crisis of so much danger and difficulty; and the jealousies of the various factions prevented anything like a firm union being formed for the defence of the kingdom on an organized scale. Further resistance, therefore,

[1] Wich, pp. 33-35. Cf. Lappenberg, *Anglo-Saxon Kings*, 106.

meant useless bloodshed; and the primate's conduct, in counselling submission to the conqueror, was neither unworthy of him as a patriot, nor inconsistent with his character as a 'minister of peace.' But having so far accepted the yoke, he was resolved to go no further. When he was invited to preside over William's coronation at Westminster, he, as we have already hinted, refused. He would not bestow his blessing on the warrior covered with the blood of patriots, on the man of treachery and guile, who had invaded a kingdom for the gratification of his selfish ambition.[1] He had advised submission because he saw no prospect of a successful resistance; but submission, in the eyes of Stigand, did not necessitate dishonour and cowardly subservience. And how could he, who had placed the crown—or at least poured the anointing oil—on the head of the gallant and English-born Harold, and afterwards on the head of a rightful scion of the ancient dynasty,—how could he be present at a ceremony which placed the sceptre of Ælfred and Eadmund in the hands of a foreign prince?

William, however, seems to have received Stigand's refusal with no ill feeling. At this time he was not incapable of appreciating a noble action,—his nature had not been thoroughly hardened by a long enjoyment of despotic power,—and it is by no means improbable that he respected the archbishop for conduct evidently dictated by the worthiest motives. It is certain that he continued for some time afterwards to treat him with peculiar distinction. He always rose when he entered his apartment; and when William took him in his train to Normandy, he ordered that wherever the primate went, he should be received with a procession.

[1] John of Bromton, i. 962.

It was in the spring of 1067 that Stigand, with Eadgar the Ætheling, the great earls Eadwine, Morkere, and Waltheof, and Æthelnoth, governor of Canterbury, attended William on his visit to his native dominions. 'The king,' says Ordericus Vitalis, 'adopted a sagacious policy in thus preventing these powerful lords from plotting a change during his absence, and the people would be less able to rebel when deprived of their leaders. Moreover, it gave him an occasion of displaying his wealth and possessions in Normandy to the English nobles, while he detained as hostages those whose influence and security carried great weight with their countrymen.

'The arrival of King William,' adds the historian, 'with all his regal pomp, filled Normandy with rejoicing. The season was still cold, and it was Lent; but the prelates and abbots began the Easter festivals wherever the king came in his progress : nor was ought omitted which is usual in doing honour to such occasions; and whatever of novelty they could invent, was gladly added. So much zeal was acknowledged on the king's part by splendid offerings of costly palls, large sums in gold, and other treasures, to the altars and servants of Christ. Those churches also which he could not visit in person, were made to share in the general joy by the gifts he sent to them.

'Easter-tide was kept at the Abbey of the Holy Trinity Fécamp, where a great number of bishops, abbots, and nobles were assembled. Earl Rudolph, father-in-law of Philip, King of France, with many of the French nobility, were also present, beholding with curiosity the long-haired natives of English Britain, and admiring the garments of gold tissue, enriched with bullion, worn by the king and his courtiers.'[1]

[1] Ordericus Vitalis, *Eccles. History*, Bk. iv. c. 2.

On Stigand's return to England, he found the land groaning under the oppression of the conquerors. Numerous insurrections had taken place, which the king's regents, William Fitz-Osbern and Odo of Bayeux, had put down with merciless severity. So full of danger, however, was the situation, and so insecure the Norman hold upon England, that William left Normandy in hot haste to take the direction of affairs into his own firm hands. As he forgot to provide for the detention of the nobles whom he had carried with him as hostages, they also made their escape to England, and the Ætheling was conveyed to Scotland under the special charge of Archbishop Stigand.

At the court of King Malcolm, who had married Eadgar's sister, the beautiful Margaret, both prince and prelate received a hearty welcome. 'Here,' says Dr. Hook, 'if the archbishop had possessed any genius for government or command, he might have organized measures for the relief of his country.' 'But although Stigand,' he continues, 'was placed under circumstances which would have raised a great mind to the highest pinnacle of power, usefulness, and glory, the archbishop had not the capacity to avail himself of it. He remained an ordinary archbishop, when the time demanded an ecclesiastical hero. And because he did not become what he had not the genius to be, while the steadiness of his principles converted the enemies of his country into the persecutors of himself, his inability to attempt what a really great man would have accomplished, left him without a partisan, perhaps without a friend.'[1]

In these remarks, we cannot help thinking that Dr. Hook does no small injustice to the archbishop. Why censure him

[1] Dr. Hook, *Lives of the Archbishops of Canterbury*, i. 520.

for not becoming 'what he had not the genius to be?' But the truth is, England in 1067 required not so much a great administrator as a mighty 'man of war,' and it could not possibly be expected that Stigand should appear in so novel a capacity. 'An ecclesiastical hero!' Of what use would such a character have been in a struggle against William the Conqueror? What could a Hildebrand or a Thomas à Becket have effected against the spears and battle-axes of the Normans? The times were 'out of joint;' and to have set them right, was a task only to have been successfully accomplished by a commander of surpassing military genius.

And at this crisis England could boast of no such commander. But when her scattered defenders rallied together under the leadership of Hereward, the 'last of the English,'[1] and the hopes of English patriotism revived among the marshes of Ely, and within the turf ramparts of the famous Camp of Refuge, the archbishop immediately stood forward to support this last supreme effort, and devoted his treasures to the national cause. An excellent judge of men, he knew that soldiers fought most valiantly when paid most liberally; and his 'moneyers' coined his gold and silver into money to supply their demands[2] (A.D. 1070-1071).

The Camp of Refuge was fixed in the Isle of Ely, which was then in very truth an island, surrounded by a perfect labyrinth of streams, and a wide waste of reeds and rushes;—in that sacred isle, described by the old chronicler as 'the inheritance of the Lord, the soil of St. Mary and St. Bartholomew;

---

[1] Osbern, *Anglia Sacra*, i. 609, 610.

[2] The story of this remarkable man is to be found in Geoffrey Gaimar's metrical *Chronicle*, and the prose *Vita Herewardi*. See Mr. Wright's edition.

the most holy sanctuary of St. Guthlac and his monks; the minster freest from all worldly servitude; the special almshouse of the most illustrious kings; the sole place of refuge for any one in tribulation; the perpetual abode of the saints, the possession of religious men, particularly set apart by the Witán of the kingdom; by reason of the frequent miracles of the most holy Confessor, an ever-fruitful mother of camphire in the vineyards of Engedi; and, by virtue of the privileges accorded by the kings, a city of grace and safety to all who repent.' Access to it by an army was almost impossible, owing to the nature of the fenny country which surrounded it; would have been impossible, had the northern army been led by any ordinary captain. But William was no ordinary captain, and his genius was never so great as when called upon to deal with what to other men seemed impossibilities.

So it came to pass that, after a heroic resistance, the Camp of Refuge was taken, partly through the treachery of the monks of Ely. Hereward escaped; and after a while, seeing that all hope of securing his country's freedom had gone for ever, he made his peace with William. Stigand was taken prisoner, loaded with chains, and flung into confinement. He had already been deposed by the legates of the Pope, and his tiara bestowed on William's able counsellor, the Italian Lanfranc. His remaining years he dragged out in captivity and sorrow, and he died a prisoner at Winchester—loaded with heavy fetters—a few months after the destruction of the camp among the rushes of Ely.

Stigand, the last of the old English primates, has been unjustly treated by our historians, who have trusted too credulously to the libels of the Norman chroniclers.

Even from these libels, it is evident that he was 'a sturdy patriot, in whose breast beat an honest English heart.' His hatred of the French never waned, and by the French he was hated with quite as firm an animosity. But, as Dr. Hook justly remarks, their hatred was more powerful than his; for they not only wielded the power of the sword, but the more enduring power of the pen.

Ordericus Vitalis accuses him of perjury and homicide; but Ordericus Vitalis was a Norman Churchman, and his accusations are unsupported by the slightest proof. Equally unsubstantial is the charge sometimes brought against him of want of scholarship. He has also been denounced as a miser; and we regret to find the calumny repeated by Lord Lytton in his brilliant romance of *Harold*. But no such charge was preferred against him by the council of Roman prelates who deposed him, and who would assuredly have availed themselves gladly of such a weapon; and it is sufficiently refuted by the liberal donations he made to the monastery at Canterbury and the church at Ely,[1] and by the noble generosity with which he distributed his gold and silver among the defenders of the Camp of Refuge. Dr. Hook observes that he was not a man of expensive habits, and that it was not for his own sake he hoarded. After his death, memoranda were found of treasures which he had buried in his various estates. Why did he not bequeath this wealth to a monastery, and so secure his canonization as a saint? Or why did he not purchase his liberty with it? 'We have only the choice,' says Dr. Hook,[2] 'of two conclusions: either he was a mean-spirited craven, which, though insinuated, his whole history denies; or

---

[1] Gervas, 1651, 1652.
[2] Dr. Hook, *Lives of the Archbishops of Canterbury*, pp. 526, 527.

he had an object both in hoarding and concealing his riches. Every act of his life seems to indicate what that object was. He never despaired of the fortunes of his country. He hoped to the last that his countrymen would rise to expel the Norman, and reassert the Anglo-Saxon dominion; and he was well aware that war could not be conducted without a well-filled treasury. If he was a miser, he was still a patriot, hoarding not for himself, but for his country.'

Thus perished Stigand,—unhappy in his life, his death, and his biographers; yet a true Englishman, stedfast in the assertion of his principles, loyal to the national cause, brave, prudent, sagacious, and inflexibly honest. Black, indeed, were the prospects of the country he so dearly loved, when he yielded up his last breath in the dungeon at Winchester. But a brighter day was ere long to dawn. The English race, the English laws, the English language, were to rise from their apparent oblivion. The Church which Hildebrand had humiliated was to recover her independence; the land which William had conquered was to throw off her bondage; and a glory was to surround the name of Englishman such as could never have been anticipated by the patriot archbishop in his wildest dreams. Where is the Norman now? Where is *not* the Englishman?

NOTES.

DEATH OF EARL GODWINE (p. 171).

THE old legend of Earl Godwine's death is thus told by the author of a Latin *Life of King Eadward* (*Vita Beati Eadwardi Regis et Confessoris*), printed from a MS. in the Bodleian Library, Oxford, by Mr. Luard, in his *Lives of Eadward the Confessor* :[1]—

> ' Ultio digna Dei Godwinum tradidit Orco.
> Proditor ille fuit, et ubertius simplicitate
> Regis, fraudi, dolo callens et fallere doctus :
> Cognatos regis et amicos expulit aulâ ;
> Eadwardi fratrem ferus ense perierat idem,
> Quod tamen ille negat testando numina cœli.
> " Haec buccella meum sic obdat guttur, ut ipsam
> Vel te prodideram :" buccellam namque tenebat,
> Quam rex suscepit, benedixit, tradidit illi.
> Ille vir ut patulo mox hanc miser intulit ori
> Gutturis in medio, vitâ spiracula clausit.
> Ejecisse foras temptat ; tamen ille meatus

[1] Luard, p. 372, lines 367-380.

Suffocat, moritur miser, et lux alma recedit;
Brachia morte rigent, frigus lethale subvenit.'

[A revenge worthy of God delivered over Godwine to Orcus. He was a betrayer, he abused the king's simplicity, and was an adept in craft and wile; he expelled the kith and kin and friends of the king from court; fiercely he put to death with his sword King Eadward's brother, which nevertheless he denies, calling the powers of heaven to witness. 'May this piece of bread choke me, if I betrayed either him or thee!' He had held a piece of bread, which the king took, blessed, and handed to him. The wretched man with a spoon placed it in his mouth; it stuck midway in his throat, and closed the breathing-tubes of life. He attempts to spit it forth; but it suffocates him,—the poor wretch dies,—soft light fades away; his arms grow stiff in death, and a deadly cold pervades his frame.]

The account given in another MS. (Harleian MSS. 526), also printed by Mr. Luard, is very different in tone, and includes nine of the above suspicious details:[1]—

'Reconciliatis ergo duce et ejus filiis cum rege, et omni patria in pacis tranquillitate conquiescente, secundo post hæc anno obiit idem dux felicis memoriæ, exequiisque suis in luctum decidit populus, hunc patrem, hunc nutricium suum regnique, memorabant suspiriis et assiduis fletibus. Tumulatur ergo condigno honore in monasterio, quod nuncupant veteris Wintoniâ, additis in eadem ecclesia multis ornamentorum muneribus et terrarum reditibus pro redemptione ipsius animâ.'

[The king being reconciled to the earl and his sons, all the country enjoyed tranquillity. But in the second year after

[1] Luard, *Lives of Eadward the Confessor*, p. 408.

this died the same earl of happy memory, and the people mourned him greatly, and commemorated him, the father and fosterer of the realm, with constant sighs and tears. With suitable honours he was interred in the monastery of ancient Winchester, many gifts of ornaments and of lands being bestowed on the same church for the redemption of his soul.]

We close our extracts with one from *La Estorie de Seint Eadward le Rei* :[1]—

> ' As says the true history,
> One day of Easter, at the great feast,
> At dinner sat the king,
> His counts and barons on the daïs ;
> Where Earl Godwine was sitting,
> A servant served out the wine,
> The cup of the king gently
> Carrying over the pavement ;
> When he mounts the steps of the daïs,
> His foot slips, which makes him ashamed ;
> He has all but fallen on the ground ;
> But the other keeps him standing,
> He holds his cup, at once rights himself,
> Nor has mishap, nor hurts himself,
> By means of one foot which aided the other.
> Earl Godwine said to the king,
> " So brings one brother to the other
> Help, who was in danger."
> The king replied, who was pensive at it,
> " So might mine [have helped me] had he been
> If you, earl, had permitted him."   [living,

[1] Luard, pp. 271-273.

'The earl changes and loses colour,
For he in truth had slain his brother;
Of which when they had reminded him,
His heart tears him with remorse,
For he had the sin and wrong of it,
Nor could he hide it, or be silent, or play the hypocrite.
'The fact makes him change colour;
And he said, " Ah ! king, good sire,
Much grief and anger hast thou caused me,
And no wonder is it if it grieved me ;
Thou hast reproached me with the death of Ælfred
Your brother; for which I am not to blame:
I will prove it openly.
The mockery much troubles me."

' Now a morsel of bread he takes and lifts up,
And says, " If I can enjoy
This morsel, which thou seest me hold,
Which I will eat in the sight of you all,
That I am not to blame for this death
All at the table will see ;
So I am either acquit or to blame for it."
King Eadward blesses the morsel,
And says, " May God grant that the proof be true."
The earl puts it in his mouth,
The morsel is fixed like a stick
In the middle of the opening of the throat
Of the traitorous felon glutton,
So that all at table see it ;
Both his eyes in his head seemed to be,

His flesh blackened and became pale.
All are astonished in the hall:
He loses breath and speech
By the morsel which sticks fast.
Dead is the bloody felon;
Much power had the blessing
Which gave virtue to the morsel;
For aye was the murder proved.
"Now," cries the king,
"Bring out this stinking dog."
By his friends by chance
Was the body placed in the sepulchre,
By the queen, with noble courage,
And his sons, and those of his lineage.'[1]

THE SEVEN SLEEPERS (p. 308).

The circumstances under which King Eadward saw the seven sleepers are thus described by the author of *La Estorie de Seint Eadward le Rei* (Mr. Luard's translation, *Lives of Eadward the Confessor*), pp. 273-275 :—

'One day of Easter it befell
That King Eadward held his court;
Great joy was there displayed
And an assembly of high chiefs;
Great and high was the service

---

[1] This Norman-French chronicle from which the above and other extracts are taken, seems to be a translation, considerably amplified, of the works of Ailred, monk of Rievaulx (died 1166), whose *Genealogia Regum Anglorum* and *Vita Sancti Eadwardi* will be found in Sir Roger Twysden's *Scriptores Decem* (ed. 1652).

Which was solemnized in the holy church.
As the season permits it,
That day the king bore his crown
At the great feast, with great nobleness.
But not on that account was the heart of the king
More lifted up or proud,
Nor more haughty or vainglorious.
On the contrary, he reflects, and keeps in mind
That of the world all the glory
Is like a flower, which opens
In the morning, and at evening withers;
Devoutly to pray he ceases not.
After the service of the mass
He went to dinner in his palace. . . .
 With head reclined for a short time
He remained in deep thought,
It had the semblance of a reverie;
Quietly and by himself he smiled,
And then like to a sage
He remained as he was before:
Thanks to God he delays not to give.
The chiefs observe it,
They understand that some secret
God has shown from heaven to the king.
But, nevertheless, at table
No one dared to ask:
They fear to anger him:
After dinner they go into the chamber;
Duke Harold follows him,
Summons a bishop to him,
And an abbot: he (the king) says, "Dear friends,

Thoughts from God bring great good,
And make one despise the vanity
Of the world, which is nought but falsity.
Know of what I was thinking, friends,
At table where I was sitting,
When I was somewhat pensive:
The seven sleepers I saw in Greece,
Who for many years that now are passed,
Have lain on their right sides;
Well I know it must be of evil significance,
That they have turned to the left.
Well I saw it distinctly,
I saw their dress, their appearance,
And know, that without lying
It is not falsity nor a dream;
It is a sign and a sentence
Of war, and famine, and pestilence:
The world is going from bad to worse.
This shall last for seventy years;
But then God shall show you His glory,
He will remember His unhappy ones."'

DEATH OF KING EADWARD (p. 318).

The remarkable scene which attended King Eadward's death is delineated with much graphic vigour in the Norman-French poem already quoted (Luard, *Lives of Eadward the Confessor*, pp. 287–290):—

'King Eadward draws to his end,
There is no one who has not great sorrow for it;

His flesh is already half dead;
His people he calls again and again comforts;
And he has been strengthened to speak,
And said to them, "Dear loyal friends,
It is a folly to lament my death;
When God wills it, one cannot remain."
Then he looks at them and raises his eyes,
Looks at the queen [to see] if she sorrows for him,
Who laments, weeps, and sighs,
Tears her hair, rends her clothes.
"Weep not," said the king, "dear one,
Grieve not for my death,
Since after this my death
I shall arrive at the sure port,
Where I shall live with my Lord,
Always in joy and happiness.
Now I pray you all who are here,
My loyal people and my friends,
To my queen who is my wife,
Whose virtues I cannot number,
Who has been to me sister and dear,
Bear loyal company.
She has been my daughter and wife,
And of very precious life:
Honour her as befits
So good and so exalted a matron;
Let her have her dowry in full;
And her manors and her people,
Be they English, be they Normans,
Honour them all their life.

"In the church of St. Peter, to whom
Of old I made my vow, let me be buried.
To him I give myself both living and dead,
Who was to me both aid and comfort."

Then Stigand gave him the Sacrament,
As befits a good Christian,
And the holy unction
Which gives pardon of sins.
And when all was accomplished,
The soul left the body;
Angels descend from above,
Singing *Te Deum Laudamus!*
All the court of heaven is full
Of glory, and of the joy which conducts him;
And St. Peter, his dear friend,
Opens the gate of Paradise;
And St. John, his own dear one,
Conducts him before the Majesty;
And God gives him his kingdom,
Who puts the crown on his head,
Makes him possessed of this great glory,
Which shall never be ended.
And thus from an earthly kingdom
He passed to a heavenly.
Truly blest was this king,
Who here and there was crowned;
And so much more is worth that (kingdom) than this,
As gold is than mire;
For the one is brief and ends soon,
The other sure and enduring.

In the thousand and sixty-sixth year
Since God took flesh,
After he had reigned twenty-three years
And a half, King Eadward
Died, the fourth day of January,
Virgin of body, pure throughout.'

English Worthies.

APPENDIX.

1. TABLE OF CONTEMPORARY SOVEREIGNS FOR THE REIGNS OF WILLIAM I., WILLIAM II., HENRY I., AND STEPHEN.[1]

2. CHRONOLOGICAL LANDMARKS.

A.D. 1061–1135.

> 'Let us not yield, like bond-men poor,
>   To Frenchmen in their pride,
> But keep our ancient liberty,
>   What chance soe'er betide:
>
> And rather die in bloody field,
>   With manly courage prest,
> Than to endure the servile yoke,
>   Which we so much detest.'
>
> <div align="right"><i>Old English Ballad.</i>[2]</div>

---

[1] These tables are intended to carry the reader on to the epoch at which the second volume of this series commences,—that of Thomas à Becket, in the reign of Henry II.

[2] Evans, *Old Ballads, Historical and Narrative,* vol. i. p. 34.

I.

TABLE OF CONTEMPORARY SOVEREIGNS.

WILLIAM THE CONQUEROR, 1061-1087.

King of Scotland.
Malcolm III., 1057-1093.

King of France.
Philip I., 1060.

Kings of Spain.
Henry I., Castile, 1061.
Sancho I., Arragon, 1066.
Sancho I., Castile, 1066.
Alphonso I., Castile, 1072.
Sancho V., Navarre and Arragon, 1076.

Popes of Rome.
Alexander II., 1061.
Gregory VII., 1073.
Victor III., 1086.

Emperor of Germany.
Henry IV., 1056.

WILLIAM II., 1087-1100.

Kings of Scotland.
Donald Bane, 1093.
Duncan, 1094.
Donald Bane, restored 1095.
Edgar, 1098.

Kings of Spain.
Sancho V., 1076.
Peter I., Navarre and Arragon, 1094.

King of France.
Philip I., 1060.

Popes of Rome.
Victor III., 1056.
Urban II., 1088.
Pascal III., 1099.

Emperor of Germany.
Henry IV., 1056.

HENRY I., 1100-1135.

Kings of Scotland.
Edgar, 1098.
Alexander I., 1107.
David I., 1124.

Kings of Spain.
Peter I., Navarre and Arragon, 1094.
Alphonso I., Navarre and Arragon, 1104.
Urraca, Castile, 1109.
Alphonso II., Castile, 1126.
Garcia V., Navarre, 1133.
Ramirez II., Arragon, 1133.

Kings of France.
Philip I., 1060.
Louis VI., 1109.

Popes of Rome.
Pascal II., 1099.
Gelasius II., 1118.
Calixtus II., 1119.
Honorius II., 1124.
Innocent II., 1130.

Emperors of Germany.
Henry V., 1107.
Lothaire, 1125.

STEPHEN, 1135-1154.

Kings of Scotland.
David I., 1124.
Malcolm IV., 1153.

Kings of Spain.
Ramirez II., Arragon, 1133.
Petronilla, Arragon, 1137.
Sancho VI., Navarre, 1150.

King of France.
Louis VII. 1137.

Popes of Rome.
Innocent II., 1130.
Celestine II., 1143.
Lucius II., 1144.
Eugenius IV., 1145.
Anastasius IV., 1153.

Emperors of Germany.
Lothaire, 1125.
Conrad III., 1139.
Frederick I., 1152.

II.

CHRONOLOGICAL LANDMARKS.

A.D.
1066. After the victory at Senlac, William continued his march along the sea-coast from north to south, burning and spoiling everything on his way.[1] A reinforcement from Normandy having landed at Romney, had been cut to pieces by the inhabitants. In revenge he destroyed the whole town. Thence he marched to Dover, the strongest fortress on the southern coast, and having set fire to the town, the garrison of the castle, either through treachery or terror, surrendered it. Here he remained eight days, erecting additional fortifications, while his fierce soldiers gorged themselves on half-raw meat, and lacking wine, drank immense quantities of water; thus inducing an epidemic of dysentery, which carried off many victims.[2]

Leaving a garrison at Dover, William now struck inland, and directed his march towards London. He pursued the line of the great Roman road — the Watling Street — which crossed the very heart of Kent. It is said that on his way he was met by a

---

[1] William of Poitiers, p. 204.   [2] Ordericus Vitalis, Bk. iii. § 14.

A.D.
1066. deputation of Kentish men, who appear to have submitted themselves to his power, and given hostages for their allegiance.

Out of this circumstance, as Mr. St. John remarks,[1] a wild legend has been constructed, in which Stigand, Archbishop of Canterbury, and Ægelsige, Abbot of St. Augustine's, are made to perform the principal parts. At the head of their followers, we are told, each with a green branch in his hand, so that, like Siward's army in *Macbeth*, they presented the appearance of a moving wood, the fantastic Jutes approached, and encircling the Norman Bastard, obtained from his hopes or fears a formal recognition of their ancient rights, which he bound himself never to infringe.

William threw forward a body of five hundred cavalry as far as Southwark, where they were encountered and defeated by a small force of the London levies. The capital at this time was in a state of deplorable disorganization. Eadgar the Ætheling had been elected king, but he excited no general enthusiasm; and the great earls, Eadwine and Morkere, considering their just claims disregarded, withdrew their army, and retired towards the north. Had the men of London been true to themselves, or been guided by a leader of resolution and ability, the Norman forces could still have been crushed; but a house divided among itself must necessarily fall, and, alarmed by the ravages which the ruthless policy of William had ordered, and which covered Surrey and

[1] J. A. St. John, *Conquests of England*, ii. 292. (See *antè*, p. 319.)

A.D.
1066. Sussex, Kent and Hampshire, with burning villages, the Ætheling's government resolved on submitting to the conqueror. William was then encamped at Berkhampstead, whither Eadgar repaired, accompanied by Archbishop Stigand and Ealdred, Wulfstan, Bishop of Worcester, the two Northumbrian earls, and other great personages, and swore allegiance.[1] The conqueror was invited to accept the crown of England. At first he made a hypocritical show of reluctance, but his feigned scruples were speedily overcome, and he marched upon London in order that his coronation might be celebrated at Westminster. The prelate

Christmas Day, 1066.
who officiated—Stigand having refused—was Ealdred, Archbishop of York, assisted by Geoffrey, Bishop of Coutances.[2] The Norman cheers which concluded the ceremony were regarded by the soldiers posted without as cries of alarm, and the latter immediately began to slay and burn, according to their secret instructions. Thus in blood began a reign, which was marked by blood throughout its entire and miserable course, and closed in blood.

1067. The new-made king, with characteristic energy, took immediate measures to consolidate his conquests,—building and garrisoning strong castles, and distributing towns, manors, and districts among his followers. He then returned to Normandy with a long train of captive nobles and prelates, leaving the charge of his new kingdom to Odo of Bayeux and William Fitz-

---

[1] William of Poitiers, p. 205.
[2] *Ibid.* p. 206; Ordericus Vitalis, iii. 14.

A.D.
1067. Osbern. In a few months, however, the patriotic spirit of resistance which began to display itself all over England — for the country had been surprised and stunned, not subjugated—compelled his sudden return. His presence in London, and his lavish promises, calmed the tumult in the capital, where he celebrated his second Christmas festival with amazing pomp.

1068. Leaving London pacified by his concessions, King William, early in 1067, proceeded to crush the formidable insurrection which had broken out in the south-western counties. In the city of Exeter, Gytha, the mother of Harold, had found a refuge, and having accumulated the wreck of her treasures, devoted them to the cause of the country for which her son had died at Senlac. She was accompanied by a patriotic priest named Blacheman, who dedicated his wealth to the same noble purpose; and in the men of Exeter they found a love of freedom and a spirit of heroic patriotism which promised to achieve great deeds for England's sake.[1]

Burning, plundering, and devastating, William approached the great city of the west, but, unfortunately, not to meet with the resistance he himself expected. The heart of the people was sound, but their leaders were treacherous and inert. The magistrates, terrified by the formidable appearance of William's army, repaired to his camp, delivered hostages, and agreed to terms of surrender. On their return to

[1] See Florence of Worcester and Roger of Hoveden under this date.

A.D. 1068.

the city, however, the citizens indignantly disavowed their pusillanimity, closed the gates, and stood to their arms. The siege lasted eighteen days, and numbers of the Normans perished; their place was supplied by fresh troops, and the miners endeavoured to sap the walls; but the citizens still thronged the ramparts. It is probable, as Thierry remarks, that they would have wearied out the conqueror, but their leaders again betrayed them. The *Saxon Chronicle* says in few words, but mournful: 'The citizens surrendered the town, because their thegns deceived them.'

William then erected a strong castle called Rougemont, from the red-coloured soil of the hill on which it was built, and entrusted its defence to Baldwin de Brionne, whom he made vice-comes of Devonshire.

At Whitsuntide, Matilda, the wife of the conqueror, came to England, and was crowned queen. As her share of the spoil, she obtained the lands of Brihtric, a Saxon earl, whose numerous possessions were scattered through all the southern counties.[1] According to an ill-supported story, Brihtric was ambassador to Flanders, while Matilda was still a maiden, at her father Baldwin's court. She fell in love with the handsome Englishman, who, however, declined the honour she would have done him; and who, twenty years later, suffered for his coldness or conscientiousness by losing all his estates, and being shut up for the remainder of his life in a fortress at Winchester.

---

[1] See Sir Henry Ellis's Introduction to *Domesday Book*; also Taylor's *Roman de Rou*, p. 65.

A.D.
1069. Birth of Henry, afterwards Henry I., who, because 'born in the purple,' was declared heir to all his father's English dominions.

Revolt of Northumbria; the insurrection spreads over all England. The Camp of Refuge is constructed in the Isle of Ely — then the most inaccessible locality in all the fen country — and is occupied by thousands of Englishmen, under the leadership of the celebrated Hereward.

William erects a strong fortress at York, which in 1069 is besieged by the citizens. He hastily marches to its relief, and having quieted the city by a terrible use of the sword, builds a second stronghold, which he entrusts to his great lieutenant, William Fitz-Osbern. He then despatches an expedition under Robert de Comines, created Earl of Northumberland, to subdue the northern counties; but the men of the Tyne Valley encountered him at Durham, and slew every man in his force.[1]

Assisted by a Danish fleet, who had entered the mouth of the Humber, the northern English marched upon York, and, after a desperate struggle, carried the town and its two castles. 'They also slew many hundred Frenchmen, and carried off many prisoners to their ships; but before the shipmen came thither, the Frenchmen had burned the city, and plundered and burned St. Peter's minster. When the king heard of this,' says the *Saxon Chronicle*, ' he went northward with all the troops he could collect, and laid

[1] *Saxon Chronicle*, A.D. 1069.

A.D.	
1069.	waste all the shire, whilst the [Danish] fleet lay all the winter in the Humber, where the king could not get at them.'
1070.	Lanfranc, Abbot of Caen, and one of William's chief advisers, was consecrated Archbishop of Canterbury. He was the ablest ecclesiastic of his age, and the future Church policy of the Norman kings was determined by his influence.

York was retaken by William, who inflicted a terrible vengeance on the surrounding country. He penetrated into Northumberland, marking his line of progress by smoking villages and hamlets reduced to ashes, by the dead bodies of men, women, and children. From the Humber to the Tyne, according to an old chronicler, not a rood of land remained under cultivation, not a single village was inhabited, not a monastery escaped profanation and spoliation. Probably in these statements the exaggeration is considerable, and much of the mythical mingles with them; but, allowing for any deduction which the sceptical historian might feel inclined to make, enough remains to show that the devastation caused by William's sanguinary policy was wide-spread and complete. A story told by John of Bromton, however, will convince the reader that these details frequently assumed a marvellous character in the hands of the early annalists.

Between York and the German Ocean, every living thing, man as well as beast, excepting those who had sought refuge in the church of St. John of Beverley,

A.D.
1070.

was put to death. St. John was of English race, and as the ruthless Normans approached, a great throng of men and women poured into his church, that he, remembering in heaven his English birth, might protect them and their property from the prey of the foreign foe. The Norman camp was then seven miles from Beverley; and tidings having reached it of the wealth which had been accumulated within the sacred walls, a party of soldiers, under one Tonstain, marched to plunder it. They entered Beverley without resistance, and broke into the graveyard surrounding the church, as regardless of the saint as they were of the fugitives who had sought shelter therein. Tonstain, the chief, observed among the terrified crowd an aged man, richly attired, and wearing bracelets of gold. He galloped up towards him, sword in hand: the old man fled into the church for shelter. Tonstain followed him, but had scarcely cleared the arched doorway before his horse slipped on the pavement and fell, crushing him in its fall. At this unexpected sight, the Normans were seized with a panic of religious terror, and hastily retreated to their camp, to noise abroad the miraculous power of St. John of Beverley. And thenceforward the territory of his church remained exempt from the spoiler's hand.[1]

This year witnessed the complete subjugation of northern England, which, like the south and east, was divided by William among his Norman followers. The City of Refuge in the Isle of Ely, and the

[1] Alured of Beverley, p. 119; John of Bromton, i. 960.

A.D.
1070. country round about Chester, alone remained unsubdued. To the latter city William accordingly directed the march of his army. It surrendered to his overpowering force; and, in pursuance of his usual policy, the conqueror erected a castle there, as he did also, on his return to the south, at Stafford and Salisbury.

1071. The Camp of Refuge in the Isle of Ely had become by this time a formidable stronghold, the insurgents having placed at their head one of the most remarkable Englishmen of the age—Hereward the son of Leofric.[1] A graphic sketch of his early and stormy career is given by Mr. St. John:[2]—

His youthful life was full of vicissitude and adventure. Confiding in his gigantic stature and almost miraculous strength, he had subdued the pretensions and provoked the anger of all the nobles and chiefs in his neighbourhood. Wherever the youths of Mercia or East Anglia assembled to indulge in wrestling or other athletic sports, Hereward was invariably present, and as invariably carried off the prize by strength or violence; for when his sinews failed him, he took to the sword, and thus extorted by force what he could not gain by address.

Hereward's hand, through the fierceness of his manners and the impetuosity of his disposition, might

---

[1] The principal authorities for his exploits are, the *Historia Ingulphi;* the chronicle *De Gestis Herwardi Saxonis* (*Chron. Angl. Norm.*); and the *Chronique de Geoffroi Gaimar* (*Chron. Angl. Norm.* vol. i.).

[2] *Four Conquests of England*, ii. 350–352. See also Canon Kingsley's historical romance of *Hereward the Saxon*, for many glowing and valuable pictures.

be said to be against every man, and every man's hand against him. Complaints, therefore, waxed numerous throughout the country-side; and Leofric, Hereward's father, was compelled to apply to King Eadward for a sentence of outlawry against his son. Expelled from his country, Hereward took refuge in Northumbria, Cornwall, Ireland, and lastly in Flanders.

This stout Englishman's soul, says Mr. St. John, was of the true heroic temper. He despised danger and death; and whether his life was long or short, determined, while he lived, to be his own master, and yield to no one. No knight-errant ever courted more earnestly the perils of the field. Wherever there was hard fighting, there was Hereward; yet, in proportion as he bearded death, it retreated from him. His name, accordingly, became the theme of popular bards and minstrels, and every palace and baronial hall in Europe rang with the praises of the Saxon hero. But the romance of his life would have been incomplete without a love episode. He saw in Flanders a noble maiden, Torfrida, who consented to soothe his exile and share his fortunes.

For reasons which are now unknown, Hereward did not return to England before the Norman invasion, during which his father Leofric appears to have died, —whether in the battle-field, or of a natural cause, is uncertain; but, at all events, his estates were confiscated, and bestowed upon one of the most infamous of the conqueror's Norman followers, Ivo Taillebois.

Learning in Flanders of the fate that had befallen

A.D. 1071.

his house, Hereward returned to England, and raising a formidable band of kinsmen and friends, swollen by English fugitives from every quarter, he attacked the Norman freebooter, drove him from the paternal castle, and regained possession of his father's estates. But his private interests speedily merged in broader sympathies, and he seems to have resolved on the desperate attempt to release his country — or perhaps the eastern counties only — from the Norman yoke. Having procured himself to be knighted, it is said, by the hands of his uncle Brand, Lord Abbot of Medeshamstede, he took command of the English forces assembled in the Isle of Ely. This act of knighthood, we must add, proved peculiarly offensive to the Normans, who were accustomed to remark, that 'he whose sword was girded on by a priest, was no true knight, but a degenerate citizen' (socordem equitem et quiritem degenerem), and who now applied the sarcasm to Hereward. But, as Thierry justly observes, in this we may see something more than their customary antipathy to the rites which connected priesthood with chivalry; they were indignant that an English 'rebel' should obtain, in any way whatsoever, the right to style himself a knight equally with themselves. Undoubtedly, for his part in the transaction, the abbot Brand would have been severely punished, if, by opportunely dying, he had not escaped the vengeance of his enemies.

To the vacant abbey was appointed Thorold, a Norman, and a true priest of the Church militant. He had scarcely taken possession of his preferment,

A.D.

1071. before he joined Ivo Taillebois in an expedition against Hereward and the English camp. The latter, leading the van, moved forward to reconnoitre among the forest of willows which covered the last asylum of patriotism, while Thorold, failing in his courage, remained on its outskirts. Hereward had vigilantly watched their movements, and whirling suddenly round the wood, surprised the abbot and his party, took them prisoners, and refused to release them, until their friends consented to pay a ransom of thirty thousand marks.[1]

1072. William now turned his arms against this formidable patriot, and proceeded to invest the Camp of Refuge both by land and water. His military genius was fertile in resources; he threw bridges over the streams and lagoons; and, to penetrate into the very heart of the morass, reared across quagmire and bog an immense and solid causeway, three thousand paces in length. This great work was by no means easily accomplished. Hereward alarmed the artisans with repeated attacks, and these attacks were so sudden and successful, that the Normans, in a panic of superstition, attributed them to the agency of the evil one. To counteract, as they thought, his spells, they had recourse to magic; and Ivo Taillebois, whom William had appointed to superintend the works of the besiegers, sent for a witch, and instructed her to thwart by her enchantments the warlike devices of the Saxons. She was posted on the summit of a lofty wooden tower, which

[1] Petri Blesensis, Ingulfi *Contin.* p. 125.

was pushed along the advancing causeway, to cast a spell over Hereward and his patriots; but they, made of sterner stuff, rushed forward impetuously, and set fire to the reeds and osiers close to the embankment; so that the spreading flames, enveloping morass and tower, and causeway and besiegers, reduced the whole to ashes.[1]

Nor was this the sole success gained by the courage and activity of Hereward, which proved in the hour of peril a sufficient counterpoise to the numbers of the enemy. For several months the Isle of Ely was closely blockaded, and received no provisions from external sources. The monks of Ely, under these circumstances, began to feel sorely pinched, and sending clandestinely to William's camp, they offered to reveal a secret pathway over the quaking morass, if he would guarantee to them their lands and privileges. The conqueror satisfied the monks, after his manner, by lavish promises, and then sent forward his troops in the track of the coward traitors, to surprise the English camp. In the desperate struggle which ensued upwards of a thousand Englishmen were slain, and the remainder, with the exception of Hereward and a few of his followers, surrendered at discretion. Among these were Earl Morkere, Bishop Ægelwin, Siward, Beorn, Abbot Ægelni, and others, who were thrown into prison in various parts of England. The common prisoners were treated with horrible cruelty. The conqueror's object was to strike

[1] Petri Blesensis, Ingulfi *Contin.* pp. 124, 125.

A.D.
1072. terror into the public mind, and therefore he tore out the eyes of some, cut off the hands and feet of others, and inflicted upon all some species of savage mutilation.

Meantime Hereward and his small band had effected their escape by winding and dangerous paths, unknown to the Norman soldiers. They reached the lowlands of Lincolnshire, and on the bank of a small river met with a small body of English fishermen, who gladly received them into their boats, and concealed them under loads of straw. Thus they approached the Norman station, where the fishermen had been accustomed to dispose of their spoil, and found the Normans seated under tents, waiting the arrival of the expected delicacy. While a bargain was being made, Hereward and his friends, battle-axe in hand, sprang from their hiding-places, attacked the Normans, cut to pieces the greater number of them, and put the rest to flight. After this exploit, they mounted the horses of the Normans and rode merrily away.

So says the chronicler:[1]

> ' Q'en dirroie? Li chevaler
> Furent surpris à lur manger.
> Cil entrent, haches en lui mains;
> De bien férir ne sont vilains,
> Normanz occistrent et desconfirent.
> Cil qui poeient s'enfuirent.
> Grant fret l'effrei par les osteaus,
> De la fuite sont communaus,

---

[1] Geoffroi Gaimar, *Chronique*, p. 26.

> Chevaus lessent enseelez.
> Les outlaghes i sont montez
> Tut à leisir et seinement,
> Onques n'eurent desturbement;
> A eise erent de fere mal.
> Chescuns choisit très bon cheval.'

For some months the great English partisan kept up a brilliant guerilla warfare; always appearing where he was least expected, and laying ambuscades for unwary Norman detachments, to whom he never gave quarter, because he had vowed that his old companions should not pass unavenged. He had with him one hundred men, well armed and of proved fidelity:

> '. . . Cent homes bien armez
> De Ereward liges privez;
> Si home crent et si fideil;'

and among these were Winter, his brother-at-arms; Geri, his cousin; Ælfric, Godwine, Leofwine, Torkill, Siward, and another Siward surnamed the Red. If one of these encountered three Normans, he shrank not from the unequal fight; while as for Hereward himself, battle-axe in hand, he would fight seven Normans at a time.

> ' Si un d'els encontront treis
> Ni s'en alasent sanz asalt . . .
> Lui setme asailli Hereward,
> Sul par son cors, n'i ont reguard,
> Les quatre oscist, les treis fuirent;
> Naffrez, sanglant, cil s'en partirent
> En plesours lius ceo avint.
> En contre vii très bien se tint,
> De vii homes avoit vertu,
> Onques plus hardi ne fut veu.'

A.D.
1072.

The fame and valour of Hereward appear, after a while, to have won the love of an opulent English lady named Æswitha. She offered him her hand, which he accepted;[1] and she then exerted her influence to persuade him to abandon a struggle evidently fruitless, and make his peace with the conqueror. According to the monastic historian Ingulphus, this he did; received as a reward his patrimonial estate; ended his days in tranquillity; and was buried in the abbey church of Croyland by the side of his wife.

Such a termination of a romantic career was, however, too tame and too commonplace for the poetical chronicler, who accordingly provides him with all the pomp and circumstance of a truly heroic death.—After he had made his peace with the king, his house, or castle, was several times attacked by the Normans; and one day they chanced to surprise him when, in the sweet summer weather, he was sleeping under a tree without his armour. His enemies were twenty in number, and no weapon had the English hero but a short pike and a sword. All resolute and fearless, he sprang to his feet, exclaiming, 'False traitors, the king has given me his peace; yet do you come against me and kill my people, and take me by surprise. But, knaves, I will sell my life dearly!'

'Triwes n'avoit doné li rois;
Mès vus venez ireement,
Le mien pernez, tuez ma gent,

---

[1] His first wife, Torfrida, became a nun at Croyland, where she was frequently conversed with by the historian of the Abbey, Ingulphus.

Surpris m'avez à mon manger;
Fel traitres, vendrai moi cher.'

So saying, he thrust his pike against the nearest Norman, and with such a doughty blow, that it went clean through his hauberk and pierced his heart. The Normans then fell upon him in a body and endeavoured to overwhelm him;[1] but he continued

[1] We quote from Geoffrey Gaimar's *Chronicle* his stirring description of the closing scene of Hereward's romantic career:—

'Donc l'assaillerent li Normant,
Traient à'lui et vont lançant,
De totes parz l'avironèrent,
En plusurs lius son cors nafrèrent;
Et il fiert eus come sengler
Tant com la lance pout durer;
Et quant la lance li faillit,
Del brant d'ascer grant coup fèrit.
Tiel le quida mult vil trover,
De son cors l'estuet achater;
Et quant le trœvent si amer,
Asquanz n'i osent arester:
Car il fèrit vigerousement,
Si's requist menu e sovent,
Od s'espée iiii en occist,
Dès qu'il fiert le bois retentist;
Mès donc brusa le brant d'ascer,
Desus l'elme d'un chevalier,
Et il l'escu en ses mains prist,
Si en fiert que ii Franceis occist;
Mes iiii vindrent à son dos,
Qui l'ont féru par mi le cors,
Od iiii lances l'ont féru;
N'est merveille s'il est cheu,
A genuillons s'agenuilla,
Par tiel aïr l'escu getta

to fight with his pike until it broke in his hand. Drawing his sword, he still laid about him so lustily, that four of his adversaries bit the dust:

> 'Car il ferit vigerousement,
> Si's requist menu e sovent,
> Od s'espée iiii en occist,
> Dès qu'il fiert le bois retentist.'

The fight continued with equal vigour, until fifteen Normans lay dead at Hereward's feet. Wounded and bleeding, he supported himself on one knee, finding strength enough to dash out, with the boss of his shield, the brains of a Breton knight, one Raoul de Dol; but at last, simultaneously pierced by four lances, he fell back and expired. The Norman leader, Asselin, then cut off his head, swearing 'by God and

> Que uns de ceus qui l'ont feru
> Fiert en volant si del escu
> Qu'en ii moitiez li freint le col.
> Cil out à non Raoul de Dol,
> De Tuttesbire estoit venuz.
> Ore sont amdui mort abatuz
> Il Ereward e li Breton,
> Raoul de Dol avoit à non;
> Mès Alselin le paroccist.
> Cil de Ereward le chef prist.
> Si jura Dieu et sa vertu,
> Et li autre qui l'ont veu
> Par meinte foiz l'ont fort jure,
> Que oncques si hardi ne fut trovè,
> Et s'il eust eu od lui trois,
> Mar i entrassent li Francois;
> Et s'il ne fust issi occis,
> Touz les chaçast fors del païs.'

Chronique de Geoffroi Gaimar (*Chron. Anglo-Normandes*), pp. 25, 26.

A.D.
1072. his virtue,' that he had never before seen so valiant a man. And it afterwards became a popular saying, as well among the Normans as the English, that had there been four such as he in England, the French would never have entered it; and that had he not thus been slain, he would assuredly have expelled them all.

Thus was destroyed the Camp of Refuge, and thus terminated the resistance of England against King William's rule.

1073. An insurrection having broken out in Maine, the conqueror visited the Continent. He speedily subdued the revolt; town and castle surrendering from fear of the terrible vengeance a prolonged defence would assuredly have drawn down upon them.

1074. A conspiracy was hatched in England among some of the Norman nobles, headed by Raulf de Gaël, Earl of Norfolk, and Roger de Breteuil, Earl of Hereford, who endeavoured to secure the assistance of Waltheof, Earl of Huntingdon and Northumbria, and other English nobles. But through the energy of the primate Lanfranc, whom William had appointed his lieutenant, the revolt was crushed before it could become general. Raulf de Gaël escaped to Brittany, and thus furnished William with a new and admirable excuse for invading the territory of his old foes, and pursuing his schemes of conquest. After besieging the town of Dol in vain, he was, however, compelled to retreat before the combined forces of the Duke of Brittany and the King of France. Then he crossed the Channel, and held his Christmas festival at London.

A.D.
1075. Waltheof, the last great English noble, was executed at Winchester for his alleged conspiracy in Raulf de Gaël's plot. His countrymen mourned bitterly for his death, and honoured him with the name of 'Martyr.'

'The execution of Waltheof,' says Thierry, 'completed the prostration of the conquered people. It would seem that the English had not lost all hope, so long as they saw one of their own race invested with great power, even though under foreign authority. But after the death of the son of Siward, there remained not in England, of all those crowned with honours and exercising political functions, a single man born in the country who did not regard the nation as enemies or brute beasts.' In due time, however, the English had their revenge. Their conquerors became absorbed in the great body of the conquered, as the Missouri is swallowed up in the great current of the Mississippi. The old English language, and institutions, and character survive— modified, it is true, but not essentially changed in spirit or in substance; while nothing of the Norman is now apparent, save a few scattered words, an obsolete custom or two, and, here and there, a feudal tradition.

1077-79. The insubordination of his eldest son Robert, and the discord in his family, clouded the latter years of William's reign. Robert demanded of his father the duchy of Normandy, and received the stern reply, 'I will not put off my clothes before I go to bed.' He then betook himself to Gerberoy, on the Norman

A.D.
1077-79. confines, and assembled a body of mercenaries, with the intent of securing to himself the domain and honours of a prince. William, ever active, speedily crossed the sea, and laid siege to the castle in which his son had taken refuge. Here a romantic incident occurred, not improbable in itself, but clothed by the chroniclers in many fictitious details. In a sally made by Robert, he engaged, it is said, hand to hand, a knight in full armour, pierced his horse, and threw his rider to the ground. Robert hastily dismounted to despatch him with his sword, when the wounded knight lifted his visor, and revealed to the son his father's face. Robert was struck with compunction, sheathed his sword, assisted his father to rise, and mounted him upon his own horse.

Such is the story told by some of our authorities, but, according to a more probable version,[1] Robert did not display the generosity with which he is here credited, and the king was furnished with another horse by an Englishman in his army named Tookie Wiggodson, who had no sooner performed this deed of loyalty than he was killed by a dart.

1079. An attempt was now made by the Norman barons to effect a reconciliation between the king and his son. A patched-up peace, however, is seldom of long duration; and Robert again misbehaving himself, drew down upon his head his father's solemn malediction, and for a third time retired to the Continent.

1080. The Northumbrians were provoked into an insurrection

[1] *Saxon Chronicle*, A.D. 1079.

A.D.
1080. by the grinding tyranny of Vaulcher, Bishop of Durham; and surprising him in the portal of the church at Gateshead, they slew him and all his train. This righteous act of retribution drew down upon them the vengeance of Odo, Bishop of Bayeux, who led a powerful army into the northern counties, and swept over them like a desolating tempest. The cruelties of which he was guilty earned him from his Norman countrymen the significant title of *Queller of the English*.[1]

'Thus,' says William of Malmesbury, writing seventy years afterwards,—'thus were cut the nerves of this once flourishing county. These towns, formerly so famous,—these lofty towers which once threatened heaven, now rent in ruin,—these pastures, once smiling, and watered by sparkling streams, now wasted and laid bare,—the stranger looks upon them with a sigh, the old inhabitant no longer recognises them.'

1082. Quarrel between William and his half-brother, Odo of Bayeux. The latter, having projected an expedition to Rome with the view of securing the Papal tiara, was seized by the king's orders, conveyed to Normandy, and flung into the prison of Rouen Castle, where he remained until William's death.

1083. Queen Matilda died at Caen, November 2d. To the industry of herself and her maids is ascribed, on no good foundation, that famous pictorial contemporary chronicle of the events of the Conquest, known as the Bayeux Tapestry. It consisted of a piece of

[1] Willelm Gemeticensis, p. 282.

A.D.
1083. linen, 214 feet long by 21 inches broad, on which a series of pictures has been very graphically executed in needlework. The compartments are 57 in number, and divided from each other by a tree or architectural design.

1086. In this year was completed the remarkable survey of the country known as *Domesday Book;* the result of a territorial inquest conducted by Henry de Ferrières, Walter Giffard, Adam, brother of Eudes the Seneschal, and Remi, Bishop of Lincoln. It shows 'how many acres of land there were in each domain, how many were sufficient for the maintenance of a man-at-arms, and how many men-at-arms there were in each province or county of England; what was the gross amount derived in various ways from the cities, towns, boroughs, and hamlets; what was the exact property of each earl, baron, knight, or sergeant-at-arms; what land, how many men holding fiefs on that land, how many Saxons, how much cattle, and how many ploughs each one possessed.' The survey occupied six years.[1]

1087. William crossed the sea for the purpose of invading France, but was detained at Rouen by an illness, which suggested to the French king, Philip, a coarse jest upon his enemy's corpulence: 'William is lying-in at Rouen; tell him that I will be present at his churching with a hundred thousand candles.'[2] When the unmannerly sarcasm was repeated to the Norman

---

[1] Thierry, *History of the Norman Conquest*, i. 299-301.
[2] John of Bromton, 980.

A.D.
1087.
king, he wrathfully exclaimed, 'By the splendour of God, I will celebrate my churching at Notre Dame, with ten thousand lances for tapers.' He entered France with a formidable army in July, laying waste the golden corn-fields and purple vineyards as he advanced, and marking his progress by the flames of burning homesteads, villages, and towns.[1] But while riding through the desolated streets of Mantes his horse trod upon some hot ashes, reared and plunged, and drove the pommel of the saddle into his rider's stomach with so much violence as to produce an internal rupture.

William immediately retreated to Rouen, where for six weeks he lay ill in a monastery outside the city. His deathbed was a gloomy one; remorse tortured him with its agonies, and he vainly endeavoured to soothe them by tardy acts of penitence, sending money to the convents and poor of England, and releasing the English and Normans whom he had flung into prison. That his conscience was at last awakened, may be inferred from the manner in which he disposed of his dominions. Normandy was his by lawful inheritance, and he left it to his eldest son, though convinced of his unworthiness. But as for the realm of England, 'I bequeath it to no one,' said the dying warrior, 'because I did not inherit it, but acquired it by violence, and at the price of blood; therefore I replace it in the hands of God, contenting myself with expressing the wish that my

[1] Ordericus Vitalis, Bk. viii. pp. 655, 656.

"While riding through the desolated streets of Mantes, his horse trod upon some hot ashes, reared and plunged," etc — LIVES OF OLD ENGLISH WORTHIES, *Page* 366.

A.D.
1087.   son William, who in all things has ever obeyed my will, may obtain it, if it please God, and prosper in it.'

Then strode forward the active and wily Harry, the youngest of the three brothers, and asked, 'What will you give to me, my father?' 'Five thousand pounds from my treasury,' replied the king. 'But what will this money avail me if I have neither castle nor lands?' 'Be patient, my son, and trust in God: permit your elder brothers to precede you, and your turn will come at last.'

Henry immediately withdrew to receive and weigh his money; William Rufus departed for England, to
Sept. 10. make sure of his crown; and at sunrise, without a mourner by his bedside, while the bells were ringing in the neighbouring church, the iron-hearted king lifted his hands, commended his soul to the Virgin, and almost immediately expired.[1]

By river and by sea, at the cost of a loyal gentleman named Herbain, the dead body of the conqueror was carried to Caen, for interment in the cathedral of St. Stephen's. All the bishops and abbots of Normandy were present at the funeral ceremony; but when the solemn mass was ended, and as the attendants were about to lower the body into the grave, a man advanced from the crowd and exclaimed:

'Prelates and priests, this land is mine; it was the site of my father's house; the great lord for whom

---

[1] Compare the narratives of John of Bromton, Simeon of Durham, Capgrave, and the *Saxon Chronicle.*

you have offered up your prayers, wrested it from me by force to build this church upon it. I never sold my land, nor pawned it, nor forfeited it, nor gave it: mine it is by right, and I demand it. In God's name, I forbid the spoiler's body to be covered with the earth which is my inheritance.'[1]

The man who spoke was Ascelin, son of Arthur, and those who were present confirmed the truth of the claim he had advanced. Therefore the bishops paid him sixty shillings for the grave, into which the attendants proceeded to thrust the king's body; but the masonry having been built with too narrow an opening, the bowels burst, and ran out into the grave, filling the church with a terrible stench. Incense and perfumes were burned, but in vain; the bystanders hurried away; and the officiating priests huddled over the remainder of the ceremony in indecorous haste.

'Oh how false, how unstable,' exclaims the Saxon chronicler, 'is the good of this world! He who had been a powerful king and the lord of many territories, possessed not then, of all his lands, more than seven feet of ground; and he who was erewhile adorned with gold and gems, lay covered with mould!'

William's character has been very variously estimated by different writers. His ability as a military commander, his sagacity as a politician, his firmness of will, his abundance of mental resources, it is perhaps impossible to deny; but we confess that in

[1] John of Bromton, 980.

every other respect he fails to command our admiration. Few men who have risen to supreme power, and secured a crown by violence, have ever exercised so ruthless a tyranny, or shown so utter a want of sympathy with the people over whom they ruled. Few have ever shown themselves so regardless of letters, and arts, and science ; few, while affecting a reverence for the Church, have ever been so utterly devoid of devout feeling. We cannot help believing, therefore, that the following portrait of the conqueror is not painted by Mr. St. John in exaggerated colours, dark and gloomy though they be :[1]—

' That William was a man of extraordinary abilities must be owned. His career from boyhood upwards, his preparation for the invasion of England, his negotiations with the Pope, with the petty princes of France, with his father-in-law the Count of Flanders, who lent him ships and money on condition of receiving a large pension, his forgeries respecting the will of the Confessor,—which thousands believed in, though no one ever saw it, — his generalship, his achievements as a statesman, his profound and subtle diplomacy,—each and all entitle him to the reputation of worldly greatness. Nothing could have been more enlarged or far-sighted than the policy by which he overcame and subjected to prolonged thraldom a free and powerful kingdom, whose inhabitants he smote with mental paralysis, so that they cowered like a vast herd of slaves beneath his sceptre. His physical

[1] J. A. St. John, *Four Conquests of England*, ii. 419, 420.

A.D.
1087. structure and personal appearance corresponded with the character of his mind: he was strong, square, and athletic, with a countenance in which, with regular and handsome features—except the mouth—was blended the expression of so much ferocity, cruelty, and falsehood, that few could regard him, especially during his paroxysms of fury, without terror and apprehension. He was addicted, moreover, beyond most men, to the habit of cursing and swearing, and his oaths and imprecations were so appalling from their blasphemous impiety, that they greatly augmented the dread excited by his truculent aspect. Among his vices, next after bloodthirstiness and cruelty, grasping avarice was most prominent. He had recourse to the most odious and disreputable means of extorting and amassing money; appropriated to his own use fourteen hundred manors from the confiscated estates of the English nobles; seized despotically on men's property, then forced them to purchase it back; and, like his brother Odo, addicted himself to indiscriminate extortion and plunder, that he might always have at his command an overflowing treasury wherewith to purchase unscrupulous agents of tyranny, or to subdue by corruption and by bribery the enemies whom he felt loath to encounter in the field. Three times a year also he applied the contents of his exchequer to the requisitions of feasting and merriment, at Winchester, Westminster, and Gloucester, where the chief nobles and authorities of the land thronged his palace and

A.D.
1087.

partook of his banquets. On these occasions he wore his crown at table, and was distinguished for courtesy and affability.

'The spirit of his government,' adds Mr. St. John, 'was precisely what might have been expected from a king of such a character. Throughout the land compassion and horror were excited by multitudes of dreadful objects upon whom the bloody laws of conquest had been exercising their tender mercies. It was impossible to walk the streets of any great city without encountering individuals whose eyes had been torn out, whose feet or hands, or both, had been lopped off, and who, thus reduced to bare trunks, owed the protraction of their wretched lives to the exercise of a dreadful charity. Other barbarities, too shocking to be mentioned, were likewise of constant occurrence. The least opposition to despotic authority immediately provoked a massacre; every attempt at the recovery of freedom was quenched in blood; executions, halters, axes, gibbets, were the daily means by which the Saxons were sought to be conciliated to their new master. If monks became unruly, they were shot down in the church, till the blood ran in streams from beneath the altar. The brave and noble were exiled for ever from their native land, the tame and submissive were reduced to servitude. It has been sometimes supposed that the slave trade, which had constituted the opprobrium of Saxon times, was prohibited after the Conquest,—erroneously, since the laws of William permit the sale of men and women

A.D.
1087. within the realm, and only repeat the ancient prohibition to export them beyond sea.'[1]

WILLIAM II., A.D. 1087–1100.

William II. crowned at Westminster, September 12.

1088. His coronation having taken place without the approval of the Anglo-Norman barons, they resolved on deposing him, and substituting his eldest brother, Robert, Duke of Normandy. At their head was Odo of Bayeux, who strongly fortified himself at Rochester, waiting the arrival of Duke Robert to march upon Canterbury and London.

In this emergency William turned to his English subjects for assistance, endeavouring to purchase their favour by many temporary concessions. With the hope, perhaps, of seeing England once more established as an independent realm, even though under a foreign king, and separated from its thraldom to Normandy, the English responded heartily to William's appeal, and with a powerful army he laid siege to Rochester. The garrison was soon compelled to capitulate, and amidst the English shouts of 'A gallows for the perjured bishop!' Odo set forth on his way to Normandy, never to return.

[1] For the details of William's reign the chief primary authorities are, John of Bromton; Ordericus Vitalis, the Saxon historian; Simon of Durham; William of Poitiers; Eadmer; Roger of Hoveden; and Florence of Worcester. Among later writers, Lingard's *History of England*, Longman's *Lectures*, Sir F. Palgrave, Roscoe's *Life of William I.*, J. A. St. John's *Four Conquests*, Dr. Vaughan's *Revolutions of Race*, etc. etc.

A.D.

1089. Lanfranc, Archbishop of Canterbury, died; a great loss to William, who thenceforth exhibited the darker features of his character, and with Ralph Flambard[1] for his chief counsellor, oppressed with equal severity both the clergy and the common people. In truth, we may justly say, that with William began that great struggle between the Crown and the Church which culminated, as we shall hereafter see, in the reign of Henry II., and in which the people were largely interested; for at this time they had little to hope from the Crown, but all and everything from the Church.

1090. Warfare in Normandy and the Cotentin, through the dissensions of William on the one hand, and Duke Robert and Prince Henry on the other. The latter purchased from his brother Robert a third part of the Cotentin.

1091. William besieged Mont St. Michael, a strong fortress into which Prince Henry had thrown himself, and compelled it to surrender. The brothers then came to a temporary agreement as to the government of their various possessions.

1092. War between England and Scotland. William seized the city of Carlisle, and built a castle for its defence; Malcolm invaded Northumberland, but was surprised and slain.

1094. The barons and knights of the northern counties re-

---

[1] So called, says Ordericus Vitalis, 'because, like a devouring flame, he tormented the people, and turned the daily chants of the Church into lamentations.'

A.D.
1094. volted against Rufus, under Roger de Mowbray, but were subdued by the king's vigour and military skill.

Rufus erected the famous hall at Westminster, strengthened the Tower, and threw a bridge over the Thames. These works, however, were accomplished at the great cost and suffering of the common people. 'Every year that passed,' says the *Saxon Chronicle*, 'was heavy and full of sorrow, on account of the numberless vexations and the ever-increasing taxes.'

1096. This year is memorable as that of the First Crusade, in which Duke Robert figured as one of the leaders, having pawned his duchy to King William to raise the necessary supplies for his expedition.

1099. Maine was ravaged by William 'with fire and sword.'[1]

1100. While hunting in the New Forest, on the 2d of August, the king was slain by an arrow, discharged, either accidentally or purposely, from some unknown bow. His death has been generally attributed, but on no good foundation, to the hand of one of his favourite attendants, Walter Tyrrel.

HENRY I., 1100–1135

1100. On receiving the news of his brother's death, Prince Henry, who was also hunting in the New Forest, hastened to Westminster, seized upon the royal treasures—in spite of the opposition of William de Breteuil, who claimed them for Duke Robert—and caused himself to be crowned in Westminster Abbey, on Sunday the 8th of August.

[1] Ordericus Vitalis, Bk. x. c. 9.

A.D.
1100.
In the thirty-five years that had elapsed since the Conquest, a great change had come over the condition and character of the country; and many circumstances prove that the English leaven was slowly fermenting in the minds even of the Norman rulers,—that the small stream of the Norman, was gradually being absorbed in the broader and fuller river of the English blood. Hence we find that Henry I., on his accession to the throne, endeavoured to conciliate his English subjects by the dismissal of rapacious administrators; and still more, by a marriage, which was purely one of affection, partly one of policy,—his marriage with Edith, daughter of Matilda (the sister of Eadgar the Ætheling), and Malcolm, King of Scotland. Her name was changed to Maud or Matilda, as more pleasing to the Norman ear,[1] or perhaps in remembrance of King Henry's mother; but neither this change, nor her many graces, propitiated the Norman barons, by whom, says Macaulay, 'the marriage was regarded as a marriage between a white planter and a quadroon girl would now be regarded in Virginia.' They contemptuously nicknamed the king Godric, and the queen Godiva;[2] but to the English this 'union of the races' was inexpressibly dear, and they continued loyal subjects of Henry Beauclerc throughout his reign.

1101. Henry I. granted a charter of rights and privileges to his English subjects.

[1] Ordericus Vitalis, Bk. viii.
[2] William of Malmesbury, *De Gestis*, Bk. v.

A.D.
1101. Robert, having returned from the Crusades, invaded England, and was supported by a Norman faction. But the English rallying round King Henry, the duke agreed to relinquish his claim to the English crown, and returned to Normandy.

Insurrection of Robert de Belèsme, Earl of Shrewsbury. It was put down by Henry's army; the earl surrendered, and, to the great joy of all England, was banished. Thenceforth, during the long remainder of Henry's reign, the country enjoyed internal peace.

1106. King Henry invaded Normandy, and defeated his brother Robert at Tinchenbrai, September 28th. The duke, taken prisoner, was conveyed to England, and confined in Cardiff Castle, where he died in 1135. From this date the crowns of England and Normandy were united; sorely to the injury of the former country, whose best interests were neglected while her sovereigns wasted her resources upon continental wars. For a century and a half, we are told, there was no English history. 'The French kings of England rose, indeed,' says Macaulay,[1] 'to an eminence which was the wonder and dread of all neighbouring nations. They conquered Ireland. They received the homage of Scotland. By their valour, by their policy, by their fortunate matrimonial alliances, they became far more powerful on the Continent than their liege lords the kings of France. At one time it seemed, indeed, that the line of Hugh Capet was about to end as the Merovingian and Carlovingian lines had ended, and

[1] Lord Macaulay, *History of England*, vol. i. c. 1.

A.D.
1106. that a single great monarchy would spread from the Orkneys to the Pyrenees. Had such been the case, it is probable that England would never have had an independent existence. Her princes, her lords, her prelates, would have been ever differing in race and language from the artisans and tillers of the earth. The revenues of her great proprietors would have been spent in festivities and diversions on the banks of the Seine. The noble language of Milton and Burke would have remained a rustic dialect, without a literature, a fixed grammar, or a fixed orthography, and would have been contemptuously abandoned to the use of boors. No man of English extraction would have risen to great eminence, except by becoming in speech and habits a Frenchman.'

We are inclined to suspect that Macaulay has not made sufficient allowance for the inherent vitality of the English nation, and that it is at least as probable that England would have asserted her independence of France as have become a mere appanage of it; but, undoubtedly, the union of the Norman and English crowns was in many respects a calamity to our island, and it is perhaps allowable to regret that Henry I. succeeded in effecting it.

1107. Henry courted the favour of the Church by an extensive creation of abbots and prelates; but as these were all of foreign birth, their influence in no wise benefited the English people.

1118. Death of the 'good queen Maud.'

A.D.

1107–1119. War between France and England. The French king was totally defeated at the great battle of Noyon.

1120. Prince William, Henry's only legitimate son, was drowned off Barfleur, in the ship *Blanche Nef.* The young prince might have been saved in a boat, had he not insisted on rowing back to save his sister, when so many drowning wretches leaped on board, that the frail skiff was capsized, and sank. It is said that the king was never seen to smile after this melancholy event.[1]

1121. Henry married Adelaide, daughter of the Duke of Louvain, by whom he had no issue.

1126. On Christmas-day, Matilda, ex-Empress of Germany, was recognised as next heir to the crown. Among the nobles who swore fidelity to her was Stephen, Earl of Boulogne, nephew of William the Conqueror.

1133. Matilda, who had married Geoffrey of Anjou, bore a son, afterwards Henry II.

1135. Death of Henry I., at the castle of Lions, about eighteen miles from Rouen, on the 1st December.

Stephen, Earl of Boulogne, making all haste to London, was crowned King of England on the 28th of December, and began a reign which, as Sir James Mackintosh says, was 'the most perfect condensation of all the ills of feudality to be found in history.' William of Malmesbury tells us that, from his complacency of manners and promptness of jest, he was a great favourite with the common people, whose champion he may be considered to have been, against the Norman-English barons.

[1] Ordericus Vitalis, Bk. xiii.; William of Malmesbury, *De Gestis*, Bk. v.

A.D.
1138. The Battle of the Standard was fought at Northallerton, August 22d. The English army was led by the Bishop of Durham; the Scotch by King David, an avowed supporter of the claims of the ex-Empress Matilda. The Scotch were totally defeated, with a loss of 11,000 men. The 'standard' was a tall cross raised on a car, and surrounded by the banners of St. Cuthbert of Durham, St. Wilfred of York, and St. John of Beverley.

1139. Stephen, supported by the large towns, endeavoured to crush the more powerful barons, and was to some extent successful. He then attempted to break the power of some of the great prelates,—especially the Bishops of Ely, Lincoln, and Salisbury,—and by so doing roused against himself the formidable hostility of the Church. The king was eventually compelled to submit to the Pope's legate, but his submission was not in time to avert his ruin. It seems allowable, we may add, to look upon Stephen as greatly in advance of his age, as a bold and sagacious reformer, who, had he been successful, would have tamed the Norman nobility and humbled the pride of the wealthy ecclesiastics; in a word, would have anticipated the revolutions worked out so bloodily in later reigns. In his courageous attempt to assert the supremacy of the State over the Church, he was followed by Henry II., his successor,— with what fortune we shall hereafter see. Throughout his reign the burgher class remained faithful to him, in the conviction that their liberties were closely bound up with his triumph over his enemies, who

A.D.	
1139.	indeed were not more hostile to the crown than they were to the rapidly rising trader class.
	The Empress Matilda landed at Arundel, and occupied the castle, where she was invested by Stephen. But the king, with his usual chivalry, suffered her to pass through his lines, and she set forward to join her brother, the Earl of Gloucester, at Bristol.
1140.	The country was distracted by the warfare between the rival factions, which grew of so intestine a character, that, as William of Malmesbury says, the neighbour could put no faith in his nearest neighbour, nor the friend in his friend, nor the brother in his own brother.
1141.	Lincoln Castle was surprised by Ranolf, Earl of Chester, and William de Rouman, his half-brother, who held it for the empress. Stephen laid siege to it, but, on the approach of the Earl of Gloucester with a powerful army, decided to give him battle. After a preliminary skirmish, in which the king's knights got the worst of it, Stephen, with his infantry, was surrounded by the enemy. 'The battle raged terribly around this circle,' says Henry of Huntingdon; 'helmets and swords gleamed as they clashed, and the terrible cries and shouts re-echoed from the city walls and the neighbouring hills. The horsemen, furiously charging the royal column, slew some, and trampled down others; many were taken prisoners. No respite was allowed, no breathing time, except where the king himself was posted, and his assailants recoiled from the unrivalled vigour of his terrible arm. The Earl of Chester seeing this, and envying the glory which the king was

A.D.
1141. gaining, flung himself upon him with the whole weight of his men-at-arms. Even then the royal courage did not blench; his heavy battle-axe flashed like lightning, striking down some, beating back others. At length it was shattered by repeated blows. Then he drew his trusty sword, with which he wrought wonders, until it, too, was broken; which perceiving, William de Kaims, a brave soldier, rushed upon him, and seizing him by his helmet, shouted " Here, here, I have taken the king!" Others came to his aid, and Stephen was made prisoner.'[1]

He was thrown into a dungeon in Bristol Castle. The Empress Matilda entered Winchester in triumph, was received by all the great prelates, and declared queen. Thence she repaired to London, but was driven forth by a sudden rising of the citizens; and from London to Oxford, where she held her court for a few short months. Stephen, meanwhile, was released for the Earl of Gloucester, who had been captured by the Londoners; and his followers speedily rallying around him, he was soon at the head of a powerful army.

1142. Stephen invested Oxford, and took it; invested the castle, besieged it for three months, and took it likewise. But the Empress Matilda escaped under cover of a deep, dark night, making her way, with three followers, over the frozen snow; and at Abingdon taking horse, she rode full speed to Wallingford.

---

[1] Henry of Huntingdon. See also *Gesta Stephani* (*Script. Rer. Norm.*), pp. 952, 953.

A.D.

1147. Finding her cause hopeless, the empress left England.

1153. Henry, son of the empress, invaded England with a large force drawn from his French provinces (he possessed Normandy, Anjou, Touraine, and Maine, in right of descent; Aquitaine and Poitou, through his marriage with Eleanor, the divorced wife of Louis of France), and besieged several castles. But no pitched battle took place. Stephen's son, Eustace, having died prematurely, terms of agreement were easily concluded between the two opponents. The king and the duke held a conference, without witnesses, across a rivulet, and this meeting opened the way to a final pacification. Henry, Bishop of Winchester, acted for the king, and Theobald, Archbishop of Canterbury, for the duke. After a brief negotiation, Stephen and the prince went in solemn procession through the streets of Winchester; and all the great nobles of the realm, by the king's command, did homage, and pronounced the fealty due to their liege lord, the Duke of Normandy, saving only their allegiance to King Stephen during his life.

1154. Death of Stephen, October 25th. Henry II. crowned at Westminster, December 19th,—the first sovereign of the Plantagenet race, which ruled England for upwards of three centuries; a race which probably produced more able men than any other royal dynasty named in history.

The principal counsellors of Henry II., after his accession, were Theobald, Archbishop of Canterbury, the Earl of Leicester, his grand justiciary, and THOMAS

A.D. 1154. A BECKET, Archdeacon of Canterbury, his chancellor (1157).

Henry II., on the mother's side, was descended from the old royal stock, and English and Norman blood was mingled in his veins. But this indeed was no uncommon case in the twelfth century. In less than one hundred years after the Conquest, the process of absorption had assumed considerable proportions; and, as Ailred of Rievaulx says, 'England had not only a king, but many bishops and abbots, many great earls and noble knights, who, being descended both from the Norman and English blood, were an honour to the one, and a comfort to the other.'

Here we pause. In our next volume we resume our story of the fortunes of England and her worthies at a stirring epoch,—the rise of the first great Englishman after the Conquest, THOMAS A BECKET, Archbishop of Canterbury, formerly called St. Thomas the Martyr.

INDEX.

A Becket, Thomas, Archbishop of Canterbury, 383.

Abingdon, chronicles of, cited, 166, 171.

Ælfgar, son of Leofric, allies himself with Gruffydd, and attacks Hereford, 173, 174; pardoned, 174; receives the earldom of Mercia, 177.

Ælfred the Great, chronology of the reign of, 6; sovereigns contemporary with, 6; the subject of universal praise amongst historians, 7; characterized by Mr. Freeman, 8, 9, 10; by Professor Pearson, 10, 11; by Sir Francis Palgrave, 12, 13; by Sir Edward Creasy, 13, 14; general summary, 14, 15, 16; his birth and early youth, 16; an old legend about, 16, 17; his skill in hunting, and love of poetry, 17; his two visits to Rome, 17, 18; his thirst for knowledge, his marriage, 18; in battle against the Danes, 19, 20; called to the throne, 20; fights ten battles with the Danes, 21; peace, and the correction of abuses, 21, 22; inaction of the first seven years of his reign, 22; meets the enemy at sea, and sets about forming a national navy, 22, 23; besieges Exeter, and defeats the Danes at sea, 23; baffled by the Danes, 24, 25; his heroic patience, 26; retires to the marshes of Athelney, 27; a popular legend about, 29, 30; in the Danish camp, 30; unfurls his banner, and is joined by a large body of followers, 31; wins the battle of Ethandune, 33; captures Chippenham, and compels the Danes to surrender, 34; approves Guthred as king of Northumbria, 40; lord paramount over all England south of the Tweed, 40, 41; defends his kingdom against the Northmen under Hastings, 42–45; close of his career, 46; his munificence, 47; analysis of his law statutes, 47, 48; characterized by Lord Houghton, 49; a codifier, not a legislator, 49; his efforts in the spread of equity and justice, 50, 51; his severe maladies, 52, 53; his children, and their education, 53, 54; amongst his people, 55; his search for helpers in good works, 56; his associates in teaching and administration, 57; his commonplace book of psalms and prayers, 58; his collection of devout quotations, and study of the Scriptures, 59; his hours of tribulation, and cares of government, 60, 61; his patronage of monasteries, 62, 63; his desire to augment his piety, 63; his division of the revenues of the year, 63–65; his desire to economize his time, 65, 66; his anxiety for the promotion of justice in his kingdom, 67, 68; his translation of the Bible, Orosius, and Bæda, 69; his version of Boethius, 69, 70; his other works, 70; an instance of his philanthropy, 71; a panegyric upon, 71, 72; some of his wise maxims quoted, 72, 73; his death, and children, 73; commemorated by Wordsworth, 74.

Ælfred, son of Æthelred, account of his career, 134, 135.

Ælgiva, wife of King Eadwig, sufferings and death of, 104.

Æswitha offers her hand to Hereward, 358.

Æthelred the Unready crowned king of England, 114; ravages the church lands, 116; endeavours to buy off the Danes, 129, 130; quarrels with Richard of Normandy, 130; marries Emma, sister of Richard, 120; collects a fleet to defend the coast against the Danes, 132; flies to Normandy, but returns and defeats Cnut, 132; his death, 132.

Æthelstan, son of Eadward, his accession to the throne, 77; wins the battle of Brunanburh, 77, 78; his death, 78.

Agricola, the Roman general, conquest of Britain by, 3.

Allectus, reign of, in Britain, 3.

Amiens, Guy of, cited, 240, 241, 298.

Amiens, William of, cited, 283.

Anderida, the city of, described, 242.

Anglia Sacra quoted, 90, 92, 102, 103, 106, 108, 124.

Anglo-Saxon Chronicle quoted, 21, 31, 34, 77, 78, 93, 113, 114, 127, 146, 151, 153, 155, 190, 191, 306, 307, 315, 347, 348, 363, 367, 368, 374.

Anlaf, revolt of the Northumbrians under, 78, 98.

Apologues, the, by Ælfred, 70.

Arundel, town of, besieged by Stephen, 380.

Ashdown, battle of, 19; described by Asser, 20, 21.

Assandun, battle of, 133.

Asser quoted, 17, 20, 21, 24, 33; his account of Ælfred's life, 52-68.

Bæda, the historian, quoted, 95; his history translated by Ælfred, 69.

Bamborough, town of, captured by the Danes, 130.

Battle Abbey, origin of, 268.

Bayeux Tapestry, the, described, 364, 365.

Benedict X., Pope of Rome, grants Stigand his pallium, 311; his deposition, 311.

Beverley, Alured of, cited, 350.

Beverley, St. John of, church of, 349, 350.

Bible, the, translated by Ælfred, 69.

Blesensis, Petrus, quoted, 354, 355.

Bourne quoted, 316.

Brand, Abbot of Medeshamstede, knights Hereward, 353; his death, 353.

Brand quoted, 316.

Bretwalda, the, of the Saxon States, 4.

Brihtric, a Saxon earl, confiscation of his estates by Matilda, 347.

Britain under the Romans, 3, 4; attacked and subdued by the Northmen, 4, 5.

Bromton, John of, cited, 321, 350, 365, 367, 368.

Brunanburh, account of the battle of, 77, 78.

Cæsar, Julius, invasions of Britain by, 3.

Campbell, Thomas, the poet, quoted, 230.

Canterbury, Archbishops of, list of, before the Conquest, 305.

Capgrave cited, 367.

Caractacus, the British prince, defeated by the Romans, 3.

Carausius, the usurper, his life sketched, 3.

Chester, city of, surrenders to William of Normandy, 351.

Childermas-day, unlucky character of, 316.

Chippenham, town of, attacked by the Danes, 23.

Christians, persecutions of, in Britain, 3.

Christianity, spread of, amongst the Northmen, 4; its decline in England during Ælfred's reign, 26.

Chronicle of Abingdon cited, 166, 171.

INDEX.

Chronicle of Peterborough cited, 147, 166, 171.
Chronicle, Anglo-Norman, quoted, 127.
Chronique de Normandie cited, 202.
Cnut defeated by Æthelred, 132; invades England, and is elected king, 132; defeated by Eadmund, son of Æthelred, 132; contests the kingdom with Eadmund, 133; his reign summed up by Mr. Pearson, 133, 134.
Code of laws drawn up by Ælfred, analyzed, 47, 48.
Comines, Philip de, quoted, 316.
Conan, Count of Brittany, refuses to assist William of Normandy against Harold; and is poisoned, 236.
Creasy, Sir Edward, quoted, 13, 14.

Danes, the, first invasion of England by, 5; second invasion by, 19–21; their division of the kingdom with the West Saxons under Ælfred, 22; attack Exeter and Chippenham, 23; besiege Kynwith, 24; their supremacy in England, 25; defeated at Ethandune, 33; and at Chippenham, 34; they settle in England under Ælfred, 35–37; invade England under Swegen and Olaf, 129; defeated at Watchet, 129; defeated by the English at sea, 129; ravage Northumberland and Yorkshire, 130; in the Isle of Wight and Kent, 130; invade Sussex, Hampshire, and Devonshire, 131; are massacred by order of King Æthelred, 131; invade England under Swegen, 131; ravage Kent, Sussex, and the Isle of Wight, and desolate Hampshire and Berkshire, 131, 132; harass the kingdom with fire and sword, 132; invade England under Lothen and Erling, 146.
De Gestis Herwardi Saxonis cited, 351.
Denewulf, Bishop of Winchester, account of, 29.
Domesday Book, survey of, completed, 365.

Dover, town of, captured by William of Normandy, 343.
Duncan, King of Scotland, invades England, 135.
Dunstan, Archbishop of Canterbury, the subject of both eulogy and detraction by historians, 82; his lineage and birth, 82; educated at Glastonbury, 84; distinguishes himself in study, 84; is attacked by brain fever, and a consequent monomania, 85; at the court of Æthelstane, 86; his wonderful powers, 87; accused of magic, 88; under the influence of Bishop Ælphege, 90, 91; again prostrated by fever, 91; is ordained priest, 91; as an anchorite, 92; returns to court, 93; becomes Abbot of Glastonbury, 93; legends concerning, 94; as a Church reformer, 95–97; improves Glastonbury Abbey, 98; becomes chief director of the kingdom under Eadred, 100, 101; his contest with Eadwig, 102; at open war with the king, 103; recalled by Eadgar, 104; made Primate of England, 105; characterized by Wordsworth, 107; rebukes the king in the matter of Wielfrida, 107, 108; achievements during his administration, 110, 111; his warfare with the married clergy, 111; crowns Æthelred king, 114; his work as writer, 116, 117; his canons, 117–123; his last sermon and dying hours, 124; his monument in Canterbury Cathedral, 125; the opening of his tomb, *temp.* Henry VII., described, 125, 126.
Durham, Simeon of, cited, 367.
Durham besieged by Malcolm of Scotland, 131; by Duncan, 135.

Eadgar the Ætheling becomes joint King of England with Eadwig, 79, 104; becomes sole king, 105; his love of magnificence, his submissiveness to Dunstan, 106; his bills, 107; at war with Dunstan and the Church, 107.
Eadgar the Ætheling elected King

of England, 320; goes to Scotland, 323.
Eadgitha, wife of Eadward the Confessor, 140, 146, 149.
Eadgyth Swanneshals, the mistress of Harold, 145; her search for his body at Hastings, 297.
Eadmer quoted, 202.
Eadmund, son of Æthelred, defeats Cnut, 132; raises the siege of London, 132; contests England with the Danes, 133; becomes king south of the Thames, and dies, 138.
Eadmund succeeds Athelstane on the English throne, 78; ravages Northumberland and Cumberland, and is slain by Leofa, 78, 99.
Eadred, accession of, 100; his death, 102.
Eadward succeeds Eadgar the Pacific, 112; is slain by Ælfthryth, 113.
Eadward succeeds Ælfred on the English throne, 77.
Eadward the Confessor called to England by Harthacnut, 135; chosen king, 135; his weak character, 140, 141; supports Eustace of Boulogne against Earl Godwine, 151; summons Godwine before the Witán, 152; is reconciled with the great noble, 154, 155; raises a large army, and summons Godwine and Harold before the Witán, 155; banishes the earl from the kingdom, 156; promises the succession to William of Normandy, 160; refuses to admit Godwine to his possessions, 166; flight of his Norman favourites, 166, 167; his last hours, 187, 316-318, 330-332; nominates Harold as his successor, and dies, 188, 318; his character, 188, 189; his burial, 200; his vision of the Seven Sleepers, 308, 309, 328-330; his foundation and consecration of Westminster Abbey, 312-316.
Eadward, son of Eadmund Ironsides, visits England, 176; his death, 176.
Eadwig, King of England after

Eadred, 78, 102; his contest with Dunstan, 102, 103; rebelled against by Northumbria and Mercia, 140; joint ruler with Eadgar, 104; death, 79, 104.
Ealdred, Abbot of Tewkesbury, 130; crowns Harold and William, 318, 319.
Ellis, Sir Henry, cited, 347.
Ely, Isle of, the camp of refuge at, 324, 325, 350, 351; treacherous conduct of its monks, 355.
England, invaded by the Danes, 5, 6; second invasion of, by Danes, 19, 20; divided between the Danes and West Saxons, 22; occupied by the Danes, 24, 25; effect of the treaty of Wedmore on, 37-39; progress of, in the reign of Eadred, 106, 110, 111; harassed by the Danes, 131-133; before the Conquest, 135-137.
Ethandune, account of the battle of, 33.
Eustace, Count of Boulogne, visits England, 150; his fracas with the burghers of Dover, 151.
Exeter attacked by the Danes, 23; again attacked, 131; besieged by William of Normandy, 346, 347.

Fitz-Erneis, Robert, a Norman knight, exploits of, at Hastings, 288, 289.
Freeman, Mr., the historian, quoted and cited, 8, 9, 10, 19, 35, 36, 129, 130, 133, 135-137, 144, 145, 153, 157, 161, 162, 171, 172, 177, 180, 198, 199, 229, 232, 241, 246, 249, 276, 298, 300, 301.

Gael, Raulf de, heads a revolt against William I., 361.
Gaimar, Geoffroi, his *Chronicle* quoted, 31, 271, 351, 356-360.
Gemeticensis, Willelmus, quoted, 364.
Gervas quoted, 326.
Glastonbury, historic associations of, 83.
Godwine, Earl, virtual ruler of Wessex, 134; receives Ælfred, son of Æthelred, and permits his death, 134, 135; accused of the murder

of Ælfred, 135; children of, described, 137, 140; his immense possessions and influence, 139, 140; his daughter Eadgitha, 140; supports Ælric as primate, 148, 149; defends the inhabitants of Dover against Eustace of Boulogne, 151, 152; accused of disobedience and rebellion, and summoned before the Witán, 152; appeals to arms, 152, 153; marches upon Gloucester, 153, 154; is reconciled with the king, 154, 155; banished with his family from the kingdom, 156; resolves to return to England, 163; joins Harold, and sails up the Thames to London, 165; parleys with the king, 166; addresses the Witán, 168; is reinstated in his possessions and dignities, 169; his death, 170; his burial, 171; his character, 171, 172; his ancestry, 178, 179; the power and wealth of his house, 179, 180.

Gruffydd, Prince of Wales, invades Herefordshire, 163; again crosses the Border, and commits ravages, 173, 174; retreats to his fastnesses, 174; crosses the Border a third time, 175; makes an incursion into England, 182, 183; beheaded by his own countrymen, 184.

Guthred, King of Northumbria, 40.

Guthrum, the Danish leader, negotiates a treaty with Ælfred, 23; attacks Chippenham, 23; defeated by Ælfred, 33, 34; becomes a Christian, 34.

Gyrth, son of Godwine, his offer to do battle with William of Normandy, 251, 252; killed by William, 282.

Gytha, mother of King Harold, her offer to ransom his body, 297; takes refuge in Exeter, 346.

Hadrian, Emperor of Rome, visits Britain, 3.

Hair, shaving the, amongst the heathen, 119.

Harold Hardrada, early career of, 136.

Harold Harefoot, King of northern England, 134; ruler over all England, 135.

Harold, son of Godwine, his birth and early years, 141; his extraordinary powers and accomplishments, 142; his personal appearance 142, 143; his character as a man and ruler, 143; his greatness as a soldier and administrator, 144; his attachment to his country, and personal demeanour, 145; raised to the dignity of Earl of East Anglia, 146; raises levies to assist his father Godwine, 152; summoned with Godwine before the Witán, 155; banished from England, 156; collects a fleet and lands at Porlock, 164; joins his father, and sails up the Thames to London, 165; appointed to the government of the West Saxons, 173; his campaign against the Welsh Prince Gruffydd, 173-175; receives an accession of territory, 177; his position as viceroy and heir apparent to the throne, 181; his pilgrimage to Rome, 181, 182; completes the minster of Waltham, 183; his career of conquest in Wales, 183-185; marries Ealdgyth, widow of Gruffydd, 184; erects a hunting-seat in Wales, 185; takes the field against the Northumbrian rebels, 185, 186; ratifies election of Morkere to the earldom of Northumbria, 187; named by Eadward his successor, 188, 318; elected King of England by the Witán, 190, 191, 198; makes a journey into Normandy, 191, 192; falls into the hands of Guy of Ponthieu, and is thrown into prison, 190; released, and splendidly entertained by William of Normandy, 193, 194; is entangled into promising the English crown to William, 194, 195; swears an oath to this effect, 195, 196; accepts the crown offered by the Witán, 199; proceeds to correct abuses, 200; receives intelligence of the Norman invasion, 248; takes counsel with his chiefs, 248,

249; collects levies of troops, and goes as a pilgrim to Waltham, 249; receives an embassy from William, 250; patriotism of his soldiery, 250, 251; advised by his brother Gyrth, 252, 253; marches for London, 253; his advantageous position on the height of Senlac, 253; his arrangement of the English army, 272; his speech to his followers, 273-275; his station by the Standard, 276, 277; his personal valour at the battle of Hastings, 279; his death, 291; his character, 294-296; the search for his body, and its burial, 297, 298; legends about, 298-300; characterized by Mr. Freeman, 300, 301; at the deathbed of Eadward the Confessor, 318; his coronation, 318, 319.

Harthacnut, King of England, 134, 135; his death, 135.

Hastings, battle of, preparations for, 258; the night before, in the English camp, 258, 259; the night before, amongst the Normans, 259, 260; the rise of dawn, 260; William's speech to his followers, 260-264; the Normans quit their entrenchments, 264, 265; William prepares to arm, 266, 267; the disposition of the Norman array, 268, 269; the bearer of the Gonfalon, 269; the advance of Taillefer, 270, 271; the English army described, 272; Harold's speech to his followers, 273, 274; the scene from the hill of Senlac, 275-277; the Normans begin the battle, 278; personal exploits of the rival leaders, 279; brave defence of the English, 279; flight of the Bretons, and confusion in the Norman ranks, 280; exertions of William and Odo, 281-283; instances of individual valour, 283-288; the Normans feign flight, 289; the English overpowered, 290; William calls out his archers, 290, 291; the death of King Harold, 291; the closing scenes of the battle, 292, 293; after the battle, 294; the field of carnage, 296, 297.

Hastings, ravages of the Northmen under, 41-45.

Hearn's *Letters* quoted, 316.

Henry I. at the deathbed of his father, 367; crowned, 374; marries an English princess, 375; grants a charter of rights and privileges, 375; quells an insurrection headed by Robert of Belèsme, 376; invades Normandy, 376; creates a number of abbots and prelates, 377; his war with France, 378; death of his son, 378; his own death, 378.

Henry II., son of Matilda, marries Eleanor of Aquitaine, 382; his meeting with Stephen, 382; his coronation, 382; his counsellors during his reign, 382, 383; his lineage, 383.

Hereward, the English hero, his youthful career, 351; is outlawed, 352; the theme of popular ballads, 352; falls in love with Torfrida, 352; returns to England and raises the standard of revolt, 324, 353; surprises Abbot Thorold, 354; his camp of refuge, 324, 325, 350, 351; is besieged in Isle of Ely by William I., 354-356; escapes, 356; keeps up a guerilla warfare, 357; his marriage to Æswitha, 358; legends about his death, 358-361.

Hook, Dean, quoted, 83, 85, 86, 87, 88, 106, 148, 149, 303, 310, 323, 326.

Hoveden, Roger de, cited, 99, 105, 151, 164, 165, 166, 200, 346.

Huntingdon, Henry of, quoted, 23, 171, 230, 381.

Ingulphus, the historian, quoted, 140, 351.

Johnson's *English Laws* cited, 110, 117.

Jumièges, Bishop Robert of, favourite of Eadward the Confessor, and virtual Primate of England, 141; created Archbishop of Canterbury,

148; quarrels with Earl Godwine, 149, 150.
Jumièges, William of, cited, 251.

Kemble, the historian, cited, 34, 95.
Kent, formation of the kingdom of, 4.
Kingsley, Canon, his *Hereward* cited, 136, 351.
Knight, Charles, quoted, 93.

Lanfranc, Abbot of Caen, consecrated Archbishop of Canterbury, 349; his death, 373.
Lappenberg, quoted, 320.
Leominster, battle of, described, 163.
Lillebonne, William of Normandy's council at, 205.
Lincoln, siege of, and battle near, described, 380.
Lingard, Dr., quoted, 96.
London attacked by the Danes under Olaf and Swegen, 138; surrenders to William of Normandy, 344.
Luard, *Lives of Eadward the Confessor*, quoted, 312, 313, 317, 328-337.
Lytton, Lord, his *Harold* referred to, 119; quoted, 142, 143, 168, 178, 179, 229, 274, 275.

Macaulay, Lord, cited, 375, 376.
Maldon, battle of, 129.
Malmesbury, William of, cited, 28, 30, 112, 114, 150, 152, 156, 171, 229, 364, 375, 378.
Matilda, wife of the Conqueror, coronation of, 347; confiscates the lands of Brihtric, 347; death, 364.
Matilda, ex-Empress of Germany, gives birth to Henry II., 378; lands at Arundel, 380; enters Winchester in triumph, afterwards holding court at Oxford, 381; besieged there by Stephen, 381; her escape and departure from England, 382.
Mercia, formation of the kingdom of, 4.
Milman, Dean, quoted, 311.

Milton, John, quoted, 75.
Montgomery, Roger of, his exploits at the battle of Hastings, 284.
Mont St. Michael besieged by William II., 373.
Morkere, son of Ælfgar of Mercia, chosen earl by the Northumbrians, 185; his election confirmed by the Witán, 187.

Norman conquest of England, first stage of, 130; early beginnings of, 135-137.
Norman influence, spread of the, before the Conquest, 141, 148, 149, 150, 156, 159, 160; its decline and extinction, 166, 167, 169.
Northern England, its resistance to William of Normandy, 348, 349, 350.
Northmen, immigration of the, 4; their progress, and foundation of kingdoms, 4, 5; ravages of, in the time of Ælfred, under Hastings, 41-45.

Odo, Archbishop of Canterbury, orders the disfigurement of Ælgifa, 104.
Odo, Bishop of Bayeux, his exploits at the battle of Hastings, 265, 281; heads a rebellion against William II., 372; quells an insurrection in Northumbria, 363, 364; quarrels with William I., and is flung into prison, 264.
Olaf Tryggwisson, King of Norway, lands in England, 129; attacks London, 130; makes peace with Æthelred, 130.
Osbern's *Life of Dunstan* (*Anglia Sacra*), quoted, 85.
Oxford, town of, besieged by Stephen, 381.

Palgrave, Sir F., quoted, 12, 13, 28, 71, 111, 168.
Pauli, Dr., cited, 17, 18, 26, 34.
Paulinus, Suetonius, his exploits in Britain, 3.
Pearson, Professor, quoted, 10, 11, 46, 47, 95, 188, 189, 196, 197.

Pevensey, arrival of William of Normandy at, 241; the neighbourhood of, described, 242; its castle, 242, 243.
Philip of France, his refusal to assist William of Normandy, 235.
Picts, the, first invasion of Britain by, 4.
Poitiers, William of, cited, 238, 247, 281, 297, 298, 343, 345.
Poitou, William of, cited, 241.

Raven, the Standard of, captured by the English, 24.
Robert of Normandy, son of William I., his rebellion against his father, 362, 363.
Rochester, town of, besieged by William II., 372.
Roman de Rou, the, quoted or cited, 194, 195, 196, 205, 206, 207, 208, 231, 233, 235, 240, 244, 248, 251, 252, 258, 259, 260, 261, 262, 263, 264, 265, 266, 267, 269, 270, 271, 273, 277, 278, 281, 282, 284, 285, 286, 287, 288, 289, 291, 292, 297.
Romney, town of, destroyed by William of Normandy, 343.
Rougemont, castle of, erected by William of Normandy, 347.

Saxons—see *Northmen*.
Senlac, Harold's position at, 253, 257; the neighbourhood described, 257; the battle of—see *Hastings*.
'Seven Sleepers,' the, King Eadward's vision of, 308, 309, 328-330.
Severus, Emperor of Rome, visits Britain, 3.
Shakespeare quoted, 119.
Sherstone, battle of, 32.
Snorro Sturleson cited, 225, 226.
St. Alban, martyrdom of, 3.
Stamford Bridge, the battle of, described, 225-228.
Stanley, Dean, quoted, 314, 316.
St. Cuthbert, Life of, quoted, 29, 30.
Stigand, Archbishop of Canterbury, counsellor of Queen Emma, 136, 137, 306; acts as mediator between Godwine and Eadward, 166; appointed to the see of the East Angles, 306; deposed from his bishopric, 307; his restoration at court, and influence with Queen Emma, 307; his contests with Robert of Jumièges, 307, 308; his alternate popularity and unpopularity at court, 309, 310; appointed primate, 310; summoned before the Papal court, 311; goes out to meet William after Hastings, 319; advocates the claims of Eadgar the Ætheling, 320; refuses to crown William, 321; is treated with distinction by the Conqueror, 321; attends William to Normandy, 322; returns to England, 323; accompanies Eadgar to Scotland, 323; supports Hereward in his rebellion, 324; is captured, imprisoned, and dies at Winchester, 325; his character canvassed, 326, 327.
St. John, J. A., quoted, 369-372.
St. Maure, Benoit de, quoted, 264, 265; cited, 281.
St. Neot, Life of, referred to, 28.
Swegen, son of Godwine, banishes himself from England, 146; returns with a large fleet, 146, 147; captures and slays his brother Beorn, 147; flees to Flanders, and returns to England, 148.
Swegen, King of Denmark, invades England, 129; attacks London, 130; again invades England, 131; last invasion by, 132; crowned King of England, 132; death, 132.

Taillefer, the Norman minstrel, his exploits at Hastings, 270, 271.
Taylor, Henry, quoted, 75, 255.
Tennyson, the poet, quoted, 1, 9, 14, 15, 19, 83.
Thierry, the historian, quoted, 75, 255.
Thorold, Abbot of Medeshamstede, attacks Hereward's camp of refuge, 353, 354; is surprised by Hereward, 354.
Thorpe's *Saxon Laws* quoted, 35, 49.

Tostig, son of Godwine, is rebelled against by the Northumbrians, 185, 186; charges Harold with complicity with the rebels, 186; is banished from the kingdom, 187.

Vaughan, Dr., quoted, 88.
Vita Eadwardi referred to, 143; cited, 149, 157, 188, 136.
Vita Haroldi cited, 299.
Vitalis, Ordericus, cited or quoted, 257, 297, 322, 343, 345, 366, 372, 373, 374, 375, 378.

Waltham, the minster of, completed and consecrated, 182; Harold's pilgrimage to, 249.
Waltheof, an English noble, execution of, 362.
Wareham, Archbishop, quoted, 125, 126.
Watchet, defeat of the Danes at, 129.
Wedmore, provisions of the treaty of, 35, 37; advantages of the peace, 37-39.
Welsh, inroads of the, under Gruffydd, 163, 173-175, 182, 183; their subjection by Harold, 183-185.
Westminster, Matthew of, cited, 308.
Westminster Abbey, foundation and consecration of, 312-316.
Wessex, spread of the kingdom of, 4; permanent supremacy of, attained, 4.—See Ælfred, King of the West Saxons.
White, Rev. James, quoted, 6.
Widon quoted, 238.
William of Normandy, early career of, 137; first visit to England, 159; is promised the succession to the throne, 160; his ambitious designs, 161, 162; demands Harold's release from Guy of Ponthieu, 193; entertains him magnificently, 194; entraps him into promising him the English crown, 195, 196; receives news of Harold's accession, 200, 201; despatches an embassy to Harold, 202, 203; decides on war, 203; seeks the aid of his barons, 204, 205; his council at Lillebonne, 205; his appeal to the Pope, 207; collects forces for the invasion of England, 231; gets together a fleet, 231-233; levies an army, 233, 234; solicits the assistance of Philip of France, 235; applies to the court of Flanders, 235; is threatened by Conan of Brittany, 236; his departure for England delayed, 237; removes his fleet and army to St. Valery, 238; murmuring in his camp, 238, 239; his anxiety, 239; at last sets sail, 240, 241; arrives in Pevensey Bay, 241; lands his army, 244; his presence of mind at landing, 244, 245; moves eastward to Hastings, 245; his systematic ravages in the neighbourhood, 246, 247; receives tidings of the battle of Stamford Bridge, 247; sends an embassy to Harold, 250; his address to his troops before the battle, 260-265; prepares to arm, 266, 267; vows to build an abbey at Battle, 268; appoints his standard-bearer, 269, 270; his personal exploits at Hastings, 282; orders his men to feign flight, 289; calls up his archers, 290, 291; sleeps on the field of battle, 294; takes Dover, and marches to London, 343; met by the men of Kent, 344; moves into Southwark, 344; is submitted to by Stigand and Eadgar, 319, 345; crowned at Westminster by Ealdred, 345; returns to Normandy, 322, 345; reappears in London to overawe rebellion, 346; crushes an insurrection in the west, 346; besieges Exeter, 347; marches to the relief of York, 348; devastates the neighbourhood, 349; attacks Chester, 351; besieges Hereward in his camp of refuge, 354-356; subdues a rebellion in Maine, 361; quells a revolt in England, 361; rebellion of his son Robert, 362, 363; quarrels with Odo of Bayeux, 364; falls ill at Rouen, 365; ravages a part of France, 366; the scene at his

deathbed, 366, 367; his burial, 367, 368; his character sketched by Mr. J. A. St. John, 369-372.

William II. at the deathbed of his father, 366, 367; coronation, 372; quells a rebellion headed by Odo of Bayeux, 372; in Normandy, 373; his war with Scotland, 373; quells a revolt of the northern counties, 373, 374; erects the hall at Westminster, and throws a bridge across the Thames, 374; his death, 374.

York, the city of, its resistance to William of Normandy, 348; captured by the Danes and English, 348; retaken by William I., 349.

Books published by William P. Nimmo.

NIMMO'S HALF-CROWN REWARD BOOKS.

Extra foolscap 8vo, cloth elegant, gilt edges, Illustrated, price 2s. 6d. each.

1. Memorable Wars of Scotland. By Patrick Fraser Tytler, F.R.S.E., Author of 'The History of Scotland,' etc.

2. Seeing the World: A Young Sailor's own Story. By CHARLES NORDHOFF, Author of 'The Young Man-of-War's-Man.'

3. The Martyr Missionary: Five Years in China. By Rev. CHARLES P. BUSH, M.A.

4. My New Home: A Woman's Diary.

5. Home Heroines: Tales for Girls. By T. S. Arthur, Author of 'Life's Crosses,' etc.

6. Lessons from Women's Lives. By Sarah J. Hale.

7. The Roseville Family. A Historical Tale of the Eighteenth Century. By Mrs. A. S. ORR, Author of 'Mountain Patriots,' etc.

8. Leah. A Tale of Ancient Palestine. Illustrative of the Story of Naaman the Syrian. By Mrs. A. S. ORR.

9. Champions of the Reformation: The Stories of their Lives. By JANET GORDON.

10. The History of Two Wanderers; or, Cast Adrift.

11. Beattie's Poetical Works.

12. The Vicar of Wakefield. By Oliver Goldsmith.

13. Edgar Allan Poe's Poetical Works.

14. The Miner's Son, and Margaret Vernon. By M. M. POLLARD, Author of 'The Minister's Daughter,' etc. etc.

NIMMO'S TWO SHILLING REWARD BOOKS.

Foolscap 8vo, Illustrated, elegantly bound in cloth extra, bevelled boards, gilt back and side, gilt edges, price 2s. each.

1. The Far North: Explorations in the Arctic Regions. By ELISHA KENT KANE, M.D., Commander, Second Grinnell Expedition in Search of Sir John Franklin.
2. The Young Men of the Bible. A Series of Papers, Biographical and Suggestive. By Rev. JOSEPH A. COLLIER.
3. The Blade and the Ear: A Book for Young Men.
4. Monarchs of Ocean: Columbus and Cook. Two Narratives of Maritime Discovery.
5. Life's Crosses, and How to Meet them. Tales for Girls. By T. S. ARTHUR.
6. A Father's Legacy to his Daughters, etc. A Book for Young Women. By Dr. GREGORY.
7. Great Men of European History. From the Beginning of the Christian Era till the Present Time. By DAVID PRYDE, M.A.
8. Mountain Patriots. A Tale of the Reformation in Savoy. By Mrs. A. S. ORR.
9. Labours of Love. A Tale for the Young. By WINIFRED TAYLOR.
10. Mossdale. A Tale for the Young. By Anna M. De IONGH.
11. The Standard-Bearer. A Tale of the Times of Constantine the Great. By ELLEN PALMER.
12. Jacqueline. A Story of the Reformation in Holland. By Mrs. HARDY (JANET GORDON).
13. Lame Felix. A Book for Boys. Full of Proverb and Story. By CHARLES BRUCE.
14. Picture Lessons by the Divine Teacher; or, Illustrations of the Parables of our Lord. By PETER GRANT, D.D.
15. Nonna: A Story of the Days of Julian the Apostate. By ELLEN PALMER.
16. Philip Walton; or, Light at Last. By the Author of 'Meta Frantz,' etc.
17. The Minister's Daughter, and Old Anthony's Will. Tales for the Young. By M. M. POLLARD.
18. The Two Sisters. By M. M. Pollard, Author of 'The Miner's Son,' etc. etc.

NIMMO'S EIGHTEENPENNY REWARD BOOKS.

Demy 18mo, Illustrated, cloth extra, gilt edges, price 1s. 6d. each.

1. The Vicar of Wakefield. Poems and Essays. By Oliver GOLDSMITH.

2. Æsop's Fables, with Instructive Applications. By Dr. CROXALL.

3. Bunyan's Pilgrim's Progress.

4. The Young Man-of-War's-Man: A Boy's Voyage round the World. By CHARLES NORDHOFF, Author of 'Seeing the World.'

5. The Treasury of Anecdote: Moral and Religious.

6. The Boy's Own Workshop; or, The Young Carpenters. By JACOB ABBOTT.

7. The Life and Adventures of Robinson Crusoe.

8. The History of Sandford and Merton. A Moral and Instructive Lesson for Young Persons.

9. Evenings at Home; or, The Juvenile Budget Opened. Consisting of a variety of Miscellaneous Pieces for the Instruction and Amusement of Young Persons. By Dr. AIKIN and Mrs. BARBAULD.

10. Unexpected Pleasures; or, Left alone in the Holidays. By Mrs. GEORGE CUPPLES, Author of 'Norrie Seton,' etc.

⁎ The above Series of elegant and useful books is specially prepared for the entertainment and instruction of young persons.

NIMMO'S SUNDAY SCHOOL REWARD BOOKS.

Foolscap 8vo, cloth extra, gilt edges, Illustrated, price 1s. 6d. each.

1. Bible Blessings. By Rev. Richard Newton.
2. One Hour a Week: Fifty-two Bible Lessons for the Young.
3. The Best Things. By Rev. Richard Newton.
4. Grace Harvey and her Cousins.
5. Lessons from Rose Hill; and Little Nannette.
6. Great and Good Women: Biographies for Girls. By LYDIA H. SIGOURNEY.
7. At Home and Abroad; or, Uncle William's Adventures.
8. The Kind Governess; or, How to make Home Happy.
9. Christmas at the Beacon: A Tale for the Young. By ELLEN PALMER.
10. The Sculptor of Bruges. By Mrs. W. G. Hall.
11. The Story of a Moss Rose; or, Ruth and the Orphan Family. By CHARLES BRUCE.
12. The Swedish Singer; or, The Story of Vanda Rosendahl. By Mrs. W. G. HALL.
13. My Beautiful Home; or, Lily's Search. By Chas. Bruce.
14. Alfred and his Mother; or, Seeking the Kingdom. By KATHERINE E. MAY.
15. Asriel; or, The Crystal Cup. A Tale for the Young. By Mrs. HENDERSON.
16. Wilton School; or, Harry Campbell's Revenge. A Tale. By F. E. WEATHERLY.
17. Percy and Ida. By Katherine E. May.
18. Fred Graham's Resolve. By the Author of 'Mat and Sofie,' etc. etc.
19. The Sea and the Savages: A Story of Adventure. By HAROLD LINCOLN.
20. Summer Holidays at Silversea. By E. Rosalie Salmon.

Books published by William P. Nimmo.

NIMMO'S ONE SHILLING ILLUSTRATED JUVENILE BOOKS.

Foolscap 8vo, Coloured Frontispieces, handsomely bound in cloth, Illuminated, price 1s. each.

1. Four Little People and their Friends.
2. Elizabeth; or, The Exiles of Siberia. A Tale from the French of MADAME COTTIN.
3. Paul and Virginia. From the French of BERNARDIN SAINT-PIERRE.
4. Little Threads: Tangle Thread, Golden Thread, and Silver Thread.
5. Benjamin Franklin, the Printer Boy.
6. Barton Todd, and the Young Lawyer.
7. The Perils of Greatness: The Story of Alexander Menzikoff.
8. Little Crowns, and How to Win them. By Rev. JOSEPH A. COLLIER.
9. Great Riches: Nelly Rivers' Story. By Aunt FANNY.
10. The Right Way; and The Contrast.
11. The Daisy's First Winter. And other Stories. By HARRIET BEECHER STOWE.
12. The Man of the Mountain. And other Stories.
13. Better than Rubies. Stories for the Young, Illustrative of Familiar Proverbs. With 62 Illustrations.

[*Continued on next page.*

NIMMO'S ONE SHILLING ILLUSTRATED JUVENILE BOOKS,
CONTINUED.

14. **Experience Teaches.** And other Stories for the Young, Illustrative of Familiar Proverbs. With 39 Illustrations.
15. **The Happy Recovery.** And other Stories for the Young. With 26 Illustrations.
16. **Gratitude and Probity.** And other Stories for the Young. With 21 Illustrations.
17. **The Two Brothers.** And other Stories for the Young. With 13 Illustrations.
18. **The Young Orator.** And other Stories for the Young. With 9 Illustrations.
19. **Simple Stories to Amuse and Instruct Young Readers.** With Illustrations.
20. **The Three Friends.** And other Stories for the Young. With Illustrations.
21. **Sybil's Sacrifice.** And other Stories for the Young. With 12 Illustrations.
22. **The Old Shepherd.** And other Stories for the Young. With Illustrations.
23. **The Young Officer.** And other Stories for the Young. With Illustrations.
24. **The False Heir.** And other Stories for the Young. With Illustrations.
25. **The Old Farmhouse; or, Alice Morton's Home.** And other Stories. By M. M. POLLARD.
26. **Twyford Hall; or, Rosa's Christmas Dinner,** and what she did with it. By CHARLES BRUCE.
27. **The Discontented Weathercock.** And other Stories for Children. By M. JONES.
28. **Out at Sea,** and other Stories. By Two Authors.